GLOBAL PERSPECTIVES ON URBANIZATION

Essays in Honor of Debnath Mookherjee

Edited by

George Pomeroy
Gerald Webster

University Press of America,® Inc.
Lanham · Boulder · New York · Toronto · Plymouth, UK

Copyright © 2008 by
University Press of America,® Inc.
4501 Forbes Boulevard
Suite 200
Lanham, Maryland 20706
UPA Acquisitions Department (301) 459-3366

Estover Road
Plymouth PL6 7PY
United Kingdom

Library of Congress Control Number: 2007936078
ISBN-13: 978-0-7618-3909-5 (clothbound : alk. paper)
ISBN-10: 0-7618-3909-7 (clothbound : alk. paper)
ISBN-13: 978-0-7618-3910-1 (paperback : alk. paper)
ISBN-10: 0-7618-3910-0 (paperback : alk. paper)

∞™ The paper used in this publication meets the minimum
requirements of American National Standard for Information
Sciences—Permanence of Paper for Printed Library Materials,
ANSI Z39.48—1984

Contents

Preface

Gerald Webster and George M. Pomeroy

This volume is dedicated to Dr. Debnath Mookherjee, Professor of Geography at Western Washington University (WWU), Bellingham, Washington. Professor Mookherjee served as advisor and mentor to both the editors during our studies for our Masters degrees at WWU. His patient mentoring was instrumental to the completion of our theses, degrees and respective decisions to continue our academic pursuits after leaving Bellingham. Dr. Webster received his Masters degree from Western in 1981, followed by a Ph.D. in geography at the University of Kentucky in 1984. Dr. Pomeroy received his Masters degree in 1995, and his Ph.D. in Urban Studies at the University of Akron in 1999. Though nearly fifteen years separate our residencies at WWU, our experiences working with Professor Mookherjee are remarkably similar. He had high expectations, but coupled these with consistent encouragement and support. We are both in Professor Mookherjee's debt for his help, loyalty, high expectations and the excellent example he set for us to emulate in our own academic careers.

Professor "Deb" Mookherjee received both his BS (1951) and MS (1953) degrees from the University of Calcutta. He arrived at the University of Florida in 1958 to begin his doctoral studies, receiving his Ph.D. in 1961. Professor Mookherjee was hired by Western Washington University in 1961 as an Assistant Professor, promoted to Associate Professor in 1967, and Professor in 1971. Between 1983 and 1992, he served as departmental chair as geography moved to Western's distinctive interdisciplinary Huxley College of the Environment. During this period he was instrumental in successfully defending the presence of the discipline at WWU. Despite his many administrative duties and obligations, Professor Mookherjee has been an active teacher and researcher at Western Washington University for over 45 years, a record unmatched by any other faculty member currently on Western's campus.

Professor Mookherjee's teaching and research interests focus on urbanization, urban and regional planning, economic geography, South Asia and world affairs. He has been recognized by WWU with faculty merit awards several times, and has been a visiting scholar at the University of Calcutta, Jawaharlal Nehru University and the University of Washington. He has published several dozen articles and book chapters, beginning with an article in the *Geographical Review of India* in 1956, and currently has a number of research manuscripts under preparation for publication. He has therefore published his work in six consecutive decades, and seems destined to add a seventh before slowing down. As he told us recently, "I get as excited with a new research idea as I did in my youth."

In addition to his first publication in the *Geographical Review of India* noted above, Professor Mookherjee has published articles in the *Professional Geographer, Ekistics, Geographica Polonica, Asian Profile, Review of Regional Studies, Geography*, the *Southeastern Geographer*, and the *Journal of Social and Economic Geography*, among others. His list of book chapters is even more substantial and includes his role as a co-author for the "Regional Development and Planning" chapter in the important 1989 volume entitled *Geography in America* edited by Gary L. Gaile and Cort J. Wilmott (Merrill Press).

Professor Mookherjee has affected the lives of hundreds of students and colleagues, likely more than he realizes. He told us that he "has always loved teaching" and that his role as a "teacher is always counterbalanced by a perennial feeling that I am a student among students, all of us linked by the same enthusiasm." Professor Mookherjee's combination of a student's enthusiasm and a faculty member's experience and wisdom in the classroom has engaged and motivated students at Western Washington University for nearly 50 years.

The editors were humbled by the affirmative response by Professor Mookherjee's academic colleagues to our request that they contribute essays to this volume. We thank the distinguished list of authors for their enthusiasm and patience as we have organized this volume, and we salute Professor Debnath Mookherjee for his decades of service to our discipline and profession. Finally, we recognize his wife Supriya ("Su") for the warmth she extended to us on our many visits to their home.

Introduction

George M. Pomeroy and Gerald Webster

Not too many years ago, several leading commentators across a handful of disciplines were lamenting the state of urban studies. The pervading thought was that urban studies, particularly urban geography, was as an area of "outmoded approaches" and too focused on empirical studies. A growing number of scholars seem to embrace the idea that a general urban theory could be developed. A vanguard of leading scholars, with converts in tow, sought out the holy grail of historically conscious structural theories that could work as general theories that would largely explain most facets of the urban world. Certainly in following this reasoning many of these theorists have made substantial contributions to understanding urban phenomena.

Eventually, however, many of them were overtaken by the reality that urban areas are far too messy to approach from such a general perspective. Cities are much more complex than many realized and the study of cities, urbanization, and their planning is appropriately kaleidoscopic in nature. Even in a world dominated by a capitalist system and with globalization evident everywhere, cities remain complex organisms that can be studied and better understood from a number of perspectives.

This book presents an invited and appropriately dedicated selection of these urban perspectives. Interestingly, most of these contributors were seasoned urbanists long before the earlier mentioned lamentations occurred. Each of these veteran researchers certainly understands, values, and appreciates the contributions made by those advocating more general theories. Furthermore, and to varying degrees, several have embraced or incorporated these ideas into their own research perspective. The point is, though, that while each chapter presented here is theoretically informed, a hallmark of each contributor's background is that they have avoided the siren call of a singular general theory.

Each has generally made the habit of keeping cities, urbanization, or urban phenomena as the focus, letting the dog wag the tail instead of vice versa.

PERSPECTIVES ON URBANIZATION

At first glance then, this collection of perspectives on urbanization appears very reasonably rather disparate in both a topical and geographic sense. A closer examination though identifies several themes across the ten chapters.

The process of urbanization and urban system development is addressed directly in three chapters and indirectly across several others. More generally, Geyer and Kontuly (chapter one) work to more finely tune the differential urbanization model. Previous models did not adequately provide for explaining the rural non-urban sector of the model, nor did they sufficiently detail earlier phases of urban development. To remedy these problems, the authors more clearly differentiate urbanization phases and better incorporate the process of counterurbanization into the model.

Within the context of a single entire country, Ianos (chapter five) takes up the challenges brought by urban system restructuring in the wake of totalitarian rule. The plight of "large habitats"—urban centers that absorbed more than their share of residential urban growth—is addressed in terms of how they came to be and the challenges they provide to planners.

In chapter nine, Aguilar and Alvarado examine a particular context for urbanization in terms of a metropolis at the top of the urban hierarchy. In "Globalization and the Restructuring of Urban Space in Mexico City," they analyze the connection between globalization and the development of a multinodal metropolis and present the implications for other large cities in the developing world.

Also in a megacity context, but more attentive to social groups is "Rich and Poor in Kolkata." Here Dutt and Halder propose a descriptive model drawing distinctions between the housing and asset ownership of slum dwellers and non-slum dwellers. The model, developed from a detailed social survey, presents a clear portrayal of the nature and character of poverty in the city.

Poverty in cities, of course, is not confined to developing countries. Tiwari (chapter ten) focuses on the interplay of ethnic and economic elements of poverty in inner city Winnipeg. He identifies two groups characterized by pervasive poverty– Aboriginals and single parent families and aboriginals – as illustrative of these ethnic and economic elements, respectively.

Bridging from Tiwari's consideration of social areas of cities, we can also find a corresponding social distinction (that is political and economic as well) between central cities and suburban areas with Akron, Ohio (chapter four). Noble, King, and Boateng use the politics of school funding to draw a clear divide between central city and suburb.

Planning activities and their impacts are central to three chapters. Pomeroy and Bennett (chapter seven), take advantage of the smaller spatial scale of municipal planning to identify a "bow wave" effect in the diffusion of land use regulations. The question they then consider is whether the wave arrives prior to or subsequent to development pressures.

Also related to planning in Pennsylvania is Benhart and Hawthorne's chapter on brownfields redevelopment. Using the case of Letterkenny Army Depot, a partially realigned military facility, they consider how reforms in state level planning activities enabled environmental planning efforts to assist in the base's redevelopment.

In chapter three, Richard Morrill considers the impact of growth management policies in fostering class distinctions and a gentrification effect in Seattle in the ten years subsequent to the state's Growth Management Act. While acknowledging the role of other forces, he concludes that growth management policies indeed "encouraged and enabled" gentrification.

Finally, and broadly in the spirit of planning for economic development, Gerhard Braun (chapter two) looks at the role universities and research activities may play in realizing the knowledge-based city. He posits that the mantra of "knowledge, knowledge, knowledge" is a bit more difficult to identify and capitalize upon but can play a positive role in the development process.

A COMMON THEME REVEALED

Happily, it must be said that there is one singular thread that very appropriately weaves all of these chapters together! As noted in the title and preface of this volume, this is a collection of essays in honor of Dr. Debnath Mookherjee. In celebrating the person and works of Dr. Mookherjee, this volume, hopefully, does indeed embody three particular facets of his character.

First, the wide-ranging nature of these chapters is a testament to the premium he has placed on intellectual diversity. A glance at his office shelves in Bellingham, Washington or the books found underarm as he leaves AAG and IGU meetings shows appreciation of a wide range of urban perspectives.

Secondly, the chapters largely speak to his keen appreciation of theory. In many a conference paper or panel session, his questions nearly always address the "theory of" aspect of a speaker's comments.

Finally, each chapter is submitted as an appreciation for his willingness, even an eagerness, to engage in intellectual debate that is balanced by genuine admiration and thoughtful respect for fellow colleagues and further tempered by a nurturing of younger scholars.

1 Historical Perspectives on Differential Urbanization

H.S. Geyer and T. Kontuly

During the early 1970s a turnaround from urbanization to counterurbanization was observed in the migration trends of a number of developed countries (Beale, 1975; Berry, 1976; Vining and Strauss, 1977; Vining and Kontuly, 1978). Later, during the 1980s, the counterurbanization trends in certain developed countries suddenly and unexpectedly started to subside (Cochrane and Vining, 1988; Champion, 1989). In certain cases the second turnaround seems to be continuing while in others it seems to be short-lived and we may once again see the return of full-fledged counterurbanization (Champion, 1989). During the same period, signs were also found of economic concentration forces in certain advanced developing countries beginning to yield to deconcentration. Originally, this process, coined as 'polarization reversal' by Harry Richardson (1977; 1980), only referred to industrial deconcentration in the Third World. Some time ago, however, the differential urbanization model was developed, tying polarization reversal as a process associated with the turning point in industrial concentration in a Third World setting to urbanization and counterurbanization as migration processes in the First World (Geyer, 1990; Geyer and Kontuly, 1996).

The differential urbanization model deals with three issues. First, it introduces polarization reversal as an intermediate phase of urban development between population concentration (urbanization) and deconcentration (counterurbanization) in the migration sequence (see Figure 1-1). Second, it shows how main and sub-stream migration can be used as indicators of the phase of development of the urban system of a country, irrespective of the country's level of economic development. Third, it recognizes the relevancy of 'productionism'[1] and 'environmentalism'[2] as forces that could drive main and sub-stream migration in First and Third World countries, irrespective of the specific combinations of factors that would create these forces in these countries.

Subsequently the theoretical foundation of the differential urbanization concept was expanded. To start, the maturing of urban systems was analyzed graphically based upon the stages of development of the French urban system (Geyer, 1996). In the analysis two sets of related findings were made. First, consistent with Fielding's (1989) view, is that there is a positive relationship between the net migration rate and settlement size during urbanization (compare Figure 1-1, stage II and Figure 1-2B) and a negative relationship during counterurbanization (compare Figure 1-1, stage VI and Figure 1-2F). Second, also consistent with trends in the French example (Fielding, 1989), is that there is a modal relationship between net migration and settlement size during the polarization reversal phase (compare Figure 1-1, stage IV and Figure 1-2D), with intermediate sized cities gaining more migrants than small or large cities overall. In addition, there are also several other relationships possible, that is, at the end of each of the intermediate stages (I, III, V, VII) of the differential urbanization model (compare Figures 1-1 and 1-2A, C, E, and G). Finally, the relevancy of the differential urbanization model to explain migration trends at the global and continental scale was investigated since the concept was initially only introduced at the national level (Geyer, 1998). The study found that certain urban agglomerations act as core cities at the global level, attracting migrants from all over the world, while lesser, but still prominent continental agglomerations serve as secondary cities. At the same time the latter also serve as core cities within their continental regions, while lesser, yet prominent national centres in these regions could be regarded as small centres in a global context.

Recently, the relevancy of elements of the concept of differential urbanization were tested positively in several countries (Bonifazi and Heins 2003; Champion 2003; Elliott, 1997; Gedik 2003; Geyer 2003; Heikkilä 2003; Kontuly and Dearden 2003; Kontuly and Geyer 2003; Mookherjee 2003; Nefedova and Treivish 2003; Tammaru, 2000, 2003). The exclusion of migration streams from non-urban to urban areas from the original model hampers its application in areas with high percentages of rural population (Pederson, 1999). In this chapter an attempt will be made to remedy the situation by looking at the role different economic and social sectors played in the evolution of urban systems, historically, and how these dynamics need to be interpreted in terms of the differential urbanization model. Referring to the development of post-industrialized societies, Kerr (1960: 358) once wrote: "This particular history gets written from the future into the present—what is currently happening comes from what is to be. The future is the cause and the present is the effect." In this chapter a similar approach is being followed, using differential urbanization patterns that are currently manifesting as a model to extrapolate backwards into the past. There are three scales of urban analysis possible, macro, meso, and micro. The macroscopic orientation in this chapter maximizes synthesis, but it also opens up new opportunities for empirical analysis.

SEQUENCES IN URBAN MATURATION

In the introduction to differential urbanization theory five propositions were made with regard to the development of urban systems (Geyer and Kontuly, 1996). In a slightly revised format it can be said that:

- Most urban systems initially go through a 'primate city phase' in which a large proportion of economic development and large numbers of migrants are attracted to one or a few primary centres.
- As the national urban system expands and matures, new urban centres are added to the lower ranks while many of those that already exist develop and move up through the ranks. In this process, economic development gets dispersed, while the urban system becomes spatially more integrated.
- Such expanding national urban systems develop various strata of territorially organized sub-systems, from the macro-level through the regional and sub-regional levels to the local level. Such urban sub-systems consist of groups of hierarchically arranged cities that normally interact more with one another inside the sub-system than with cities collectively in sub-systems elsewhere in the national system.
- The sequence of tendencies observed in the development of urban systems, first toward concentration and then toward dispersal is not limited to systems at the national level only, but can also manifest at each of the lower levels of territorially organized subsystems.
- In an expanding urban system, the odds normally favor the development of larger centres closer to primary centres, unless an outlying centre is located in an area with exceptional locational attributes.

Based on these propositions differential urbanization can be described as a sequence of urban development cycles, each cycle consisting of consecutive phases of urbanization, polarization reversal and counterurbanization. During urbanization, large cities gain proportionally more migrants than intermediate- and small-sized cities in a country. This phase is characterized by large-scale migration from peripheral regions, although intermediate sized and smaller cities in and around the core areas of a country usually also benefit from this first phase of mainstream migration. The urbanization phase is followed by polarization reversal when the growth of larger cities tend to taper down, due to factors associated with agglomeration diseconomies, while a larger proportion of migration is directed to secondary or regional cities than before. Secondary cities closer to the urban core areas still tend to gain more migrants during this phase than those located in the periphery during this phase, except in cases where new resources have been discovered or where areas have gained new strategic importance due to changing social and political circumstances. Finally counterurbanization sets in when more migrants tend to migrate to smaller cities than larger cities in the system. Here, the mainstream migration trend of the urbanization phase is reversed, although sub-stream migration to large cities may still continue.

The spatio-temporal model (Figure 1-1) shows how small, medium-sized and large cities are impacted by net internal migration over centuries[3]. It forms the backbone of the differential urbanization theory. The equality in the urban phases and the smooth and proportional tapering off of the curves in the model is an indication how groups of large, medium sized and small cities would evolve under fairly homogenous environmental conditions over time. Different methods of development intervention by governments due to different political, social, economic, and physical circumstances in countries would obviously result in distortions in the curves on the graph in real-life situations. In the spatio-temporal model, it is assumed that small, medium sized and large cities already exist. Also, rural (non-urban) areas are disregarded in the theory thus far, which leaves a gap in the theory. Two of the issues that remain to be addressed in this debate, therefore, are how urban settlements develop from the beginning and what their relationship is with the rural non-urban society.

THE ORIGIN OF URBAN SYSTEMS

Layers of human activities

Early in this century Weber (1929) developed a conceptual model explaining how different layers of economic activities of people affect the location of industries. Expanding on his conceptual model to include all the economic, social and organizational activities that are necessary to sustain human life, Figure 1-3 serves as an exploded diagram depicting the multi-dimensional character and complexity of community life as it unfolds over time (Geyer, 2001). Urban settlements originate from these activities. As Hauser (1965: 1) said: "It seems clear that the emergence and development of the city was necessarily a function of four factors: (1) the size of the total population; (2) the control of natural environment; (3) technological development; and (4) developments in social organization."

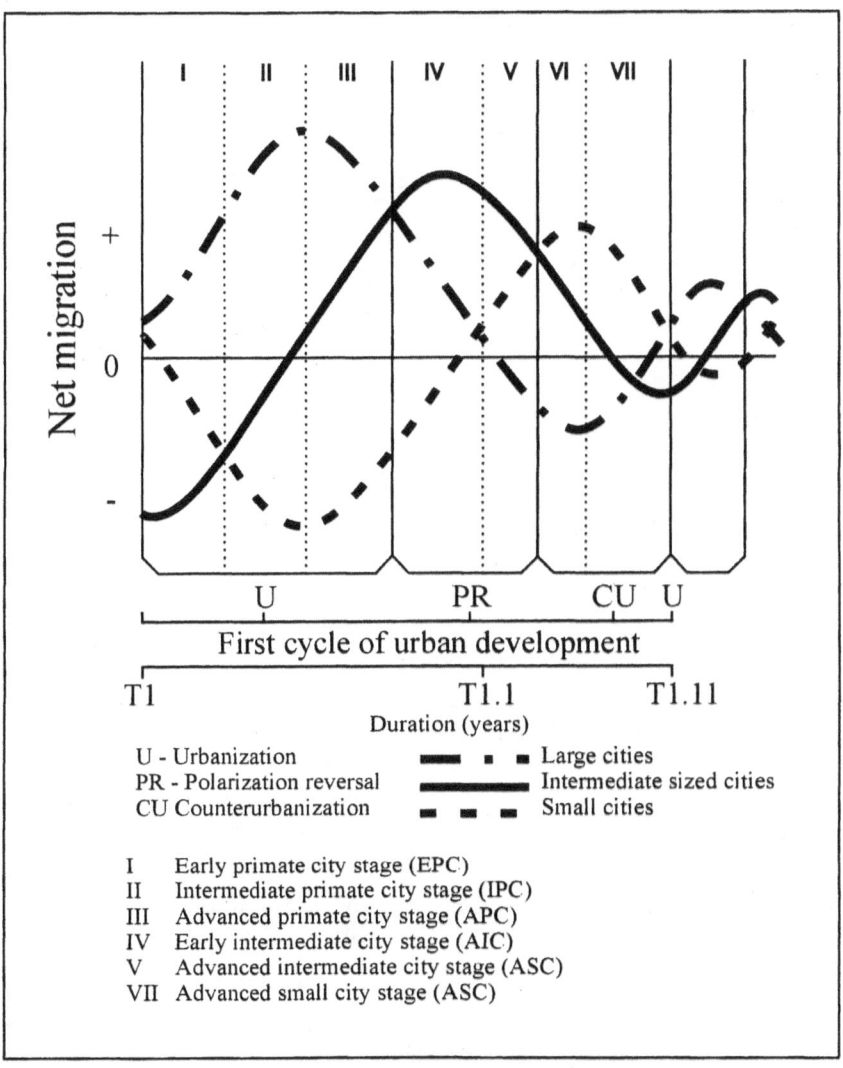

Figure 1-1
Cycle of Differential Urbanization in Middle and Advanced State of
Development of an Urban System

H.S. Geyer and T. Kontuly

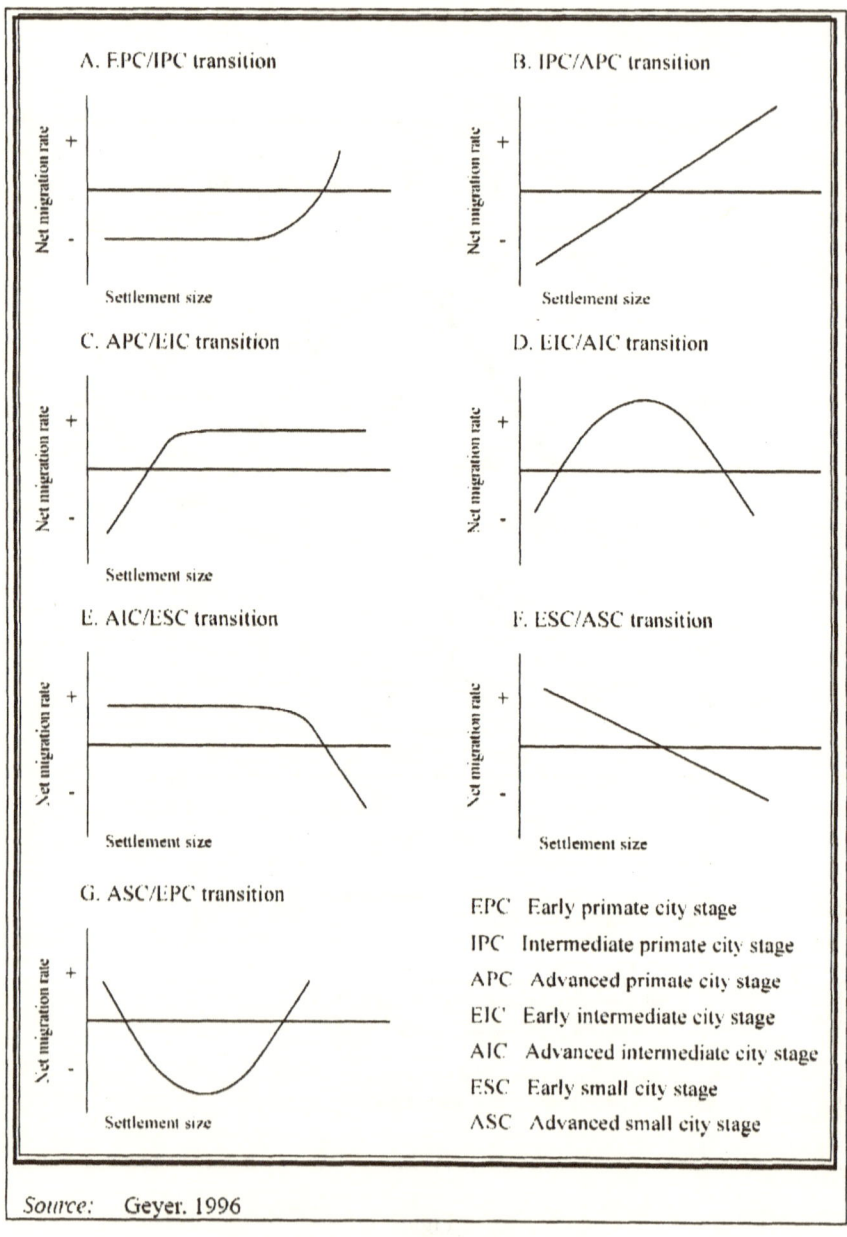

Figure 1-2
Changing Relationships between Net Migration Rates and Settlement Size
During Different Stages of Development in Differential Urbanization

The figure gives an indication of the range of social, economic and organizational factors that make up the constituting elements of a community's activities. Looking at the construct from the top downwards, it gives one an overall picture of the geographical location and density of human settlement patterns in an area, for example, the picture one sees when looking at an atlas superficially. As such, the map itself does not reveal much of the patterns of activities of the people living in that area, or the reasons why they settled in that particular fashion in the first place, unless one analyses the factors that influenced their decisions to migrate to the area. To be able to understand the logic behind the settlement patterns and the social and economic dynamics that drive the settlement process, one needs to study the layers of interrelated human activities shown in Figure 1-3. Only then can one comprehend the complexity of the settlement patterns on the map.

First the land's potential to sustain human life is a limiting factor. The resource potential of the land, combined with the ability of the people to utilise those resources in any of the levels of activities indicated in Figure 1-3, to a large extent determines the distribution and well-being of the people in that area. Three concepts, Zelinsky's (1971) 'mobility transition' and Hart's (1983) 'productionism' and 'environmentalism' cut across these layers as important factors determining the kinds of activities in which communities engage themselves and the settlement patterns that result from these activities. According to Zelinsky there is a direct relationship between the level of development of people, the level of control over their social, biological, economic, and demographic environment, and their mobility, physically and intellectually.

Applying this relationship to the early history of human settlement, settlements tended to be non-urban in character and spatially dispersed (Doxiadis, 1970). As technology improved, people acquired the ability to produce more food than they could consume. In the process, labour that was previously needed for hunting and food collection became increasingly redundant. Alternative non-agricultural occupations started to develop, spatial specialisation started occurring, and settlements began to acquire an urban character (Mumford 1961). Throughout history, urban settlements that emanated from first level activities in the human activities-model (Figure 1-3) served as market areas and places of social gathering, providing goods and services to local rural communities. In terms of Christaller's (1966) and Lösch's (1954) models these settlements would be regarded as 'central places.' Usually they are relatively small, widely dispersed, and local oriented, similar to the market place in von Thünen's (1966) 'isolated state.' Urban areas that arose from this first wave of the division of labour could be regarded as 'first wave' migration - the beginning of urbanization.

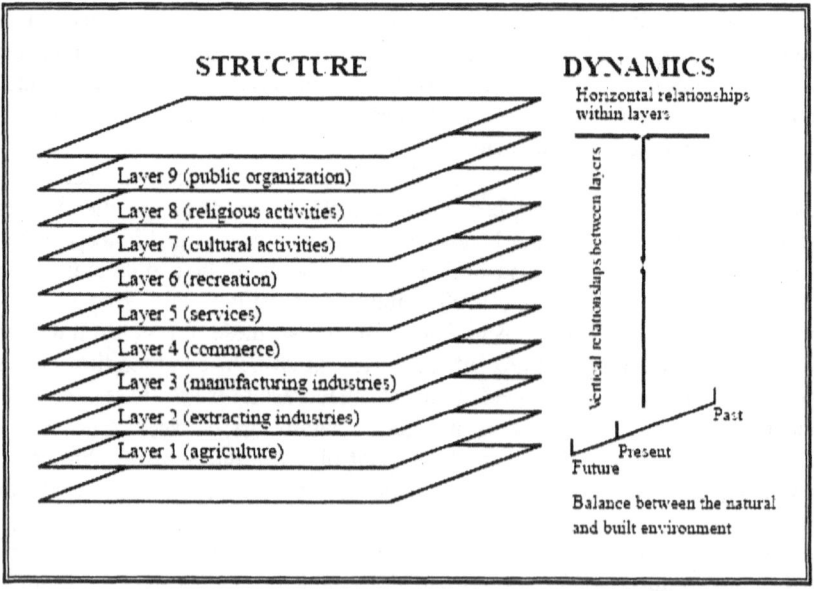

Figure 1-3
A Human Activities Model

Throughout history, settlements resulting from second layer (mining) activities (Figure 1-3) typically started out as 'non-central places' (Richardson 1973) because such mining activities occurred where the mineral deposits were located, not necessarily where the people lived at the time. However, large mineral deposits often led to large-scale mining activities that, in time, resulted in the development of prominent urban agglomerations that are dominating the urban scene in many parts of the world today.

The third (manufacturing) layer consists of factories that derive their input from the first two layers. Production and consumption goods are produced by this layer for businesses and for individuals operating in the other layers in the model, and thereby it enhances urban development resulting from activities in the first two layers. Over the past century, the factors that determine the location of industries and the positive and negative spin-offs industrial development had on almost all spheres of human existence have been an extremely fruitful area of research in many disciplines (Smith, 1971). In most cases it is the activities in this layer, combined with activities in the second layer, that transformed urban centres from ordinary local rural service centres into higher order centres of attraction.

Commerce is a fourth-layer activity. It is shown as a separate layer in the human activities model because trading most visibly occurs through formal and informal commercial activities that are associated with business districts and shopping centres in cities. But in actual terms commercial activities are not limited to commercial districts and shopping centres only. Economic exchange amongst business enterprises and people in all layers of the model forms part of commercial activities right from the beginning of civilisation. Wherever outlets are located that sell products (goods or services) originating from the other layers in the model, commercial activities occur. Although commerce is therefore indicated as a fourth layer activity, trading, as an activity occurs in all layers of the model all the time. Only when trading becomes concentrated enough to become visible, i.e. when central business or suburban shopping centres develop in urban areas, commercial activities become a distinct layer in the arrangement of human activities.

The professional services layer is a transitional layer bridging the lower four layers, where consumer goods are produced and sold, with the upper four where social needs are fulfilled. It covers a wide range of personal and professional services that are needed to sustain community life such as health, financial, intellectual, and civil services. Because most of these services are used directly by the public, they are spatially associated with activities in the commercial layer.

Activities in the upper four layers are all of a social nature, some spatially more exclusive than others. The uppermost layer, public organization, refers to all kinds of organisations that are designed to spatially, systematically, quantitatively and qualitatively keep society intact. They include activities such as organised politics, commerce, industry and agriculture, all of which are necessary to ensure order.

Continuity and scale of human activities

In the preceding discussion it is not suggested that there is necessarily chronology in the development of the layers in the model of human activities shown in Figure 1-3[4], although there often is. The exploded diagram does, however, give one a holistic view of the range of human activities that shape our urban systems. Running through the layers of activities in any particular study area enables one to better comprehend the factors that influence the spatial distribution of urban settlements in an area (Geyer, 2002b).

The organisation of economic space in the first (agricultural) layer and that of social space in the last (institutional) layer of the model are generally easily reconcilable with the concept of formal or homogenous regions. Social and economic organisation of activities in the layers in-between is more often spatially punctuated, and therefore, more readily associated with the concept of functional or nodal regions. The widely distributed rural population of the first layer serves as a market for the establishment of rural local service centres which provide goods and services to the local rural population—that is, non-basic activities (Alexandersson, 1959) in Christaller's central places. Activities in the other layers, especially mining and manufactured products are often produced for a market that is larger than the local centre, and as basic activities (Alexandersson, 1959), they increase the potential for urban explosion. For instance, the Industrial Revolution caused many people to leave rural areas to become involved in activities in the second, third and fourth layers in the human activities model (Figure 1-3). This migration was essentially productionism oriented (Hart, 1983; Geyer and Kontuly, 1996) causing unprecedented urban explosions in many parts of the world at the time. Urban pressures caused by the Industrial Revolution triggered the expansion of transport services, i.e. activities in layer five, which, in turn, augmented urban sprawl. The development of the department store around the 1960s, i.e. fourth layer activities revolutionised commerce and multi-nodal urban structures worldwide. More recently, the industrial shift from fordism to post-fordism (especially in third layer activities) and explosions in the information and communication technologies had an equally dramatic effect on urban development globally (Castells, 1993; 1996; Graham, 1998; 1999).

As mentioned earlier migration induced by the second to fifth layers are traditionally productionism oriented. Agricultural and recreational induced activities, in contrast, are often environmentalism oriented. If one really wants to understand the dynamics of differential urbanization and of main and sub-stream migration, especially questions about when and how pull and push factors work under different circumstances, one needs to take those activities into account that impact significantly on the urban and rural environment on all the layers on the human activities model (Figure 1-3) (Geyer 2002a; 2002b).

Due to large core-peripheral differentials in developing nations, urban areas often exert exceptionally strong forces of attraction onto rural areas that are lagging behind the more economically advanced communities in core areas (Todaro, 1982). Different streams of rural-urban and urban-rural migration within such countries are normally determined by productionism and environmentalism driven considerations respectively. In productionism driven migration the younger and/or less developed section of the population often tend to migrate from rural or lagging regions to urban areas in search of better prospects of a livelihood (Hart, 1983). Affluent people who previously lived in large Third World cities, areas that are now being targeted by the production oriented migrants from lagging regions, tend to migrate to environmentally more serene or safer areas inside the cities or to less urbanized areas elsewhere, where they can escape from the hustle and bustle of city life.

Similar productionism and environmentalism-driven migration patterns are observable in developed countries, but where productionism-driven trends are dominant in developing countries, simply because the proportion of less affluent people in such countries are higher than in developed countries, environmentalism-driven migration is becoming a more prominent trend in the latter than previously. Large scale productionism driven migration in developing countries tend to augment spatial conversion, while counterurbanization in developed countries tends to reduce regional differences. Due to the high levels of spatial and economic integration between urban and rural land uses in certain parts of Western Europe and North America, some of the traditional differences between them have largely been eradicated in recent decades (Geyer, 1996). In fact, in large parts of these industrialised regions, especially in Western Europe, rural and urban land uses are intermingled to such an extent that the question could well be asked whether the traditional meaning of the term 'rural' or 'periphery' still applies to these areas. This observation was already made by Kötter (1964: 27) as early as the 1960s when he wrote: "In the modern mass society the old rural-urban dichotomy is being replaced increasingly by the rural-urban continuum, with the metropolis at the one end and the remote village at the other. . . . Tourism is a typical phenomenon of our mobile, industrial society, characterized by a growing amount of leisure time. Vacation seasons in Western Europe bring about a real 'migration of the nations', with millions crossing national borders toward regions with scenic landscapes and recreation facilities. More and more in this time previously isolated areas are opened by this process."

In general terms one can conclude that, the effect of the often opposing concepts of productionism- and environmentalism-driven migration can be clearly observed at higher levels of spatial aggregation, i.e. at the national and international levels. Whether one deals with a developed or developing nation, rural-to-urban migration and migration from smaller to larger urban areas is usually productionism oriented, while urban-to-rural migration and migration from large to smaller centres is often environmentalism driven. Globally, similar productionism and environmentalism driven tendencies can be observed between the more developed components of nations migrating from less to more developed countries, and from countries that are environmentally less attractive to more attractive areas (Geyer, 1998).

At the micro scale migration trends tend to be much more complex, but migration inside the metropolitan areas that is directed towards the outskirts of the city often tends to be environmentalism-driven. Housing in exclusive areas inside large cities remains popular but because its availability is often limited and expensive it can only be afforded by a small percentage of the people. Even older areas inside cities that are 'rediscovered' and upgraded from time to time, soon fall in the exclusive category—housing that can be afforded by only a few (Bourne, 1992). Good housing is normally more readily available at more affordable prices in outlying rural oriented service centres on the perimeter of the city, converting them into dormitory areas of metropolitan areas. Environmentalism-driven migration at the local level, therefore, results in higher income groups deconcentrating towards affluent areas inside the cities and to satellite cities closer by, while lower income groups originating from rural areas often tend to settle in sprawling low-cost suburban areas closer to areas of employment inside the perimeter of the large cities.

Following on the analysis of the relationship between population redistribution patterns and the human activity model in this section, one of the outstanding issues that still needs to be addressed, is what the likely patterns of rural-to-urban migration are that would have preceded the idealized patterns of differential urbanization shown in the spatio-temporal model (Figure 1-1). Likely answers will be sought from an analogy between the early history of urban evolution in Europe and the human activities model depicted in Figure 1-3.

URBAN DEVELOPMENT IN HISTORY

There is evidence of the existence of *Homo sapiens* dates dating back to the Upper Paleolithic period, about 50,000 years ago (Easton, 1955). In his synopsis of early human settlement Hauser (1965) maintains that there could have been between five and ten million people in the world by the end of the Neolithic period, increasing to between 200 and 300 million by the beginning of the Christian era. By the beginning of the modern era in 1650 the population increased to approximately 500 million. It took all the millennia up to the 1850 for the world population to reach the first billion mark. The second billion took only seventy-five years, the third, thirty-seven years, and, increasing faster and faster all the time, the six billionth baby was born at the turn of the third millennium (Geyer, 2002b).

It took a long time for humans to learn how to live together in urban agglomerations. The first cities appeared around the middle of the fourth millennium B.C. and it took two thousand five hundred years before most of the urban functions, depicted in the layers in Figure 3, were operative (Mumford, 1961). Throughout history urbanization occurred in waves as and when different peoples pioneered uninhabited areas or conquered new territories (Wallerstein, 1974; Tellier, 1997). In West and Central Europe most urban settlements developed between 1250 and 1350 (Pounds, 1994). It is estimated, according to Hauser (1965), that by 1800 about 15 million people lived in cities of more than 100,000, about 21 million in cities of 20,000 and over, 27 million in cities larger than 5,000, with the majority living in rural areas and rural villages. Between 1800 and 1950, the world population increased by over 250 per cent, but over the same period the population of urban areas of 5,000, 20,000, and 100,000 or more inhabitants, increased by approximately 2,600, 2,300, and 2,000 per cent respectively. As a consequence, approximately 36 per cent of the world's population was rural, while 30 per cent lived in urban places of 5,000 inhabitants and more, about 21 per cent in places of 20,000 and over, and 13 per cent in places of 100,000 and over by the middle of the twentieth century. Even by 1950 only approximately four per cent of the world's population lived in places of a million or more inhabitants (Geyer, 2002b).

To understand the fundamentals of urban development, a question that needs to be answered is why and where urban settlements developed and whether there is chronology in the process.

As an answer to the first question many reasons are offered in the literature. Right in the beginning, developments such as the domestication of animals and food growing helped transforming the Neolithic peasant village into centres with an urban character (Easton, 1955). Other important incentives included the establishment of common centres for religious worship and administrative control, shelter from natural elements and from attacks from other people. Later on, after the beginning of the Modern Era, agricultural productivity, crop yields, energy sources, and transport costs became important factors influencing the location of centres, the former tending to lift the ceiling on urbanization, the latter two constraining urban progress. Fuel supplies, for instance, severely limited urban development during the nineteenth century (Van der Woude, et al., 1990).

In many areas in Europe intensive urbanization was initially limited to locations that could be reached by water transport. Urban nodes developed at crossroads, at river fords, in sheltered bays, at the foot of passes, and at strategic locations such as fortified castles. The Rhine and the Danube effectively marked the limits of Roman colonization in central Europe. Peripheral areas such as England and northern Gaul (France) only had small urban populations. Even at the height of the Roman Empire most urban settlements were no more than villages, housing only a few hundred people (Hohenberg and Lees, 1985). Advances in transport technology reduced these locational limitations later on. As a result improved access to products, and gains from trade, increased spatial options for urban settlement.

As time went on, factors influencing urbanization became more and more complex, making it sometimes difficult to distinguish between the causes and location of urban development in specific areas. Limiting factors included gross national product per head, the level of industrialisation, export and import, international migration, population density, population size, urban-rural population ratios, dominant cultures, forms of consumption, the form of government, availability of human and natural resources, topography, and climate (Bairoch, 1990; Kötter, 1964)

Advances in industrial technology and organisation remain important factors in the growth and decline of urban development throughout history. According to Pounds (1994), important changes occurred in the scale and organisation of manufacturing during the millennium preceding the beginning of the modern era. Production became a specialised activity resulting in a large increase in output, and as a consequence, the trading of goods. Industrial development could not, however, have flourished without a rural population at the time. Cities and towns (and the needs for manufactured products) grew as a result of immigration from rural areas, and most were maintained only by continued migration from rural areas (Pounds, 1994). Referring to 19th century migration, Bengtsson (1990: 192) says:

> Students of migration have often distinguished between 'push' and 'pull' factors. The industrial demand for labour could be regarded as a structural 'pull' factor and fairly insensitive to short-term fluctuations. Similarly, the increase of productivity on agriculture could be characterized as a structural 'push' factor.

The decrease in the farm population during the early urbanization phase of the Modern Era was not only a result of technical progress, however. Unfavorable circumstances and low farm incomes in an otherwise prospering economy, and a 'desire to participate in a more urban way of life' motivated many people to leave for the cities, despite the apparent lack in employment opportunities for most at the time. Urbanization was, therefore, a 'movement induced by certain values common to society as a whole', and a need of people from the farming communities, to 'attain a living standard corresponding to that of the industrial population' (Kötter, 1964). This view is still being held in the Third World where there is an obvious gap between rural and urban living conditions (Todaro, 1982).

Industrial development in the Modern Era in Europe went through three phases according to Pounds (1994). Initially, production was aimed at self-sufficiency. This was the period of 'economies of no markets'. Between the 10th and 12th centuries manufacturing shifted from monasteries and rural areas to the expanding urban areas, and from non-specialised to specialised production. Towards the Middle Ages, a gradual movement of craft industries occurred from the towns to the countryside. According to Pounds (1994), the latter trend continued through the sixteenth and seventeenth centuries, which partially explains why most towns failed to grow significantly after the 14th century.

By 1330 most urban settlements in Western Europe were still small market towns and villages because medieval society was predominantly agricultural. People working the fields around these towns lived there and sold their produce in the market in town. At that time, 3,000 of the 3267 urban areas were small towns and villages. Only nine cities were regarded as 'very large' with populations exceeding 25,000, 38 were 'large' centres with between 10,000 and 25,000 inhabitants, and 220 were intermediate sized centres with up to 10,000 inhabitants (Pounds, 1994).

By 1500 people producing specialised industrial goods could be found in most small towns. "Many failed to attract enough settlers and trade to survive the economic contractions of the later Middle Ages, but others developed more complex economic structures and extended the size of their marketing region over time" (Hohenberg and Lees, 1985: 51). Regional administrative functions distinguished intermediate-sized cities from local market towns. Most of the former only occurred in the core areas of Europe.

The counterurbanization phase that started in Europe in the 1970s (Beale, 1975) was not the first in the region's history of urban development. The first slump in urbanization occurred during the end of the Roman Empire when technical insufficiency, civil strife, and attacks from Germanic tribes led to the unraveling of urban development (Pounds, 1994). New advances in agricultural production technology between the Sixth and Eighth centuries led to the beginning of the next wave of European urbanization, but it took another two centuries of improvement of technology and trade before the economic viability of towns was secured. The second slump occurred during the latter stages of the Middle Ages (Hohenberg and Lees, 1985). Throughout the early history of civilization, technical advancements had a positive effect allowing urban development to progress. Only social repression such as religious closure during the Middle Ages and political invasions earlier on, hampered urban progress. If one were to disregard the inhibiting effects social repression had on progress in urban development over the ages, a relatively clear picture can be formed in the mind's eye of how unabated urban development would have evolved over the years. This is what will be attempted in the next section.

DIFFERENTIAL URBANIZATION IN HISTORY

Drawing from the human activities model (Figure 1-3) and Doxiadis' (1970) phases of human interaction patterns which are based on the history of human settlement patterns[5], a number of postulations can be made about urban development early on in the human settlement process.

Beginning with Doxiadis' (1970) second phase of human interaction patterns, people were almost exclusively dependent on the land for their existence. Most of the human activities at this stage occur in the first layer in Figure 1-3. Many human settlements at this time are not permanent, and those that are permanent are non-urban in character. These settlements are also still very small and sparsely dispersed because the prevailing agricultural and transport technology do not yet allow for large groups of people to coexist in the same area. Socially, the communities tend to be xenophobic, isolated and even hostile towards one another, because they are mostly engaged in a subsistence economy. If trade does occur, it occurs almost exclusively amongst members of own communities. Very little interaction occurs between communities, a situation that resembles the pre-industrial phase in Friedmann's (1966) core-periphery model.

Later on, as agricultural practices improve, the kinetic fields of people (Doxiadis, 1970) become smaller, and food production increases significantly. This, together with excess labour that increasingly becomes redundant in the agricultural sector, gradually stimulates urban oriented industrial, commercial and service activities. These urban activities are still unsophisticated and mostly locally oriented at this time, resembling perhaps early signs of Rostow's (1960) traditional society[6].

The increase in the numbers of people involved in non-agricultural activities leads to the transformation of the rural settlements of the previous era into urban settlements, but because the activities are mostly local in character at this stage, the settlement sizes do not tend to vary significantly. The distribution of settlements in this phase of urbanization therefore largely represents the central place distribution of low order settlements in accordance with Christaller's (1966) and Lösch's (1954) models. Early on in this phase it seems logical to assume that most migration occurred between rural areas and local urban settlements. At this stage the 'urban establishment phase' comes to an end.

The second phase signifies the beginning of the 'urban differentiation' period, the beginning of which could perhaps be associated with the mercantile period. People are now entering the Modern Era. Advances in agriculture, industry and transport make trade possible over longer distances than before. The urban system now gets transformed from a local oriented Christaller-like central place system to a more open network-oriented urban system (Gradman 1916; Pottier, 1963; Janelle, 1968; Whebell, 1969; Vance, 1970; de Vries; 1984;

and Hohenberg and Lees, 1985) which also contains non-central places (Christaller, 1966) located in areas where there are viable economic, strategic, social and other locational attributes (Richardson, 1973). Migration from the agricultural sector to the urban sector continues to be determined by technological advances in both sectors. The division of labour broadens and the urban and rural society becomes culturally, socially, and economically more structured. A fully-fledged urban hierarchy of small, intermediate sized, and large cities begins to develop, a situation that is reflected in the first phase of urbanization in the temporal model of differential urbanization (Figure 1-1).

While most migration occurred from rural (non-urban) areas to small urban settlements nearby during the period of urban establishment, differential urbanization patterns start occurring during the phase of urban differentiation. Interurban migration begins to appear on a visible scale. In net migration terms, small and intermediate sized urban areas that have gained population over extended periods of time now start losing migrants to larger urban centres.

Throughout the period of urban evolution, but especially during the first two periods of urban settlement—i.e. the phase of urban establishment and the phase of urban differentiation—people keep on leaving the agricultural sector to settle in urban areas. There does not seem to be an apparent lower limit to the depopulation of the agricultural sector at this stage. Although indications are that the depopulation of this sector has been declining during the latter phases of urban system maturity in most developed countries, increasing production output of agricultural holdings due to advances in agricultural and transport technology—that is, processes that are associated with the concept of 'factory farming'—keep on pushing the farming population down in even the most advanced countries of the world.

The urban differentiation period comes to an end when the urbanization period winds down. At this stage the urban development process has reached a turning point; it has started from a position of maximum divergence to one of maximum convergence. The onset of polarization reversal followed by counterurbanization signifies the beginning of the return from maximum convergence to a state of increasing divergence – i.e. the turning point in an inverted U-curve of urban concentration over time. During the period of convergence the urban society becomes transformed from Zelinsky's (1971) 'premodern traditional society' to his 'advanced society'.

It is anticipated, however, that during the super advanced stage of urban maturity, i.e. a stage that coincides with Zelinsky's (1971) fifth phase of super mobility, highly mobile members of advanced communities (the economic *élite*) may move into non-urban areas for the sake of improving their living environment. Evidence of this form of environmentalism can now be observed on a visible scale in the most advanced sectors of society in countries in Western Europe, North America and on a smaller scale elsewhere in the world. This is a disguised form of 'ruralization' however, because these newcomers are economically still very much linked to the urban sector. They have very little in common with the agricultural communities, except their places of residence. The association seems to be generally mutually beneficial, however, because the urban invasion of rural areas generally leads to an inflation of rural property prices and capital that flows into such areas often leads to the upgrading of civil infrastructure in the areas.

The process of urban invasion of the rural areas of super advanced societies is often associated with subsequent wave-like population redistribution processes[7]. (see Geyer, 2002d for a more explicit description). First, people (most of them the economic *élite*, i.e. those that have moved from more central city locations to suburbanized areas during an earlier phase of urban development) start moving to satellite centres on the fringe of core areas (Gordon, 1979). A variety of factors such as improved transportation technology and infrastructure, high immigration to certain large centres (Frey, 2002), and an increasing crime rate (Berry, 1976), induces this deconcentration process. Most people that move out of the cities maintain strong direct economic and social ties with the city centres causing the commuting areas of such large centres to expand significantly (Pumain, 2002). Later on, deconcentration occurs beyond the outer limits of the expanded commuting areas of large centres. First the larger, but later on also the smaller rural centres in the outer periphery now start gaining migrants (Vining and Strauss, 1977). At this stage core areas may start losing population in absolute terms, but this does not necessarily signify an economic dissociation between the people that deconcentrate and the core regions. Information technology may allow people in this category to maintain strong indirect economic ties with the core regions despite the larger physical distances between them (Castells, 1993; Graham, 1998; 1999).

This stage of system wide deconcentration is often associated with an increase in the cosmopolitan content of the central core cities. Immigrants move into ethnic neigbourhoods that are becoming commonplace in high immigration metropolitan areas while the less qualified sector of the local population (i.e. those that have followed the economic *élite* to the core cities during the convergence phase) start suburbanizing. Eventually, the latter may follow the economic *élite* to inner and outer peripheral regions (Frey, 2002) for the same reasons they have followed the *élite* to the core regions during the convergence phase. At this stage, well-established immigrants that are being undercut by new international migrants in low wage jobs in the cities may start moving to suburban neighbourhoods (Geyer, 2002d).

SUMMARY

In his assessment of the differential urbanization model (Geyer and Kontuly, 1993), Pedersen (2000) suggested two areas in which the model could be improved, (i) the inclusion of the rural non-urban sector in the model and (ii) an explanation of the earlier phases of urban development. Subsequent tests of the model (Geyer, 2003; Kontuly and Geyer, 2003) confirmed this weakness of the model. An attempt has been made in this chapter to address these two outstanding issues. Looking at general patterns of urban evolution worldwide over the ages, this chapter suggests two phases of urban development. First an urban system starts from a position of maximum divergence, that is the phase of urban establishment when rural settlements gradually turn into urban areas. Later on the urban system advances to the urban differentiation phase when certain urban areas grow faster then others. As a result of the impact of main and substream migration in the process of differential urbanization (Geyer, 2002a; 2002c; 1996; Geyer and Kontuly, 1993) an urban hierarchy, consisting of large-, intermediate-, and small-sized urban settlements, develops. The urban differentiation phase ends when the urbanization phase (see Figure 1-1 and Figure 1-2B) comes to an end, i.e. when the urban system's condition of convergence reaches a relative maximum. Subsequently, polarization reversal and later on, counterurbanization sets in to begin the process of urban divergence. When the growth path of an urban system that has gone through the sequence, is plotted on a graph indicating urban concentration over time, it forms an inverted U-shaped curve, from divergence to convergence and back towards divergence.

1. Productionism driven migration occurs when employment is a higher priority to migrants than good living conditions.
2. In environmentalism driven migration the environment and good living conditions are a higher priority than good employment.
3. The reader is reminded that the vertical (y) axis in Figure 3 is linear, while the horizontal (x) axis reflects time in an inverted log scale, compacting time towards the left of the graph.
4. This was demonstrated in the discussion of the commercial activities above.
5. Here the *ceteris paribus* conditions have to apply because factors such as hostile invasions, cultural and climatic differences and many other variables could affect the duration of change in the model.
6. Although the sequence of Rostow's model has been questioned, many of the characteristics of the phases in his model are accurate.
7. These migration waves are by no means the only migration patterns to be discerned. In addition to major migration patterns a variety of minor (substream) migration patterns may occur simultaneously (Geyer, 1996; 2002a; 2002b)

REFERENCES

Alexandersson, G. (1959). "City-Forming and City-Serving Production." in Mayer, H.M. and Kohn, C.F. (eds.) *Readings in Urban Geography*. Chicago: University of Chicago Press.

Bairoch, P. (1990). "The Impact of Crop Yields, Agricultural Productivity, and Transport Costs on Urban Growth Between 1800 and 1910." In Van der Woude, A. D., Hayami, A .& de Vries, J. (Eds.) *Urbanization in History: A process of dynamic interactions*. Oxford: Claredon Press. pp.134-151.

Beale, C.L. (1975). "The Recent Shift of United States Population to Nonmetropolitan Areas, 1970-75." *International Regional Science Review* 2:113-122.

Bengtsson, T. (1990). "Migration, Wages, and Urbanization in Sweden in the Nineteenth Century" in Van der Woude, A. D., Hayami, A. & de Vries, J. (Eds.) *Urbanization in History: A process of dynamic interactions*. Oxford: Claredon Press.

Berry, B.J.L. (1976). "The Counterurbanization Process: Urban America Since 1970." *Urban Affairs Annual Review* 11:17-30.

Bonifazi, C. and F. Heins (2003). "Testing the Differential Urbanization Model for Italy." *Tijdschrift voor Economische en Sociale Geografie*, 94:23-37.

Bourne, L. S. (1992). "Population Turnaround in the Canadian Inner City: Contextual Factors and Social Consequences." *Canadian Journal of Urban Research*, 1:66-89.

Castells, M. (1993). "European Cities, the Informational Society, and the Global Economy." *Tijdschrift voor Economische en Sociale Geografie*, 84:247-257.

Castells, M. (1996). *The Rise of the Network Society*. Oxford: Blackwell.

Champion, A.G. (1989). "Counterurbanization: The Conceptual and Methodological Challenge," in Champion, A.G. (ed.) *Counterurbanization: The Changing Pace and Nature of Population Deconcentration*. London: Edward Arnold. pp.19-33.

Champion, T. (2003). "Testing the Differential Urbanization Model in Great Britain." *Tijdschrift voor Economische en Sociale Geografie*, 94:11-22.

Christaller, W. (1966). *Central Places of Southern Germany*. Baskin C.W. (Trl.) Englewood Cliffs, NJ: Prentice-Hall.

Cochrane, S.G. and D.R. Vining, Jr. (1988). "Recent Trends in Migration between Core and Peripheral Regions in Developed and Advanced Developing Countries." *International Regional Science Review*, 11:215-243.

de Vries, J. (1984). *European Urbanization, 1500-1800*. London: Methuen.

Doxiadis, C.A. (1970). "Man's Movement and His Settlements." *Ekistics*. 29:296-321.

Easton, S.C. (1955). *The Heritage of the Past: From the Earliest Times to the Close of the Middle Ages*. New York: Rinehart & Co.

Elliott, J. R. (1997). "Cycles Within the System: Metropolitanisation and Internal Migration in the U.S., 1965-90." *Urban Studies*, 34:21-41.

Fielding, A.J. (1989). "Migration and Urbanization in Western Europe." *The Geographical Journal*, 155:60-69.

Frey, W.H. (2002). "A History of Recent Urban Development in the United States," in H. S. Geyer (ed.), *International Handbook of Urban Systems: Studies of Urbanization and Migration in Advanced and Developing Countries*. Cheltenham, Glos.: Edward Elgar.

Friedmann, J. (1966). *Regional Development Policy: A Case Study of Venezuela*. Cambridge, Mass.: MIT Press.

Gedik, A. (2003). "Differential Urbanization in Turkey." *Tijdschrift voor Economische en Sociale Geografie*, 94:100-111.

Geyer, H.S. (1990). "Implications of Differential Urbanization on Deconcentration in the Pretoria-Witwatersrand-Vaal Triangle Area (PWV), South Africa." *Geoforum*, 21:385-396,

Geyer, H.S. (1996). "Expanding the Theoretical Foundation of Differential Urbanization." *Tijdschrift voor Economische en Sociale Geografie*, 87(1):44-59.

Geyer, H.S. (1998). "Differential Urbanization and International Migration: an Urban Systems Approach," In C. Gorter, P. Nijkamp, and J. Poot (eds.) *Crossing Borders: Regional and Urban Perspectives on International Migration*. Aldershot: Ashgate.

Geyer, H.S. (2001). "Development Planning Transition in South Africa," in H.C. Marais, Y. Methien, N.S. Jansen van Rensburg, M.P. Maaga, G.F. de Wet, and C.J. Coetzee (eds), *Sustainable Social Development: Critical Dimensions*. Pretoria, Network Publishers.

Geyer, H.S. (2002a) "An Exploration in Migration Theory," in H. S. Geyer (ed.), *International Handbook of Urban Systems: Studies of Urbanization and Migration in Advanced and Developing Countries*. Cheltenham, Glos.: Edward Elgar.

Geyer, H.S. (2002b) "On Urban Systems Evolution," in H. S. Geyer (ed.), *International Handbook of Urban Systems: Studies of Urbanization and Migration in Advanced and Developing Countries*. Cheltenham, Glos.: Edward Elgar.

Geyer, H.S. (2002c). "The Fundamentals of Urban Space," in H. S. Geyer (ed.), *International Handbook of Urban Systems: Studies of Urbanization and Migration in Advanced and Developing Countries*. Cheltenham, Glos.: Edward Elgar.

Geyer, H.S. (2002d) "The Urban Future" in H. S. Geyer (ed.), *International Handbook of Urban Systems: Studies of Urbanization and Migration in Advanced and Developing Countries*. Cheltenham, Glos.: Edward Elgar.

Geyer, H.S. (2003). "Differential Urbanization in South Africa: A Further Exploration." *Tijdschrift voor Economische en Sociale Geografie*, 94:89-99.

Geyer, HS and T.M. Kontuly. (1996). "A Theoretical Foundation for the Concept of Differential Urbanization," in N Hansen, KJ Button and P. Nijkamp (eds.), *Regional Policy and Regional Integration*. Vol. 6 of Modern Classics in Regional Science. Cheltenham: Edward Elgar.

Gordon, P. (1979). "Deconcentration Without A 'Clean Break'." *Environment and Planning A*, 11: 281-290.

Gradmann, R. (1916). *Schwäbische Städte*. Gesellschaft für Erdkunde zu Berlin. April, 8.

Graham, S. (1998) "The End of Geography or the Explosion of Place? Conceptualizing Space, Place and Information Technology." *Progress in Human Geography*, 22:165-185.

Graham, S. (1999) "Global Grids of Glass: On Cities, Telecommunications and Planetary Urban Networks." *Urban Studies*, 36: 929-949.

Hart, T. (1983) "Transport and Economic Development, the Historical Dimension," in K.J. Button and D. Gillingwater (eds.). *Transport, Location and Spatial Policy*. Aldershot, Hants: Gower.

Hauser, P.M. (1965). "Urbanization: An Overview," in Hauser, P.M. and L.F. Schnore (eds.) *The Study of Urbanization*. New York: Wiley.

Heikkilä, A. (2003). "Differential Urbanization in Finland." *Tijdschrift voor Economische en Sociale Geografie*, 94: 49-63.

Hohenberg, P.M. and H.L. Lees (1985). *The Making of Urban Europe, 1000-1950*. Cambridge, Mass.: Harvard University Press.

Janelle, D.G. (1968). "Central Place Development in a Time Space Framework." *The Professional Geographer*, 20:5-10.

Kerr, C. (1960). "Changing Social Structures" in Moore, W.E. and Feldman, A.S. (eds.) *Labor Commitment and Social Change in Developing Areas*. New York: Social Science Research Council.

Kontuly, T. and B. Dearden. (2003). "Testing the Temporal Characterization of the Differential Urbanization Model in Western Germany, 1939-2010." *Tijdschrift voor Economische en Sociale Geografie*, 94:64-74.

Kontuly, T. and H.S. Geyer. (2003). "Lessons Learned from Testing the Differential Urbanization Model." *Tijdschrift voor Economische en Sociale Geografie*, 94:124-128.

Kötter, H. (1964). "Changes in Urban-Rural Relationships in Industrial Society," in Anderson, N (ed.) *Urbanism and Urbanization, Volume 2 in International Studies in Sociology and Anthropology*. Ishwaran K (2nd. ed.) Leiden, Netherlands: Brill.

Lösch, A. (1954). *The Economics of Location*. New Haven: Yale University Press

Mookherjee, D. (2003). "Differential Urbanization Model: The Case of a Developing Country, India 1961-91." *Tijdschrift voor Economische en Sociale Geografie*, 94: 38-48.

Mumford, L. (1961). *The City in History: It's Origins, It's Transformations, and It's Prospects*. San Diego: Harcourt Brace Jovanovich Publishers.

Nefedova, T. and A. Treivish. (2003). "Differential Urbanization in Russia." *Tijdschrift voor Economische en Sociale Geografie*, 94: 75-88.

Pedersen P.O. (1999) (Book review) H.S. Geyer and T.M. Kontuly, *Differential Urbanization: Integrating Spatial Models*. London: Arnold. *Development and Change*, 30: 403-404.

Pottier, P. (1963). "Axes de Communication et Developement Economicque." *Review Economique*. 14: 58-132.

Pounds, N.J.G. (1994). *An Economic History of Medieval Europe*. London: Longman.

Pumain, D. (2002) "The French Urban System" in H. S. Geyer (ed.), *International Handbook of Urban Systems: Studies of Urbanization and Migration in Advanced and Developing Countries*. Cheltenham, Glos.: Edward Elgar, pp.

Richardson, H.W. (1973). *Economic Growth Theory*. London: MacMillan.

Richardson, H.W. (1977). *City Size and National Strategies in Developing Countries*. World Bank Staff Working Report, Washington.

Richardson, H.W. (1980). "Polarization Reversal in Developing Countries." *Papers of the Regional Science Association*, 4:67-85.

Rostow, W.W. (1960). *The Stages of Economic Growth: a Non-Communist Manifesto*. London: Cambridge University Press.

Smith, D.M. (1971) *Industrial Location: An Economic Geographical Analysis*. New York: Wiley.

Tammaru, T. (2000). "Differential Urbanisation and Primate City Growth in Soviet and Post-Soviet Estonia." *Tijdschrift voor Economische en Sociale Geografie*, 91:20-30.

Tammaru, T. (2003) "Urban and Rural Population Change in Estonia: Patterns of Differentiated and Undifferentiated Urbanization." *Tijdschrift voor Economische en Sociale Geografie*, 94:112-123.

Tellier, L. (1997). "A Challenge for Regional Science: Revealing and Explaining the Global Spatial Logic of Economic Development." *Papers in Regional Science*, 76:371-384.

Todaro, M.P. (1982). *Economics for a Developing World: An Introduction to Principles, Problems, and Policies*. Harlow: Longman.

Vance, J.E. (1970). *The Merchant's World: The Geography of Wholesaling*. Englewood Cliffs: Prentice-Hall.

Van der Woude, A.D.; de Vries, J. and Hayami, A. (1990) "Introduction: The Hierarchies, Provisioning, and Demographic Patterns of Cities," in Van der

Woude, A. D., Hayami, A. & de Vries J. (Eds.) *Urbanization in History: A Process of Dynamic Interactions.* Oxford: Claredon Press.pp.1-19.

Vining, D.R. Jr. and A. Strauss (1977). "A Demonstration that the Current Deconcentration of Population in the United States is a Clean Break with the Past." *Environment and Planning A*, 9:751-758.

Vining, D.R., Jr. and T. Kontuly. (1978). "Population Dispersal from Major Metropolitan Regions: An International Comparison." *International Regional Science*, 3:49-73.

Von Thünen, J.H. (1966). *The Isolated State.* Wartenberg CM (Trl.)   Oxford: Pergamon Press.

Wallerstein, I. (1974). *The Modern World-System.* Academic Press: New York.

Weber, A. (1929). *Theory of the Location of Industries.* CJ Friedrich (Trl.). The University of Chicago Press.

Whebell, CFJ. (1969). "Corridors: A Theory of Urban Systems." *Annals of the Association of American Geographers*, 59: 1-26.

Zelinsky W. (1971). "The Hypothesis of the Mobility Transition." *Geographical Review*, 16: 219-249.

2 The Role of Universities and Research in Future Urban Economic Development

Gerhard Braun

INTRODUCTION: KNOWLEDGE, KNOWLEDGE, KNOWLEDGE

2002 was a year of bankruptcies and insolvency that affected almost all levels of societies in advanced economies. However, there were exceptions:

- private firms were hard hit, but small and young businesses seemed to fare better;
- private households were affected, but while middle income households suffered the most, lower-income groups fared better;
- communities were also impacted, but peripheral and "fordistic" cities suffered less while leading capitals and major cities were harder hit.

Most of these effects resulted from an inability to adjust in a timely manner to transformational processes. In the period of transformation towards post-fordism, "location, location, location" appeared to be the most important element in determining further overall development.

While the game of global networking continues apace and cities are divided into a few winners and a large number of losers - either affected by new forms of dependency or by exclusion - we should get back to basics and ask ourselves what cities "are for" as we search for new answers to the economic development question. Indeed, cities have an innate capacity to concentrate development potential through economies of scale and scope. Today, "knowledge, knowledge, knowledge" and, as a consequence, "education, education,

education" are the "post-fordist" slogans most often heard in connection with urban economic development.

However, there are important discrepancies in the implications of both "fordist" and "post-fordist" notions of development. Location per se (1) already incorporates attributes such as "hard" location factors, as these are either pre-existing or can be created easily within a short time (2), and - most importantly - (3) these "hard" inputs are real and spatially fixed.

Education and knowledge production, however, are much more difficult to identify as inputs and spatial phenomena. The reasons for this are:

(1) investment in education demands large inputs in terms of money, ideas, discussion, assessment and action before outputs become available that can serve as new inputs for future cumulative development effects;

(2) output in terms of investment in education can not be expected to have exclusively local effects due to processes of brain-drain;

(3) investment in education is accompanied by uncertainty. Rather than making direct investments for training purposes, many companies outsource training and compensate for more limited employment periods through higher salaries (knowledge has its price, but how to make use of knowledge is the secret of a company's success).

At the same time, there is no question that adjusting to a "state of the art" economy - when not exclusively based on capital - can be facilitated by endogenous development and, furthermore, through education and a production of knowledge supported by training in entrepreneurship.

This could be a message to all cities that find themselves unable to play a leading or important role in the global context. The best strategy at present would seem to be an application of the first transformation law of cyberspace in which money is transformed into knowledge and, consequently, knowledge translated back into money, and so forth.

CHANGING CONDITIONS AND RESULTING PROFILES OF CITIES

Rising complexity and uncertainty in the urban macro-environment (politics, economy, society, etc.) as well as in the urban microenvironment (urban governance, urban housing, etc.) lead at present to various different development paths of urban regions and agglomerations. These paths of development are conditioned by several processes like globalization, de-regulation, space- and time-compression of innovation via diffusion, but also regionalization, that is, the growing importance of regional milieus as complements to the global world.

At the beginning of the 21st Century, characteristics of urban development paths presage general shifts in urban political and spatial organization. This fundamental restructuring of cities can be seen in:

- spatial and structural shifts in the national and global urban system hierarchies;
- de-nationalization due to economic competition;
- restricted capacities of urban governance.

These processes create a massive potential for structural differentiation and the urban agglomerations will follow divergent, polyvalent future developments, revealing divergent structural phenotypes.

THE CHANGING ROLE OF UNIVERSITIES IN A KNOWLEDGE-BASED SOCIETY

Within these changing conditions and their resulting urban-regional profiles, many new challenges confront knowledge producers such as universities and non-university research institutions. At present, societies have become fragile not because of globalization or the economization of societal conditions, but rather through the loss of power due to the changing role of knowledge (Stehr, 2000). Knowledge creates new ranges of activities and potential for action.

The extraordinary economic role of knowledge is not merely rooted in the fact that research-based knowledge is necessary for growth and continued high-performance development. Knowledge is more than this: it is an activator, an enabler; knowledge changes the manner of productivity and serves as the basis for complex restructuring. In this respect there is little difference between knowledge based on common sense, religious belief or on scientific analysis. Similarly, the specific role of science or technology-based knowledge is not due to the "fact" that research or findings are more truthful, objective, real, or significant. The new specific role of knowledge results from the fact that it permanently creates, more than any other locational factor, new ranges of activities and possibilities for action (Stehr, 2000).

Still, it is not high levels of investment, for example, in information and communication technologies, which causes higher productivity and creates knowledge regions. The so-called productivity-paradox describes a situation where, despite heavy investment, discrepancies between economic expectations and measurable progress in productivity occur (Stehr, 2000).

However, this process does not yet explain why the number of qualified workers is increasing. The answer that new technologies induce higher demand for skilled workers seems to be superficial. The opposite answer can be also true, that is that the increasing number of skilled persons shapes the character of modern societies. As in a self-inducing process, it appears that the supply of rather than the demand for skilled workers makes the working world increasingly knowledge intensive. This is the reason why, despite structural persistence, today's knowledge-based society changes with unusually high speed (Stehr, 2000).

The productivity paradox, therefore, indicates that an immense investment in information and communications technologies does not directly correspond to an increase in productivity. An increase in productivity rather results from the growing qualifications of graduates who push their way in the job market. Therefore, the decisive characteristics of a modern job market are the uncertainties and the missing predictability to determine the required qualifications for the working world (Stehr, 2000). These are, at the same time, the challenging objectives and targets for which universities should aim.

TRANSFORMATIONAL PROBLEMS: PERSISTENCE OF PERCEPTION AND BEHAVIOR

Both institutions, that is:

1) cities as actors, catalysts and locations in this post-fordistic socio-economic restructuring process; and

2) research institutions as the producers of knowledge and providers of content, are (and indeed must be) interdependently linked. Their strategic behaviors can result in either growth or decline and both cities and research institutions are currently at a decisive point where either scenario is possible. Monetary investment does not play the only and/or a central role here, political responsibility and regional reputations are also of paramount importance.

At present it seems that weaker regions are able to learn this lesson easier due to greater pressure to adjust to the new urban system and locational competition. Stronger regions, in contrast, often try to resist change because of their hitherto successful fordistic and sometimes hegemonic behaviors. In particular, the more that major cities capitalize on their present concentration of wealth and functional specialization in order to maintain their previous course, the earlier and probably more often they will fail.

The Freie Universität Berlin represents this situation quite well, both in 1948, the year of its foundation, and at present. In spite of post-war hardships and an acute lack of resources, those who invested in the intellectual potential of the Freie Universität Berlin understood the sign of the times and the need to develop a sound and independent scientific research base in Berlin West. However, in times of surplus, convincing people to change their behavior and think strategically is quite difficult as long as there is no formal need or socio-economic pressure to do so - a situation like the one characterized by the Malthusian dispute.

The German satirist Klaus Staeck caricatured this situation of complacency in his typical way: A society cheering its boxing champions, soccer players, tennis heroes, Formula I racers, is easily able to do without universities.

MULTIPLYING EFFECTS DUE TO CIRCULAR AND CUMULATIVE CAUSATION

Goddard's (2000) elaborations on "the response of higher education institutes to regional needs" defines two, not necessarily interdependent but more often separate and therefore not value-added systems, representing on the one side the university and, on the other, the region. A third system results in the case that both systems adjust to each other, interact and multiply their input: this is called the university-regional-interface. This interface-system has many interdependent complex facets that will be analyzed in the following.

That learning region interface works as a coordinating intervening opportunity within an input-output relation interacting system between universities and cities. This is where university restructuring and cooperation/competition correspond to urban restructuring respectively urban competitiveness via multiplying effects (Figure 2-1). This interface stands for a complex set of socio-economic processes which structure in circular cumulative causation both the attractiveness and competitiveness of cities and universities. However, the relational effects are not complete, that is, that one input unit of either the university or the city does not necessarily create an output unit of the same scale and so on.

Corresponding to the productivity paradox, all the interrelated effects are not necessarily compelling and complete, because one university or city input unit does not necessarily cause a comparable output unit and vice versa. On the other hand, there is at least a five to ten year time-lag between input and output effects, for example, economic and educational research progress take a long time before they can influence each other. In addition to incompleteness and time-lag, a third dimension, one defined by general uncertainty, influences the intensity of the input-output-relation system. All three components explain why politicians as well as other actors representing cities and universities have difficulty making use of the endogenous potential inherited in the input-output-system between the city, research organizations and institutions of higher learning.

In knowledge-based societies every sector within the urban socio-economic environment is directly or indirectly affected by university related influences. Further, each sector is at least a part of the input-output system in a significant manner, even if the time lag varies from sector to sector.

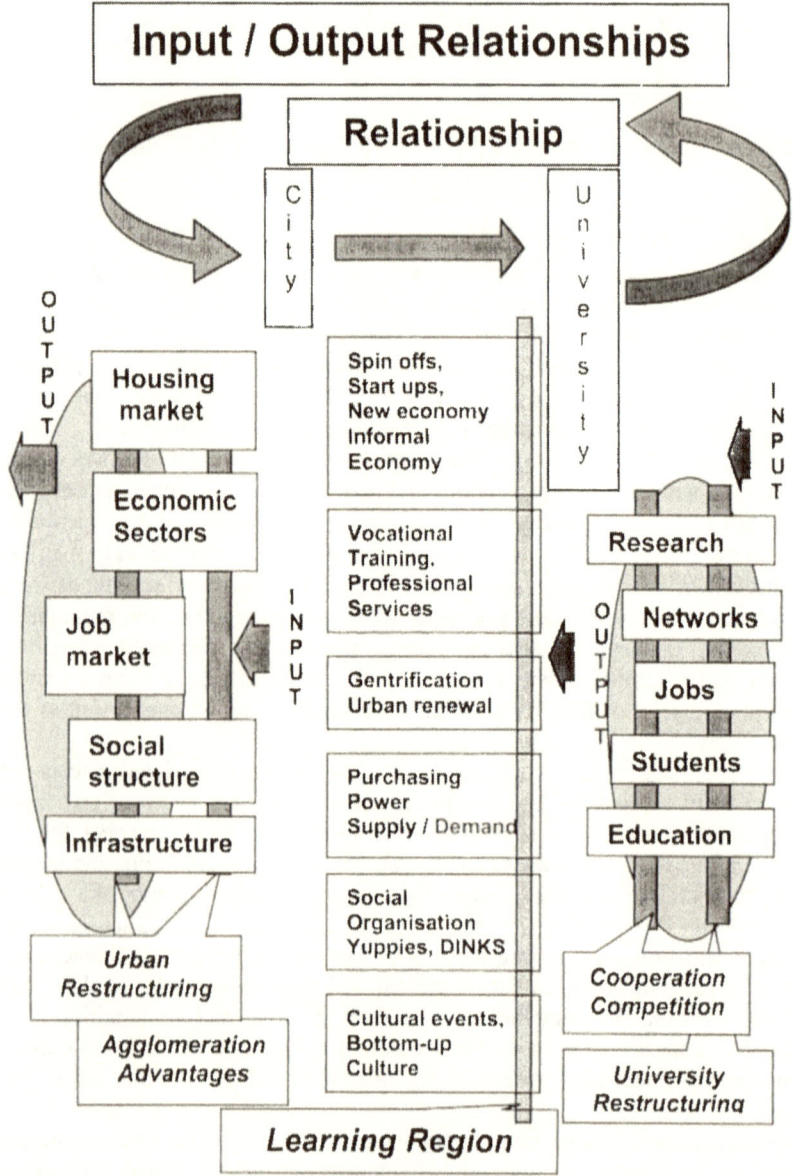

Figure 2-1

Altogether, in such circular and cumulative systems it seems to be inevitable that time loss or poor decisions will force the system into a negative cycle while timely and correct decisions induce positive cycles (in other words, positive multiplying effects). Quite obviously, investment in positive cycles is, in the long term, less costly than suffering from and repairing damage caused by wrong decisions.

All these aspects will be integrated into a model that combines elements of the basic / non-basic concept and those of growth pole theory (Figure 2-2). The key element in both concepts is the multiplying effect which enables description of the regional growth potential as an interdependent regional demand- and regional supply-system in which external demand and external supply support respectively, hinder the internal cumulative effects. Backwash effects, like income tax, value added tax, consumption taxes, social security contributions, or disadvantageous consumption ratios slow down the structural and spatial effect of circular accumulation while forward linkages via indirect and direct effects accelerate. The multiplier k, therefore, takes all these backwash effects into consideration.

The German Institute for Economic Research (DIW) has designed a model that expresses the k multiplied by regional demand J as the change in development of regional demand in a specific period of time. With regard to public investment into universities, the model has been applied to the financial situation of Berlin for the year 2000 (Figure 2-3). The data set collected by DIW for expenses, income, direct and indirect effects generated by university, non university research institutions and students, allows calculation of both the multiplier k as k = 1.35 and the regional demand as ΔJ = 5.087 (Mil.DM). A Δk = 1.35 means that an additional demand of DM 1000. induces an additional demand of DM 350.

The product of k and J reproduces the developmental change of regional demand as ΔJ = 6.868 (Mil. DM). This ΔJ expresses that the Berlin specific expenses for universities and non university research institutions reproduce a 3.1 times higher regional demand as output in relation to their input (in total 2.232 Mio DM). In advanced economies this coefficient demonstrates that investment into science and research induces one of the best input-output relations within a regional economy.

Gerhard Braun

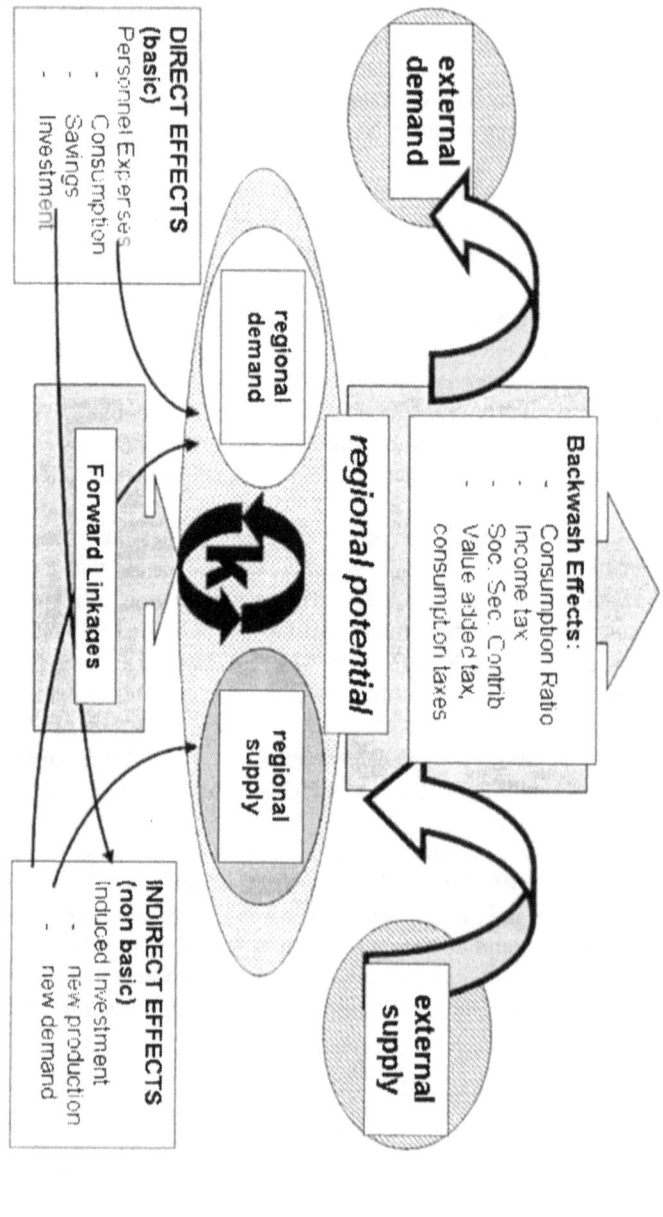

Figure 2-2

Spatial and Structural Concept of the Multiplying Analysis

Figure 2-3

Finance Situation and Regional Economic Effect, Berlin 2000 (in mil. DM)				
	Non-University Research Institutions	*Universities*	*Students*	*Total*
Expenses				
personnel	710	1.568	2.217	
investment	494	876		
construction	55	37		
subtotal	*1.259*	*2.482*	*2.217*	
Income				
Berlin	282	1.950		2.232
Government	585	4		
funding	259	283		
Add. sources	159	287		
subtotal	*1.285*	*2.524*		
Direct Effects				
Personnel expenses	710	1.569*		
deductibles	139 (19.4%)	*		
Balance	*570*	*2.366**		
Indirect Effects				
investment	549	913	2.217	
External share	324 (59%)	539 (59%)	665 (30%)	
Balance	*225*	*374*	*1.552*	
Total Effects		*2.740**	*1.552*	*5.087*
k = 1.35		3.700*	2.095	6.868
				3.08

* inconsistent and / or missing sources.

Source: Deutsches Institut für Wirtschaftsforschung (DIW): *Wochenbericht* 39/2001, pp. 599-605

RELATIONS BETWEEN CITY AND UNIVERSITY: EMPIRICAL EVIDENCE

In the following, out of that complex system only two modules ("students" and "scientists") will be taken to reflect multiplying effects in greater detail. The first module gives some insight into the network of the cumulative supply- and demand-causation that students create or depend upon (Figure 2-4). Direct relations between university and city with only minor contributions to the overall GDP are represented in the center of the model. However, as pointed out earlier in the transformation concept before, most relations, including structurally decisive ones, act indirectly and create, via detouring multiplying effects, added value. Not only the students' supply of innovation, culture or jobs but also their demand for consumption and investment goods, jobs - especially in the informal economy - and housing facilities change and/or contribute to the adjusting development of the urban structure.

Most of these direct contributions and their GDP contribution are well known, but structurally more important are the indirect circular cumulative effects which help the urban economy to adjust to the competitiveness of leading centers. In general, students as producers and suppliers of knowledge not only contribute to the overall urban renewal and restructuring process but also function as catalysts of urban revitalization.

The network of the second module presented here involves "scientists" within the city-university relationship and is of a similarly complex nature (Figure 2-5). In general, within their supply and demand system, scientists contribute to the general stability and high development potential of the local and regional economy. The demand part of the system, therefore, creates in a circular and cumulative manner qualified housing, a deeply specialized division of labor, a demand of high-quality cultural events, qualified personal services and, in addition, all kinds of agglomeration advantages. With their supply network they support not only the basis for the development of a knowledge region but also they contribute to the future development of professional services, research based occupational advantages and, most importantly, to the development of national and international networks necessary for the endogenous ability for permanent structural adjustment.

The effects of these regional and structural agglomeration advantages can be tested when the locations of university and non-university research institutes are mapped in the case of Berlin. Three major clusters can be identified representing the campuses of the three Berlin universities. The strongest agglomeration is found in the Dahlem region (high income sector in SW) with the Freie Universität of Berlin as its center.

When interpreting the spatial pattern of 77 start-ups founded within a three year period in Berlin (Wichitill, 2000), and which were successful in the business plan competition, a special type of incubator, we will find clusters of

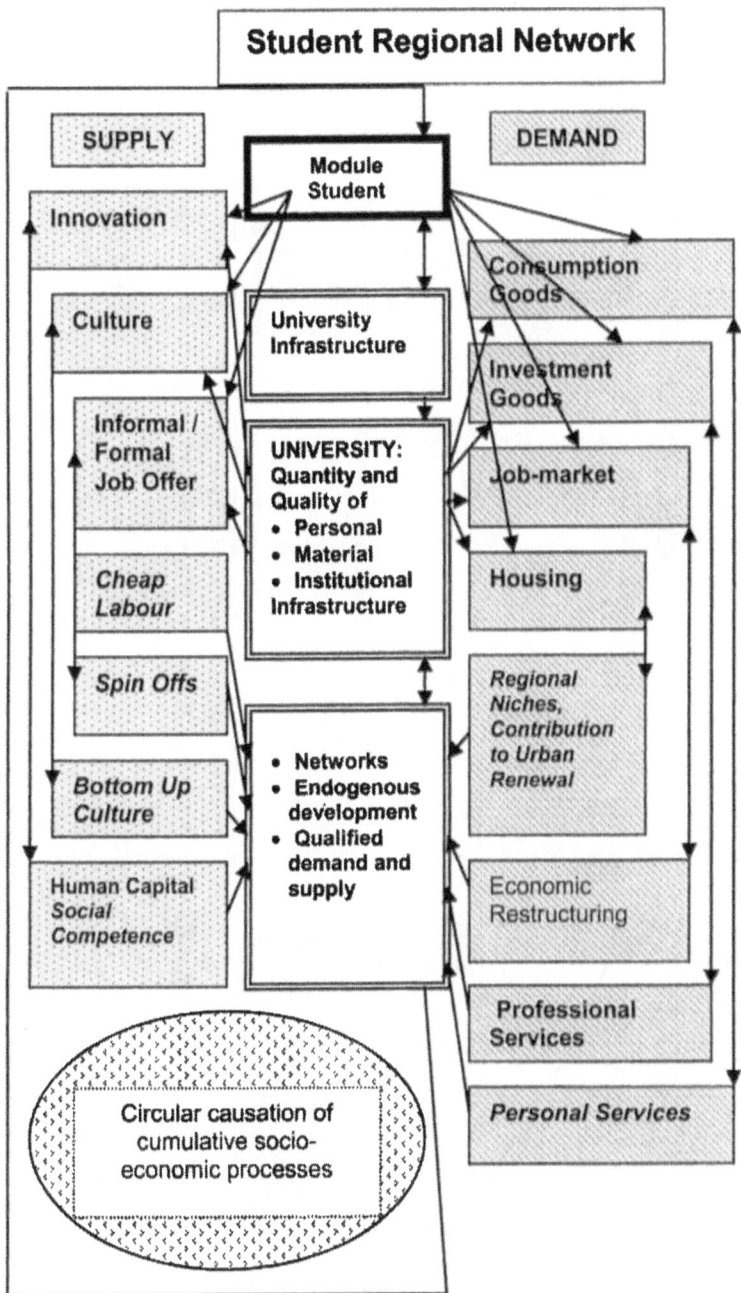

Figure 2-4

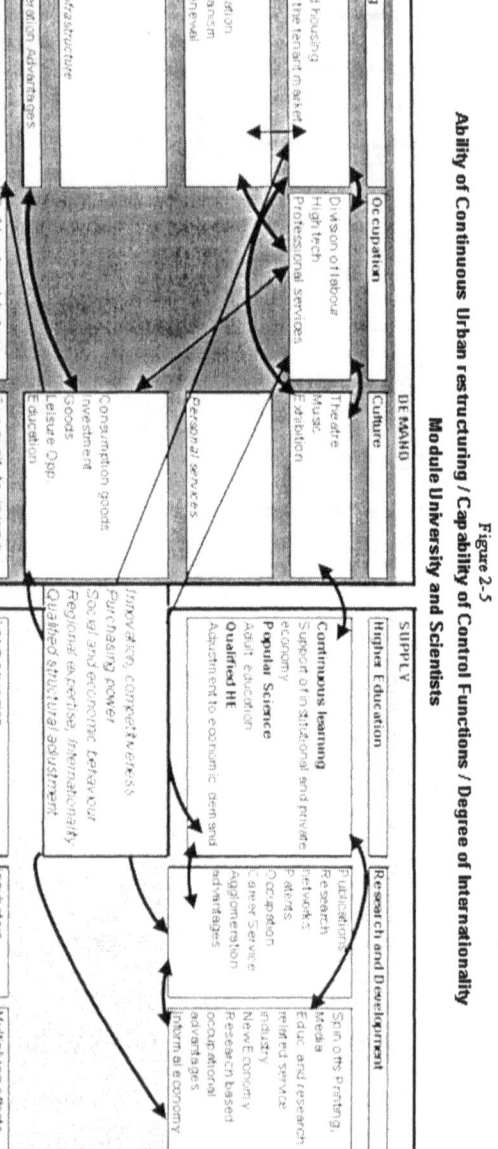

Figure 2-5
Ability of Continuous Urban restructuring / Capability of Control Functions / Degree of Internationality
Module University and Scientists

spatial concentration where the universities and non-university research institutions (Steglitz, Zehlendorf, Charlottenburg, Treptow) and the gentrified areas (Kreuzberg, Mitte) are located. The rest of the pattern seems to be more randomly distributed.

Most of these start-ups are knowledge-producing and/or knowledge- based production sites (high tech, internet, bio-med-tech, I&CT, multi-media, professional services like consulting and education). Their customers are, to a large degree, not private persons but other enterprises that use the output as input for further multiplying effects. Companies having passed through an incubator show a significantly lower death rate than those without the help of incubators. Within that three year period the young entrepreneurs increased their average size from 1.5 to 3.4 jobs per start-up. The small size of these start-ups is related to the degree of specialization and to their locations which are preferably residential or mixed residential areas. The average time worked is above 50 hours weekly, a factor that also explains the close vicinity to the urban scene.

ERRORS IN THE SYSTEM IN THE TRANSFER OF KNOWLEDGE IN VIABLE START-UPS

According to a study by the consulting company McKinsey, a set of decisive errors, mistakes and shortcomings within that learning-region-concept are analyzed when academic knowledge is going to be transferred in viable start-ups in practice (Figure 2-6). The elements within the circles indicate the basic players within a learning-region like basic research, university, scientists, industry, financing, transfer-offices, and start-ups. Within these conditional players there is a core cycle consisting of the elements like research, grants and subsidies, venture capital, professors, transfer-offices and start-ups (shown in italics within select boxes). Conditional to a functioning of that cycle are factors like Early Stage VC, Tenure, Disclosures, Proof of Concept, conditions to license and patent as well as governmental interventions like the Bayh-Dole Act.

That act regulates that all inventions financed with public money have to be licensed by patents while the government facilitates licensing free of charge and the universities are in receipt of the right of use. The McKinsey analysis indicates all the necessary links to make the model functioning. In reality, however, many links between important factors are either not existing or are restricted in their functions. For example, there are only little interrelations between markets and basic research, research activities and start-ups hardly receive venture capital, never in an early stage of development, or professors have their specific scientific interest in the invention and not in the introduction of their findings into markets. Even if there are inventions in remarkable quantity and even if there are disclosures to the university, only a few of these inventions

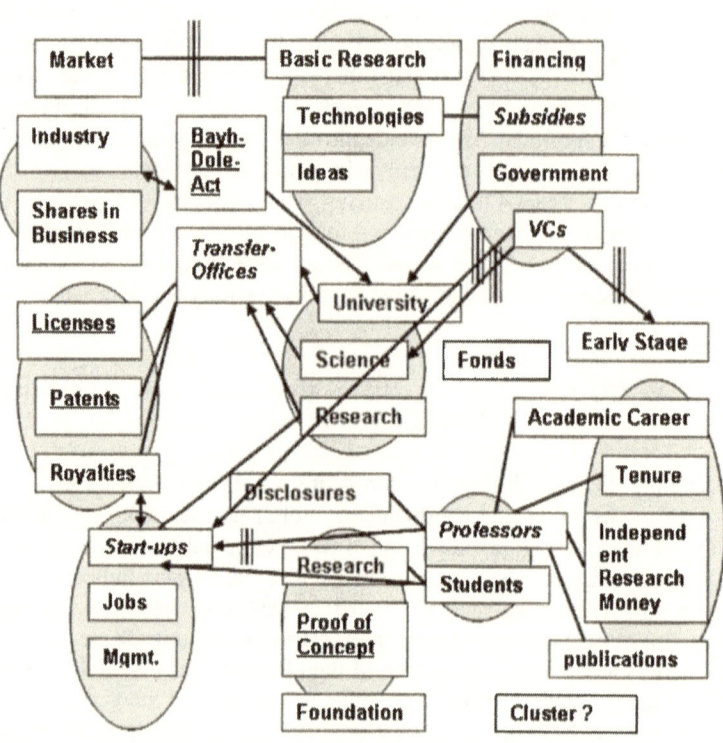

Figure 2-6
Errors in the System in the Transfer of Academic Knowledge
Into Viable Start-ups

Source: McKinsey Wissen 04 2. Jg. 2003, S. 57.

flow into start-ups. Reasons for such an inflexible behavior can be seen either in poor regional economic and entrepreneurial milieus but also in view of, how universities understand their task at present. Another aspect can be found in the understanding of transfer offices which are more interested in the maximization of income via selling licenses rather than in the transfer of patents into start-ups via foundation.

Summing up these, universities should be interested in, especially for their own existence, to think about their own contribution to the progress of learning-region-systems' development (Figure 2-2). In that view, the decisive element of such a concept is not the start-up but the readiness and ability of universities to re-think and to-conceptualize what the universities' task should be. Links between research and education are up to now only practiced in basic research but not in the application of science. For example, many professors and students do not realize the present and future market relevance of their specific research findings. Therefore, all the curricula have to be changed that way, not only to understand the point of research but also to identify its story for the transfer into markets.

There are many concepts to bridge the gap of commercializing between money and knowledge, for example, between venture capital and university research. Based on that new understanding and based on either the help of foundations or university operated incubators, the most active and effective scientists should get all the support to develop their findings up to the readiness for marketing. The model (Figure 2-6) shows some of the parameters and their interdependent links to make incubators successful. In practice, these incubators will not work without the implementation of an adaptive framework, which mainly consists of basic conditions like trust, open competition, and excellent education and training but also the necessary institutional infrastructure, such as a specific regional milieu. Only from a certain level of increasing complexity onwards will the hoped for high scale of multiplying effects occur. Up to now, only a few universities enjoy the effects of incubators.

CONCLUSIONS AND THE SPECIFIC ROLE OF CAPITAL CITIES

In conclusion, two points can be added with regard to the regional and structural effects of circular and cumulative causation within the university-city relation. First, development within capital cities gives reason for an additional dimension of the discussed complexity of the city-university-relational network. Indeed, more important than the localized expertise represented by universities in all kinds of political areas is the international focus of the networks that emerge within the existing regional pattern.

Secondly, and this is not a satiric comment but rather concluding evidence stressing the importance of transformational processes in the inter-city-university relation: A society cheering its universities is easily able to excel in sports as well.

REFERENCES

Bögenhold, D. (1997). "Gründungsforschung aus soziologischer Sicht." in *BIFEGO-Tagung*, Bonn: Bad Godesberg.

Braun, G.O. (1991). "The Process of Multipolarisation," In: M.J. Bannon et al., *Urbanisation and Urban Development. Recent Trends in a Global Context*. Dublin: University College Dublin, pp. 216-226.

Braun, G.O. (2000). "Inter- and intra-university competition and co-operation," In: *METAR*, Vol. 41, Berlin.

Breßler, Chr. (1992) *Das Wohnungssuchverhalten von Studenten* Berlin: der Freien Universität Berlin. Diplomarbeit.

Carsten, St.(1999). *Antizipation von Agglomerationstypen*. Diplomarbeit, Berlin. *Der Spiegel* (2000) "Studieren lohnt sich." In: *Der Spiegel* 46, pp.54-94.

Deutsches Institut für Wirtschaftsforschung (2001). "Berliner Ausgaben für Wissenschaft und Forschung: Kräftige Impulse für die Stadt." In: *Wochenbericht* 39.

Goddard, J. (2000). "The Response of HEIs to Regional Needs." Manuscript presented at Transborder Universities Conference, Copenhagen.

Hall, P. (1988). *Cities of Tomorrow: An Intellectual History of Urban Planning and Design in the Twentieth Century*. Oxford: Blackwell.

Harmens, S. (1992). *Ursachenanalyse der studentischen Wohnsituation und Wohnungsnot in Berlin*. Diplomarbeit, Berlin.

Henton, D.; J. Melville and K. Walesh (1997) *Grassroots Leaders for a New Economy: How Civic Entrepreneurs are Building Prosperous Communities*. San Francisco: Jossey-Bass.

Heuer, St. (2003). "Fehler im System." In: *McKinsey Wissen* 04, 2. Jahrgang, pp. 56-63.

Hochschul-Informationssystem (HIS) (2000) *Sozialstudie 1999*. Hannover.

Krätke, St. (1995) *Stadt - Raum – Ökonomie: Einführung in aktuelle Problemfelder der Stadtökonomie und Wirtschaftsgeographie*. Basel: Stadtforschung aktuell, Bd. 53.

McKinsey (see Heuer, St.)

O'Toole K. and D. Manuel, (2002). "'Knowledge Network' Founders Strive to Preserve, Pass Along What is Known." In: www.stanford.edu/dept/new/...rt/ news/august11/knexus-811.html

O'Toole K. (1997) "Successful Entrepreneurs Talk About How It's Done." In: www.stanford.edu/dept/new/...rt/news/july16/entrepreneur.html

Ripsas, S. (2000). "Ten propositions to foster the culture of entrepreneurship at German Universities." In: *Science Next Wave*. http://nextwave.sciencemag.org/ cgi/content/full/2000/07/06/1.

Ronzheimer, M. (1998). "Gründerboom an den Unis." In: *Berliner Morgenpost*, 2.8.1998. Berlin.

Senatsverwaltung für Stadtentwicklung, Umwelt und Technologie, Technologiebericht Berlin (Auszüge), Informations- und Kommunikationstechnologien/ Medien, Berlin 1999.

Senatsverwaltung für Wissenschaft, Forschung und Kultur, Forschung in Berlin. Politik - Potenziale - Projekte. Berlin 1999.

Silber, J. (2000). "Triumph des Unternehmergeistes." In: *Forum*, pp. 36-43.

Stehr, N. (2000). "Die Neue Ökonomie: Informationstechnologien, Wissen und der Arbeitsmarkt." In: *Informationsdienst HRK*, November. Bonn.

Welter, F. (1997). "Das Gründungspotenzial in Deutschland: Konzeptionelle Überlegungen, empirische Ergebnisse. Rheinisch-Westfälisches Institut für Wirtschaftsforschung, Forschergruppe." *Handwerk und Mittelstand*. Essen.

Wichitill, G. (2000). "Evaluierung des Businessplan Wettbewerb." Berlin: Brandenburg der Jahrgänge 1996 bis 1999. In: *Existenz-Gründer-Institut Berlin e.V.*, Berlin.

3 Gentrification, Class, and Growth Management in Seattle, 1990-2000

Richard Morrill

During the 1990-2000 decade, not only the greater metropolitan area, but the central city of Seattle experienced significant growth in population, jobs, and income. The year 2000 also marks ten years of planning under state-mandated growth management. Comparison of geographic patterns of characteristics of population and housing reveals a marked transformation of the urban landscape, including a surprising degree of gentrification and displacement within the core city of Seattle. This paper analyzes this social and demographic change and tries to evaluate the possible role of growth management.

Was this gentrification or revitalization or what? Who gained and who lost, within the city of Seattle, and between the city and its suburbs? What was the nature of gentrification? Was it in the form of displacement of the poorer by the richer? Of Blacks by Whites? Of the older by the younger? Or was gentrification more a redevelopment of relatively unused areas with minimal social impact? This paper has four parts: first, gentrification and revitalization are defined, attempting to sort out the competing interpretations. Second, change in Seattle is compared to that of the rest of the metropolis; third, a set of maps is used to illustrate the geography of demographic change within the city; and fourth, a limited multivariate analysis (factor and cluster analyses) is used to discover different forms and spaces of change, in an attempt to better understand the varieties of gentrification, the actors and the winners and losers.

The comparison of Seattle with its suburbs reveals a very substantial real net shift of poorer households, lower valued housing, and racial minorities from the city to the suburbs. The map analysis is used to convey, through a set of indicator variables about race, age, households, housing and income, the parts of the city and the relative settings that moved up or down in status, and the actors associated with these changes.

The factor analysis rather neatly distinguished three forms of social change: gentrification—displacement; revitalization—gentrification— replacement; and gentrification—redevelopment. Finally the cluster analysis grouped tracts, based on their scores on the three dimensions of change, permitting the identification of areas of the city characterized by the different kinds of change. The downtown core emerged as the locus of redevelopment and rapid growth; areas east of downtown as the locus of gentrification by professionals, often non-family, and displacement of Blacks; and the areas between downtown and the University of Washington as the locus of rejuvenation, replacement and likely gentrification.

The results of the study support a multivariate conception of social change as both gentrification and revitalization. It does overall reinforce gentrification as a class and capital reclaiming of the core by higher class households and businesses.

GENTRIFICATION AND REVITALIZATION

There is a large and spirited literature on gentrification. I prefer the simple definition: a significant rise in the mean status OR the degree of inequality in the status of residents (and of businesses) and in the value of residential and non-residential property—in other words, an upward shift in class. At least within an only moderately dense but fully built-up city like Seattle, such change necessarily means either a large addition to population and business via partial redevelopment, or succession/replacement of those dying or leaving voluntarily, or displacement of the weaker (lesser status and value) by the stronger (higher status and value). Succession may be rejuvenation when a younger population replaces an elderly population, and does not necessarily result in short term gains in income although it may in other measures of class such as education or occupation. Displacement can be from condominium conversion, evicting renters, from existing owners and renters being outbid by households wanting to move into the area, or from major upgrading and replacement of structures, as in replacement of small homes and businesses by high rise mixed use developments.

If we view gentrification as a shift in status via new residents and businesses, we can conceive of revitalization as a concerted improvement in communities on the part of mainly existing residents. Finally we may distinguish agents of gentrification by what we may call "gentrification A" and "gentrification B." Via Smith (1996), gentrification A is a result of organized conscious public and private planning and coordinated investment and development, often quite large scale and involving marked densification, replacement and enlargement of structures, and perhaps public institutions and infrastructure, for example, stadiums, operas, theaters, museums, and perhaps rail transit. This form often occurs downtown or in university or hospital districts, involving "new economy" jobs, creating a supply of office space and core urban living to be filled mainly by childless professionals of all ages. Such core resurgence obviously responds to industrial restructuring, the burgeoning business services and information jobs that take advantage of access to the core and of agglomeration economies, and represents a new cycle of higher land rents and municipal revenues.

A key characteristic is that government, even as in Seattle a 'liberal' Democratic regime cooperates with land owners and developers to displace the poor from 'underutilized" and hence undervalued areas, to be reclaimed by people and jobs of a higher economic class. Growth management and 'smart growth' provide a planning and environmental justification for this recentralization of 'better' jobs and residents.

Via Ley (1996) gentrification B while also enabled or encouraged by planning policies of smart growth including upzoning, the designation of "major urban centers" and of "urban villages", and transit routing, is at least somewhat more a consequence of individual decisions of buyers and renters, who for job, lifestyle or other reasons, desire to live in the central city, reasonably close to but not necessarily in the core itself. These 'agents' are very likely to be of higher 'social class', that is, by occupation, education and family connection, but are not necessarily of higher income than current residents, at least at first. Of course the downtown core also attracts 'lifestyle' residents, young singles and couples, empty nesters who prefer or want to try high rise living, and who thereby displace or simply overwhelm preexisting SRO populations, who are often shifted into 'homelessness'.

This broader zone of change—gentrification and possible revitalization— is likely to surround the core, possibly leaving a least desirable sector for the displaced, poor downtown population. Depending on their relative position—for example to major institutions, pre-existing racial and ethnic enclaves, or kinds of housing stock, the degree of gentrification may vary from moderate rejuvenation to more radical displacement of the poor and of racial minorities. But most of the zone will be characterized by rising rents, housing values and reinvestment.

One would have to be contemptuous of both theory and fact to choose between broad 'economic' or 'cultural' interpretations of gentrification, or to deny the possibility of revitalization as an alternative to gentrification. There are powerful constituencies for gentrification, which may indeed conspire to reclaim parts of the urban core for higher classes and uses, or which may conveniently reinforce each other's distinct agendas, to the same effect. At least ten interests contribute to gentrification. Most prominent are the private-public partnerships between (1) developers, (2) city governments, and (3) land owners, all interested in "closing the rent gap", on the economic side, and the urban lifestyle converts, actually a somewhat diverse group of (4) young, childless singles and couples, straight and gay, who seek an urban experience, even though some reverse commute to the suburbs; (5) empty nesters, often coming back from the suburbs, and (6) a smaller number of families usually with dual downtown or near downtown professional positions. This public-private alliance is supported as well by (7) planners, academic as well as professional, in the apriori belief that high density urban village living is good, by (8) construction trades and public employee unions, for job reasons, and even though housing price inflation and taxes may adversely affect them; by (9) most of the media, because of advertisers and perhaps a belief in a more grandiose city, and by (10) the powerful and articulate environmental movement, again because high density urban redevelopment is necessary to save the countryside from evil middle class sprawl (but still allow 20 acre estates for the rich).

Some of these interests *intend* to upgrade the class of the city; the uncompetitive can go somewhere else. Besides developers and presumably land owners, city, county and state government, even if Democratic and avowedly liberal, planners and the regional media are in this camp, the latter two (government and media) convincing themselves that the added wealth generated by gentrification will more than pay for the necessary income transfers, public housing or housing subsidies and added services for the displaced—some actually believe this trickle down theory! While the unions and public employees may appreciate that there will be winners and losers and that upward shifts in wealth and power will result, they evidently feel powerless to challenge the system.

Other interests, the young and unmarried, the empty nesters, urbanist families, environmentalists and some planners do not intend to gentrify in the sense of displacing the poor, or reducing the average quality of housing; they may extol class diversity and even be willing to pay to subsidize some households who can no longer compete for housing and business space in the revitalized areas, but in the end, over time, the effect is usually to gentrify and displace—because of the inflated values of land and housing—and further separate the winners and the losers. Resistance and grass-roots revitalization and rejuvenation does occur, without marked gentrification, but probably in areas beyond the most desirable, attractive and accessible core areas.

The initial gentrification or revitalization in the US occurred in the 1970s and into the 1980s, impelled by both the 'economic' and the 'cultural' constituencies, often in connection with the new wave of CBD high rise offices related also to economic restructuring toward professional and business services, and major public investments (rapid transit, stadiums), and peopled by the vanguard of urban lifestyle devotees. Evaluation in the late 1980s of such redevelopment revealed a political, ideological and social science polarization concerning the meaning and effects of gentrification, even if that were too loaded a word for what happened. Thus the familiar debate between a more negative economic-based assessment, emphasizing displacement and the windfall gains to developers and landowners (and city coffers); and more positive cultural-lifestyle assessments, emphasizing the recovery of core housing, population and business, the return of vibrant city life, and the offering of an alternative to the sterile suburbs of endless sprawl. Many authors, including Smith (1992) and Ley (1996) themselves, understood that reality was a more complex mixture. Some like Lees (1994) and Clark (1991, 1994), Badcock (1995) and Beauregard (1990) have argued for a broader theory that recognizes both kinds of forces. Others, Knopp for example (1990), offered case studies that illustrated the economic consequences of a culturally-driven process.

Florida (2002) identifies the rise of the "creative" class (gays, artists, highly-educated migrants) as key components of the revitalization of the urban core. Using his composite measure, Seattle ranks 2nd only to San Francisco in the share of these new cosmopolitans.

LOCAL BACKGROUND

Growth: Metropolitan Seattle grew fairly rapidly in the 1990s, at 20 percent, changing from 3,000,000 to 3,600,000. The core city grew moderately, at nine percent, from 518,000 to 563,000; but considering that the city's population had declined significantly from around 1955 to 1980, and that it was fairly fully built out by 1970, the current recovery is noteworthy.

Regional growth was impelled primarily by an even faster rise in employment, fueled by good performance of the traditional mainstays of transportation equipment (aerospace, trucks) and the Port of Seattle, but even more by the accelerated growth of the information and technology sectors, dominated by Microsoft. Significant to the story of gentrification is that the Seattle economy has been radically transformed since 1970 from a relatively egalitarian one to one of startling income inequality, as higher rates of return to education, and property sources of income became more prominent.

Social change and gentrification did not begin in the 1990s. In the 1970s some rejuvenation and revitalization and reinvestment occurred on Capitol Hill-First Hill, both east of downtown and on Queen Anne, just northwest of downtown, owing to their proximity to downtown or to the University of Washington campus (please see Figure 3-1). Hodge (1979, 1981) and Hodge and Lee (1981) studied the degree of displacement and found it of modest scale and relatively benign in this period. In the 1980s the coordinated redevelopment of the downtown core began, with incipient residential high rises following large scale skyscraper office development. Thus by 1990 displacement and homelessness of the downtown and near downtown poor became noticeable, as well as a hint of displaced Black households from the "central area" or CD east of downtown. Yet the establishment, 100 percent liberal Democratic, undertook to pursue policies of redevelopment ever more vigorously, promising to build more public housing to deal with displacement and homelessness.

GROWTH MANAGEMENT

Washington state passed the Growth Management Act in 1988 (based on Oregon's earlier act) and it was effectively implemented in the Seattle area in 1990. The goals of growth management include (1) imposition of an urban growth boundary to induce in-filling and urban redevelopment (or intensification/densification); (2) imposition of concurrency development impact fees on new construction, mainly at the urban fringe; (3) encouragement of the concentration of jobs and population in major urban centers, and also smaller urban villages; (4) requiring of jurisdictions to take their 'fair share' of higher density and moderate income housing; and (5) creation of a rail rapid transit system connecting the major centers to downtown Seattle. The central city of Seattle volunteered to accept a large amount of housing, population and jobs, and upzoned accordingly.

A key component of Seattle's planning under the GMA has been to complete the transition of the Lake Union area, between downtown and the university, from an industrial and underdeveloped cityscape to a high density city-within-a-city. Although public-subsidized development plans ("Seattle Commons") were twice voted down by city voters, it is of course happening anyway, because of a three-way partnership of the city, the University of Washington and Microsoft billionaire Paul Allen, to build a 20,000 job biotech complex. Preview to what follows: this area is precisely the center of gravity of Seattle gentrification in the 1990s!

An evaluation of ten years of growth management reveals substantial impacts, both in line with and against hopes and expectations. On the one hand, the urban growth boundary was effective at encouraging infill and redevelopment; the vast majority of new housing has been in the form of apartments rather than single family homes; and there has been some concentration of jobs and people in major centers, especially downtown. On the other hand, the large majority of growth (80 percent) continues to be at the urban fringe, hard up against the urban growth boundary; and significant growth has leapfrogged out to independent standing 'rural' satellite towns and even adjacent counties (Central Puget Sound Real Estate Research Committee, 2001, 2003). But the greatest impact has been severe inflation in the land and housing markets, and a decline in the real quality of, and/or a rise in the cost of housing, for probably the less affluent majority of the population.

Data and Scope

The map review will cover only the central city of Seattle. A vast amount of social change has occurred in the "suburbs" including, for example, a substantial increase in immigrants, a rise in less affluent especially single-mother households in South King county, and even a relative decline of 'status' in parts of the generally affluent east and north side suburbs, in part an exchange with Seattle, which overall gained higher status and displaced lower-status households. But a detailed analysis will be confined to Seattle for four reasons (1) it is one jurisdiction and school district, with reasonably uniform policies; (2) it is a manageable area and population; (3) since the city was fully built, the focus can be on the effects of redevelopment, unaffected by new subdivision; and (4) there has been minimal change in census tract boundaries, so that comparison between 1900 and 2000 is subject to only a moderate error.

Variables used from STF1, the 100 percent count, include population by age, by race and by household type, and housing by tenure, for 1990 and for 2000; and from STF3, the sample data, include occupation, education, income and poverty. Discussions will mainly be of maps of change in numbers and proportions of persons with varying characteristics, but in a few cases maps of 1990 and 2000 values of the variables may be referenced. Figure 3-1 includes neighborhood names to ease discussion of the maps. Because of space and costs, the maps here are both limited in number and are simplified black and white versions of originally more nuanced and visibly useful color maps. Thus the reader is invited, better instructed, to go to the author's website, to examine the color version of these maps, as well as of some additional maps (http://faculty.u.washington.edu/morrill/gentrify).

SEATTLE AND SUBURBS—COMPARING CENTRAL CITY CHANGE TO THAT IN THE REST OF KING COUNTY

Just as Seattle varies internally from very affluent to very poor areas, as we shall see, so does suburban King county. Indeed the 'average' conditions in Seattle are far 'better' than the actual conditions in many suburban places. The gentrification of Seattle has resulted in the displacement of minority, single parent, single, and other poor households to close-by suburban cities and even farther satellite cities. Table 3-1 summarizes values for Seattle and for suburban King county for 1990 and 2000 for selected indicator variables.

Population and Race

While the suburbs received far more growth, the city's addition of over 47,000 was an impressive indication of substantial urban redevelopment. Racial composition begins to tell the story of city gentrification. The city's white

Table 3-1
Seattle Versus Surrounding King County

Characteristic	Seattle							King County (except for Seattle)						
	1990	1990%	2000	2000%	Change	% change	Ch. in %	1990	1990%	2000	2000%	Change	% change	Ch. in %
Population	516,259		563,375		47,116	9.1		991,060		1,173,659		182,599	18.4	
White	377,817	73.2	382,532	67.9	4,715	1.2	-5.3	872,787	88.2	892,805	76.0	19,818	2.3	-12.2
Black	57,948	10.1	47,541	8.4	-10,407	-18.0	-1.7	24,341	2.5	45,268	3.9	20,927	86.0	1.4
Minority	138,447	26.8	180,843	32.1	42,396	30.6	5.3	118,268	11.9	281,208	24.0	162,940	137.8	12.1
25-34 old	112,028	21.7	122,282	21.7	10,256	9.2	0.0	188,700	19.1	272,161	14.7	-16,539	-8.8	-4.4
45-64	85,689	16.1	123,447	21.9	37,748	44.0	5.8	191,848	19.3	277,216	23.6	85,368	44.6	4.3
Over 65	78,971	15.2	87,807	12.0	-11,164	-14.1	-3.2	88,341	8.9	113,917	9.7	25,576	29.0	0.8
HW families	81,719	34.6	84,649	32.7	2,930	3.6	-1.9	228,341	60.1	245,122	54.1	16,781	7.3	-5.7
Singles	94,207	39.8	101,542	40.8	7,335	7.8	1.0	85,889	22.6	116,620	25.8	30,751	35.8	3.2
Non-family (2 plus)	28,846	12.7	39,558	16.3	10,713	37.1	3.6	25,963	6.8	34,231	7.6	8,268	31.8	0.8
Own	115,689	48.9	125,181	48.4	9,492	8.2	-0.5	246,000	86.0	300,275	66.0	54,275	26.7	0.0
Single Fam detached	139,594	55.4	132,988	49.1	-6,826	-4.1	-6.3	290,400	84.9	290,400	61.4	44,420	18.1	-3.5
Multiple	110,500	44.6	136,267	50.9	25,767	23.3	6.3	133,000	36.1	162,595	38.6	29,595	22.2	3.5
Med House Value	$137,900		$259,600		121,700	88.3	0.0	$141,140		$227,700		86,560	61.3	0.0
Median Rent	$483		$721		258	55.7	0.0	$548		$789		243	44.5	0.0
College graduate	140,248	37.9	193,322	47.2	53,074	37.8	9.3	193,462	30.1	281,036	35.1	87,574	45.3	5.0
Professional/Mgr	103,016	36.8	155,834	49.4	52,818	51.1	12.6	170,800	32.5	247,847	40.2	77,047	45.2	7.7
Services	36,683	13.1	44,533	13.9	7,840	21.4	0.8	65,300	10.5	75,237	12.2	19,937	36.1	1.7
Median HH Income	$29,363		$45,736		16,383	55.8	0.0	$40,498		$57,404		16,906	41.7	0.0
Poverty	61,681	12.4	66,478	11.8	4,797	7.8	-0.6	55,908	5.6	79,433	6.8	23,525	42.1	1.2
Inequality	0		0		0	23.1	0.0	0		0		0	32.4	0.0
Not at one	213,350	44.6	236,918	44.1	23,568	11.0	-0.5	413,000	44.7	540,940	49.6	127,940	31.0	4.9
Migrant	117,828	24.5	112,412	20.9	-5,416	-4.6	-3.6	177,750	19.2	176,778	15.9	-972	-0.5	-3.3
Foreign Born	67,535	13.1	94,952	16.9	27,317	40.4	3.8	72,544	7.3	172,551	14.7	100,007	137.9	7.4
Public Transit	44,381	15.9	55,652	17.6	11,291	25.5	1.7	22,050	4.2	31,648	5.3	9,598	43.5	1.1

note: change in % = %2000 - %1990

population grew for the first time since the 1950s, while the Black population fell absolutely, as a net of over 10,000 were displaced, as the suburban Black population almost doubled. Both city and suburbs experienced huge gains in other minorities- Asians and Hispanics, but the gains were vastly greater in the suburban county.

Change in selected age cohorts continues the story. While the 45-64 year old group increased rapidly everywhere, from the aging of the baby boomers, the change in the proportion 45-64 was greater in the city (5.8%) than in the suburbs (4.3%), an indicator of the city's job vitality and overall attractiveness for living, and despite the reputation of the city as less desirable for raising and educating children than the suburbs. But it is the increase in the 25-34 year old cohort, despite the baby bust, that distinguishes the city from the rest of the county, which experienced an absolute decline. The city was extraordinarily attractive to young households and workers, who were key agents of gentrification.

Kinds of households are a further indicator. While the city has long been relatively unattractive to traditional husband-wife families—percentage-wise, their share was 34.6 compared to 60.1 in the county in 1990!—it actually gained such families and their proportion of all households fell far less than in the suburbs, which now experienced very large gains in singles and single parent families, both relatively poor and seeking more affordable housing. In contrast the city gained most in non-family households with two or more persons, mainly young unmarried partnerships, key contributors to gentrification.

Housing

Seattle experienced only a slight decrease in home ownership, but a significant decline in single family homes—the share dropping below 50 percent; the retention of ownership was from condominium construction or conversion of rental apartments. Condos and apartments in larger buildings (over 10 units) increased 23 percent, and their share of housing rose 6.3 percent. Because of the prevalence of new, high-rise, more upscale buildings, even the rentals contributed to gentrification in and around downtown Seattle and some in the University district. Another measure of relative city gentrification was the 85 percent increase in the median value of housing, compared to 61 percent in the rest of the county, and the remarkable shift from the city median value being under the suburban value in 1990 ($138,000 to $141,000) to well above in 2000 ($260,000 to $228,000). Excessive housing costs are universally argued as the main reason for displacement of less affluent households out of the city. Rents also rose more in the city than in the suburbs.

Education and Occupation

These variables are at the core of an understanding of the gentrifiers. The share of college graduates in the city rose from 38 to an astounding 47 percent of persons over 25, compared to 35 percent in the rest of the county, which corresponds almost exactly to the equally extreme high share of professional and managerial occupations in the city, at 48 percent, compared to 40 percent in the suburbs.

Income and Poverty

Given the high levels of education and the structure of occupations, it is not surprising that the median household income rose more steeply in the city, at 56 percent, than in the suburbs, at 42 percent. This is equivalent to a displacement of at least 10000 less affluent households. Consequently, the share of poor persons fell in the city but increased in the suburbs. Indicative of the severe gap between the educated and professional affluent and the less educated, poorer and more minority population is the very high level of inequality (measured here as the difference in the mean and median household income, divided by the median) in the city compared to the suburbs, although inequality increased relatively more in the suburbs, because of the displacement of many poor households into a changing suburbia.

The variable "foreign born" is interesting, as it shows that the suburbs, not the city, took the lion's share of the large influx during the 1990s. Finally, the share using public transit is of interest, as it underscores the difference in character, with public transit use inside the city quite high for a western city.

Map Analysis and Discussion

Population Change

Virtually all growth in the city was accommodated in high density apartments or condominiums. Seattle has an extremely low average household size, only 1.8, comparable to that of San Francisco. The population change map (Figure 3-1) tells a simple story: Most of the net growth, about 30,000, was right downtown, where the population more than doubled—ironically a level similar to what it had been at the end of World War II—but quite different in character! Secondary areas of growth, at a moderate 10-25 percent, include the extreme south of Seattle, the extreme north of Seattle, and selected areas or corridors in between, coinciding with urban redevelopment along major urban arterials, in miles of three-story apartments replacing 1920s to 1940s cottages and one story businesses. Areas of population decline (quite small in number) were almost entirely areas of older, white family housing in fairly affluent areas.

Race and Ethnicity

Seattle remains a central city with white residents in the majority and has never had a large underclass ghetto. But race is part of the gentrification story (Figures 3-2a and 3-2b).

Figure 3-2a shows change in the "non-Hispanic white population." Both absolute numbers and white shares of the population declined in the majority of tracts, in both north and south Seattle. Many are precisely the same majority of tracts in which absolute numbers and nonwhite shares increased, while the population totals remained almost constant (Figure 3-1). Except for a very few tracts in the southeast, these are not "majority minority" areas, but rather are unusually integrated. In most of downtown Seattle, and in some close-in neighborhoods to the north, Queen Anne, Fremont-Wallingford, absolute numbers of whites grew even as their shares fell, and as minority populations grew in numbers and shares; these areas experienced moderate to rapid overall growth, and revealed a mixture of gentrification, revitalization and redevelopment. Most important, in a sizeable contiguous area east of downtown, (Capitol Hill, Madrona, Leschi and the "CD" or "central area") the white population grew substantially in absolute numbers and in shares, while the minority population declined in both numbers and proportions—again in areas that were stable in total population. This is the primary area of white "reclamation" and minority "displacement," the more classic form of gentrification.

Figure 3-2b of the change in the Black population gives more detail about the composition of this racial restructuring. As background the reader should know that the northern part of the area of decline in the Black population is what is called the "CD", the historic Black community of Seattle, and the southern part, the "Rainier Valley" is the area of extension of Black settlement, 1960-2000. The entire area, but preeminently the original core settlement, has been astoundingly diminished, as whites have aggressively integrated the area (because of its desirable location, not out of a social agenda to integrate). Even the tracts with large public housing projects are affected, as the projects are being rebuilt with shares of "market" housing to attract middle class white residents. The Black population increased slightly in the far north, the far south, and the less affluent edge of downtown. The Asian population (not mapped) grew markedly, fueled by substantial immigration. Asians, too, were displaced from the northern part of the "CD", gained moderately downtown, significantly in the far north end, and dramatically in south Seattle, overlaying and intensifying (via new apartments) the traditional area of Asian settlement, and also displacing many Black households. In these areas it is too soon to tell if substantial reinvestment and gentrification are likely to occur.

Age

Seattle is unusually attractive to young adults and relatively less attractive to those of middle age and their children. Change in persons 25-34 (Figure 3-3) is positive and significant (except in the affluent view and waterfront areas), and is clearly the main constituent of the growth downtown, in Capitol Hill (including the CD), Queen Anne, and in Fremont, Ballard and Green Lake.

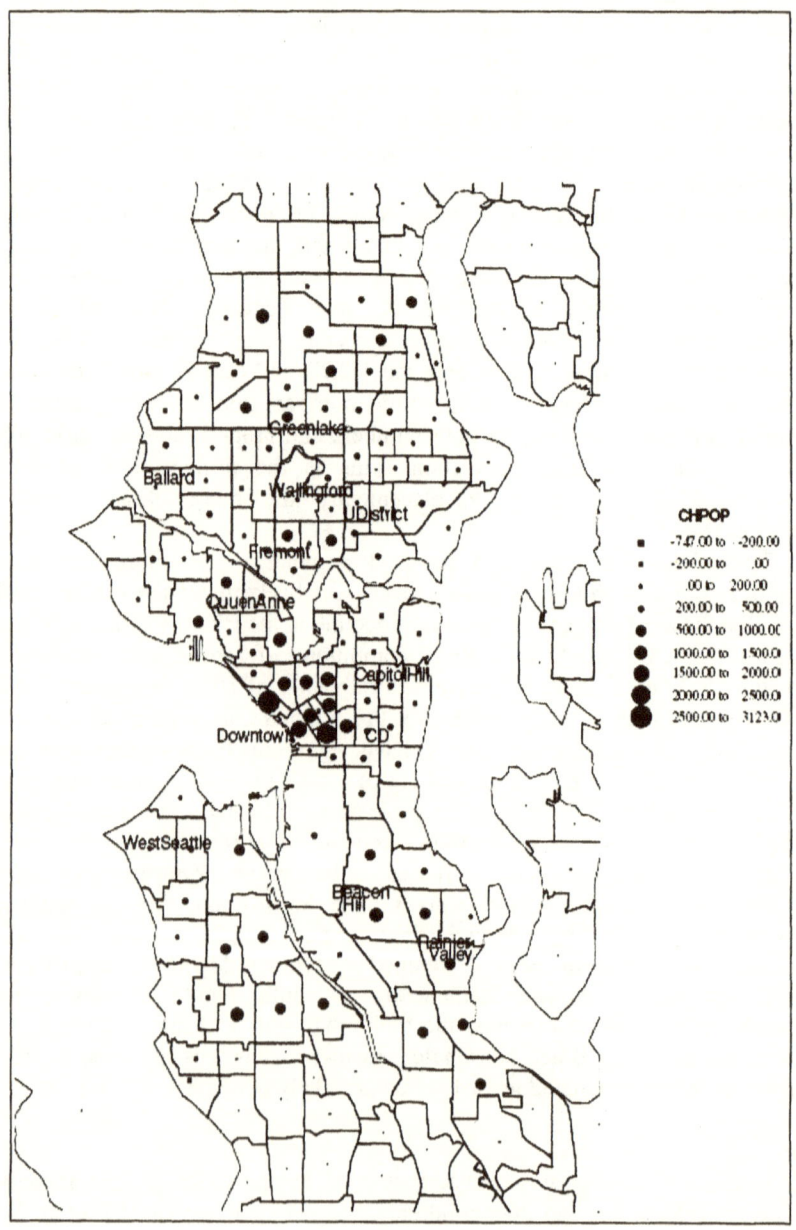

Figure 3-1
Seattle: Change in Population, 1990-2000

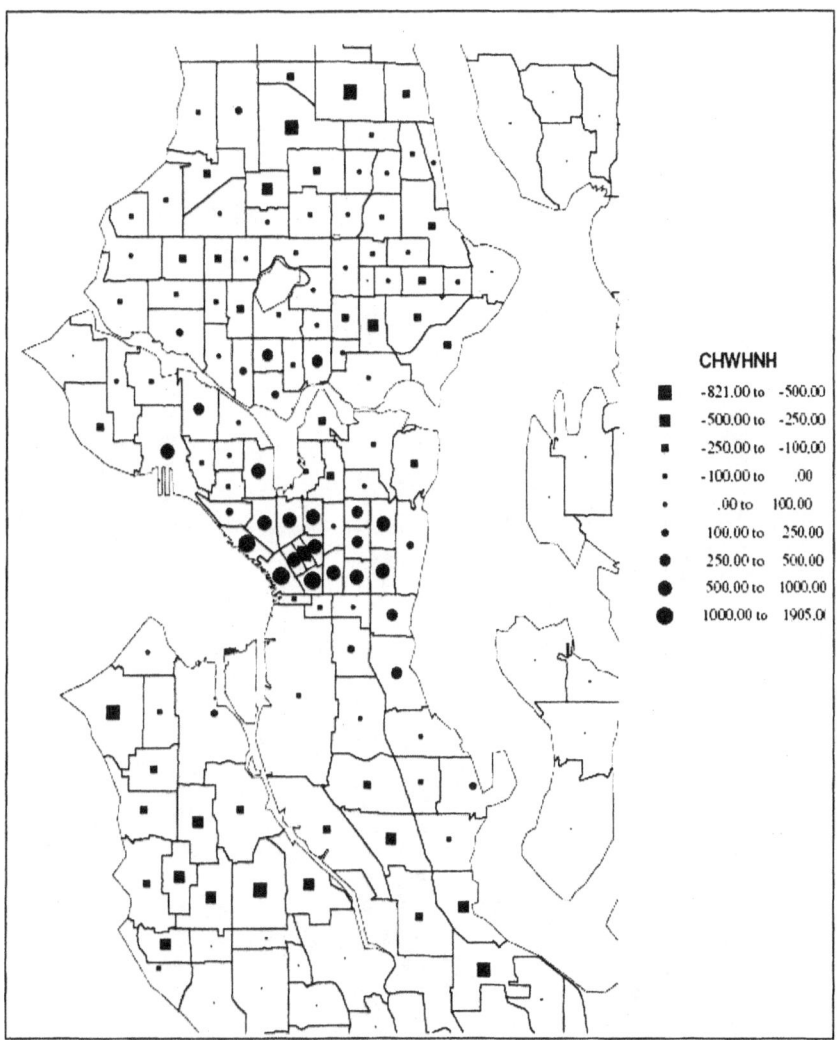

Figure 3-2a
Seattle: Change in Non-Hispanic White Population

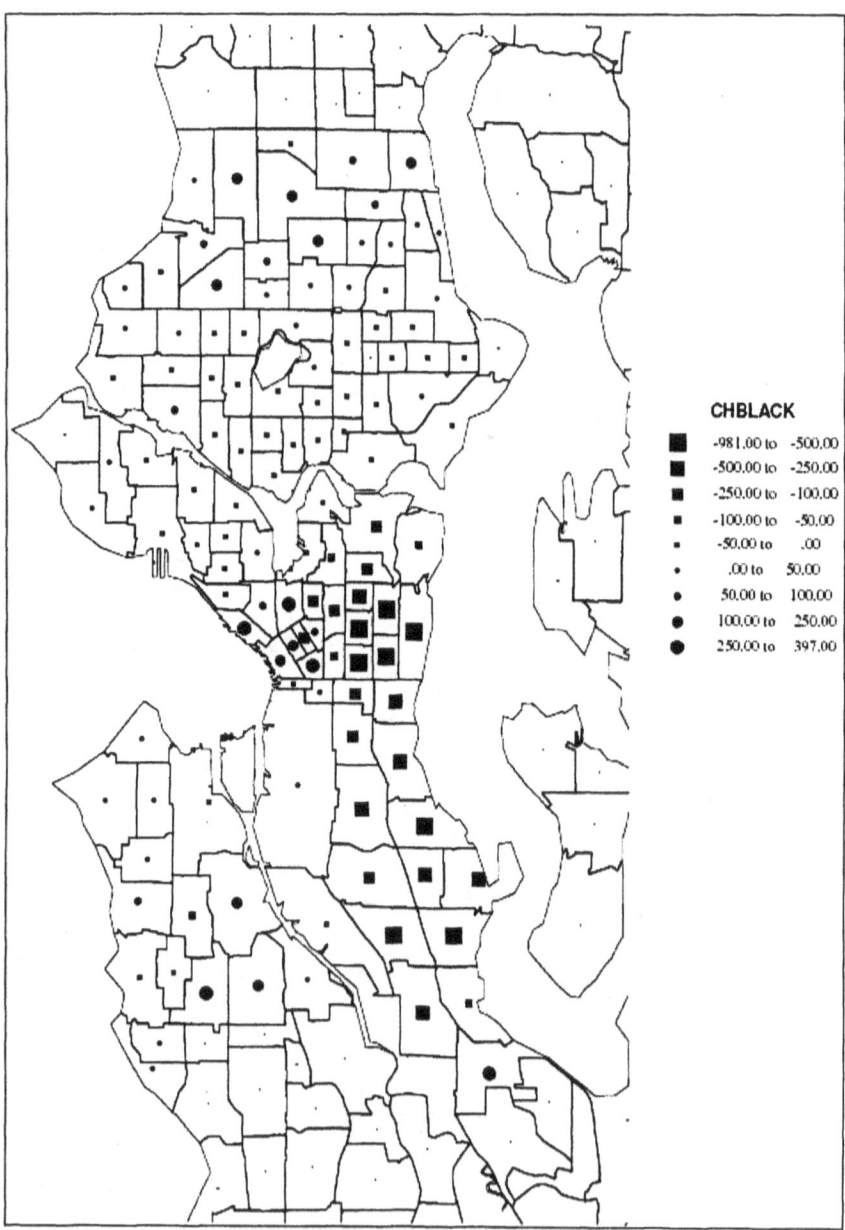

Figure 3-2b
Seattle: Change in Black Population

Many are students at the University of Washington or Seattle University, and a substantial number are employed in the burgeoning engineering, professional and technical firms dominating the sub-region. But many may also work in the high tech industries in the eastside suburbs, but prefer the in-town older city lifestyle. Persons 45-64 (not mapped), show a general pattern of gain, partly what may be expected from aging-in-place of the baby boomers. As a relatively educated and affluent age group, with high growth in the high amenity, single family, waterfront and view edges of the city, they tend to displace their parents' generation. They contributed to gentrification in two sub-regions: filling downtown's condominiums and in the Green Lake area. The over 65 population (Figure 3-4) generally declined absolutely and relatively, except in strongly Asian areas. The decline was greatest in areas where the younger 20-aged household growth was greatest, suggesting modest displacement and replacement by that gentrifying group (the older population grew in the far outlying areas with lower housing costs and less 'stress').

Types of Households

Families

Families (not mapped) declined in most of the city, except downtown and in the area of recent Asian immigration in the far south. The movement downtown of families, both younger and older couples without children, while small in absolute numbers, is high relatively and a fascinating component of gentrification. Looking at families of different types, the pattern for the most traditional family (husband and wife with children) is quite different, as these increased slightly in the richer, whiter single family view parts of the city, replacing an older generation. They were displaced from gentrifying areas, both on Capitol Hill- the Central area, and from Fremont to Ballard. Husband-wife families without children, both new young couples and empty nesters, declined in the very areas where the younger families with children replaced them, but increased in two areas, in downtown Seattle and east of downtown, contributing to gentrification.

Single Parent Families

Single parent families (not mapped) are very common in Seattle and increased everywhere, often replacing husband-wife families. The increase was very small downtown and on Capitol Hill and other areas of gentrification (presumably housing was too expensive) but was substantial in the far north and very rapid in the main minority areas of south and southeast Seattle, in Asian even more than in Black areas. Single households are by far the most common kind of household in Seattle—over 40 percent. During the 1990s their numbers and shares increased in much of north Seattle, in Queen Anne and West Seattle, often in newer apartments in what were single family home areas, but they

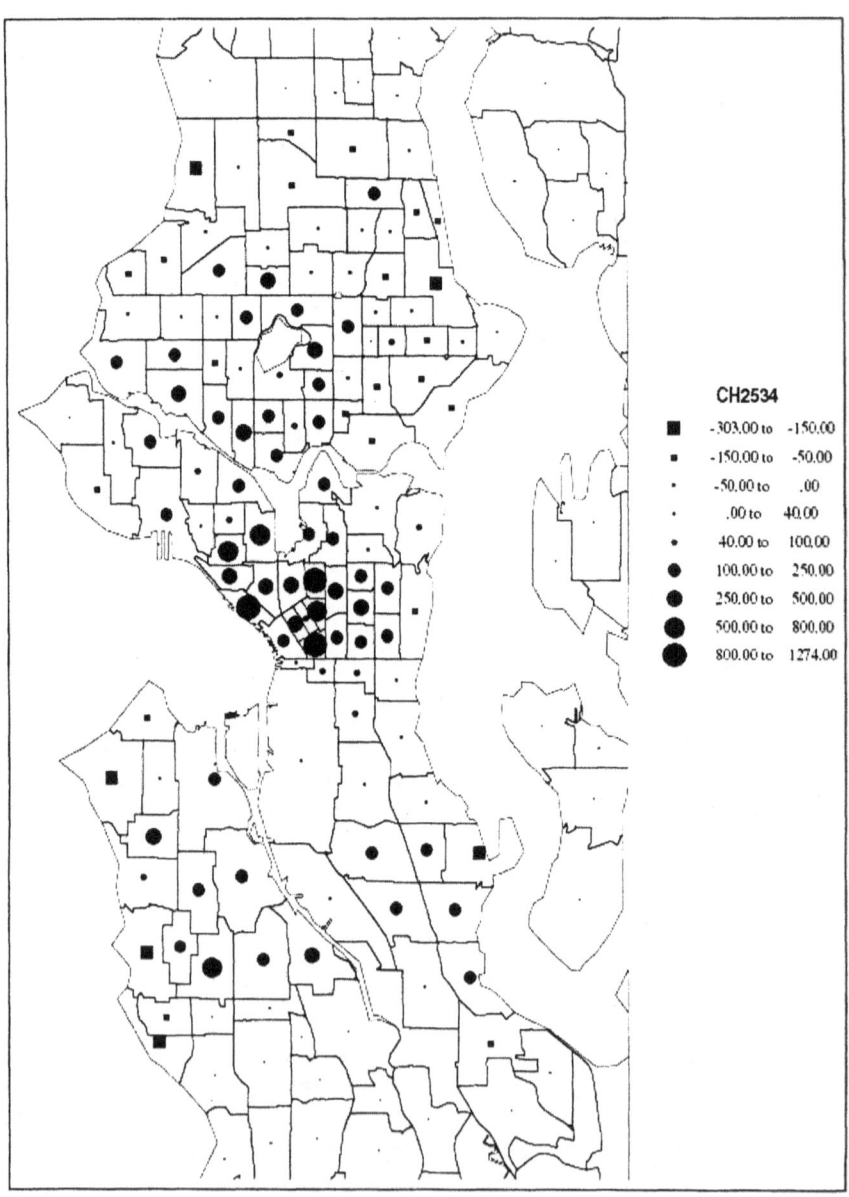

CH2534

- ■ -303.00 to -150.00
- ■ -150.00 to   -50.00
- · -50.00 to   .00
- ·   .00 to   40.00
- · 40.00 to   100.00
- ● 100.00 to   250.00
- ● 250.00 to   500.00
- ● 500.00 to   800.00
- ● 800.00 to 1274.00

Figure 3-3
Change in Persons, 25-34

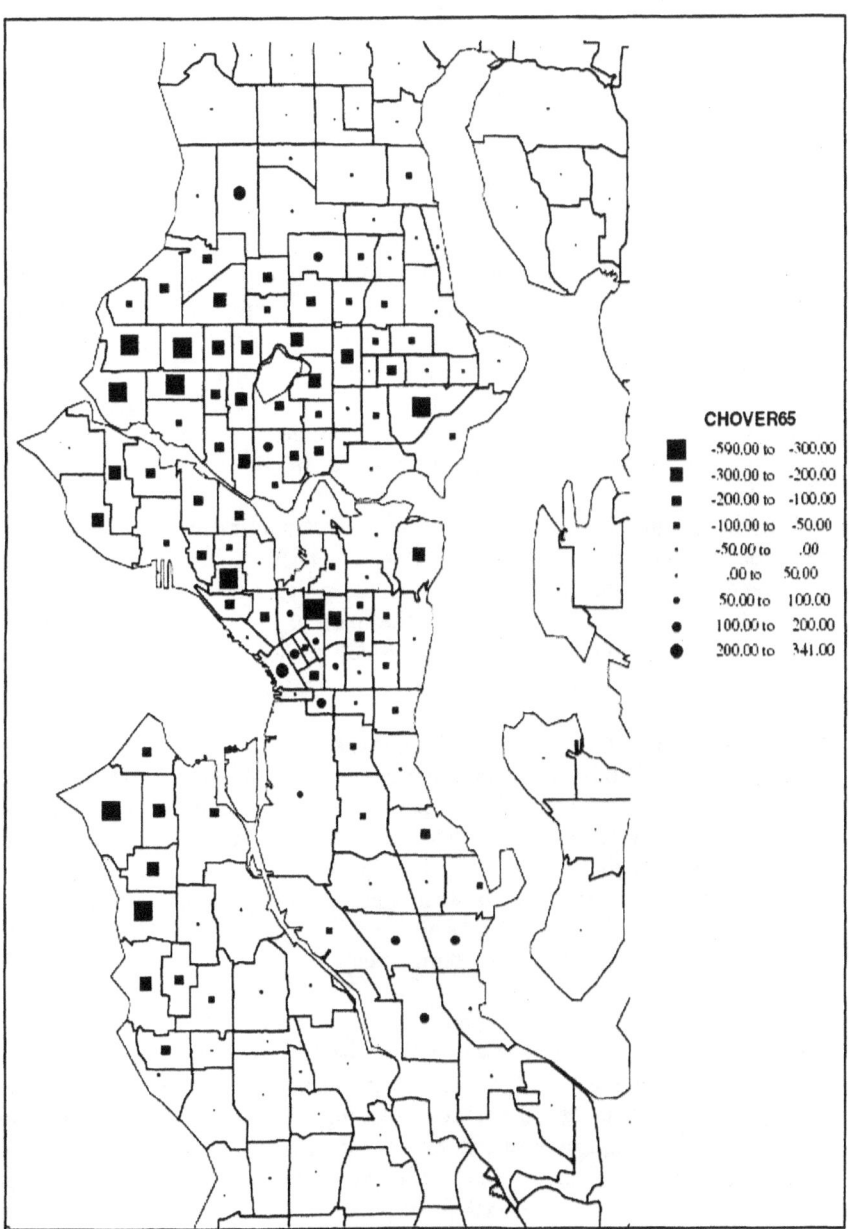

Figure 3-4
Change in Persons Over 65

decreased (were outbid?) in the new downtown high-rise market (often condo), both by families and by partners. The gains contributed to gentrification and displacement mainly rather far east from the downtown in what was the core CD, and in Fremont and Queen Anne.

Non-Family Households
    Non-family households (Figure 3-5), with two or more persons, which are about two-thirds opposite sex and one-third same sex partners or roommates, are the kind of household which grew by far the fastest, even considering that some of the change may be from more people willing to say so than in 1990. The increase was small but real in the affluent, single family view areas, but was higher in three kinds of areas: (1) moderate in the minority Black and Asian but somewhat integrated areas in Rainier Valley (and many are of multiple ethnicity), (2) rapid and in large numbers in Queen Anne-Interbay, Fremont-Ballard, Greenlake and Greenwood, in both apartments and in smaller houses, with people employed downtown, in Fremont and in the Lake Union and University districts.
    This is certainly a zone of some degree of reinvestment or gentrification, and probably of replacement of older married couples and widows (revitalization). But the most impressive area of growth was (3) downtown, Capitol Hill into the CD (central area), the main area of gentrification, and of displacement of poorer white as well as of Black households.

Housing
    Although Seattle has a majority of renters, and almost all construction in the 1990s has been in multi-household structures, enough of these have been in the form of owned condominiums (and there was substantial conversion from rental to condo status) that there was an increase in the number and share of owned housing in much of the city (Figure 3-6), in the minority and new immigrant areas of south and southeast Seattle, in Interbay and Fremont, but mainly in downtown, the south of Queen Anne, and north Capitol Hill, areas of reinvestment and gentrification, dominated by young and middle aged professionals.
    Although there were small increases in the number of *single family homes* (not mapped) in a few tracts, shares fell in the large majority of tracts. Little change occurred in north and central Seattle, and gains were mainly in the minority areas of southeastern Seattle, including much public-assisted housing construction. The highest proportions of single family houses are on the periphery of the historic city of Seattle (before 1955)—a swath of high numbers and proportions half way up in north Seattle.
    There were very large increases in the numbers of apartments in larger structures (10 units or more). By far the largest additions were in greater downtown Seattle, followed by far northern Seattle (the Greenwood and Aurora

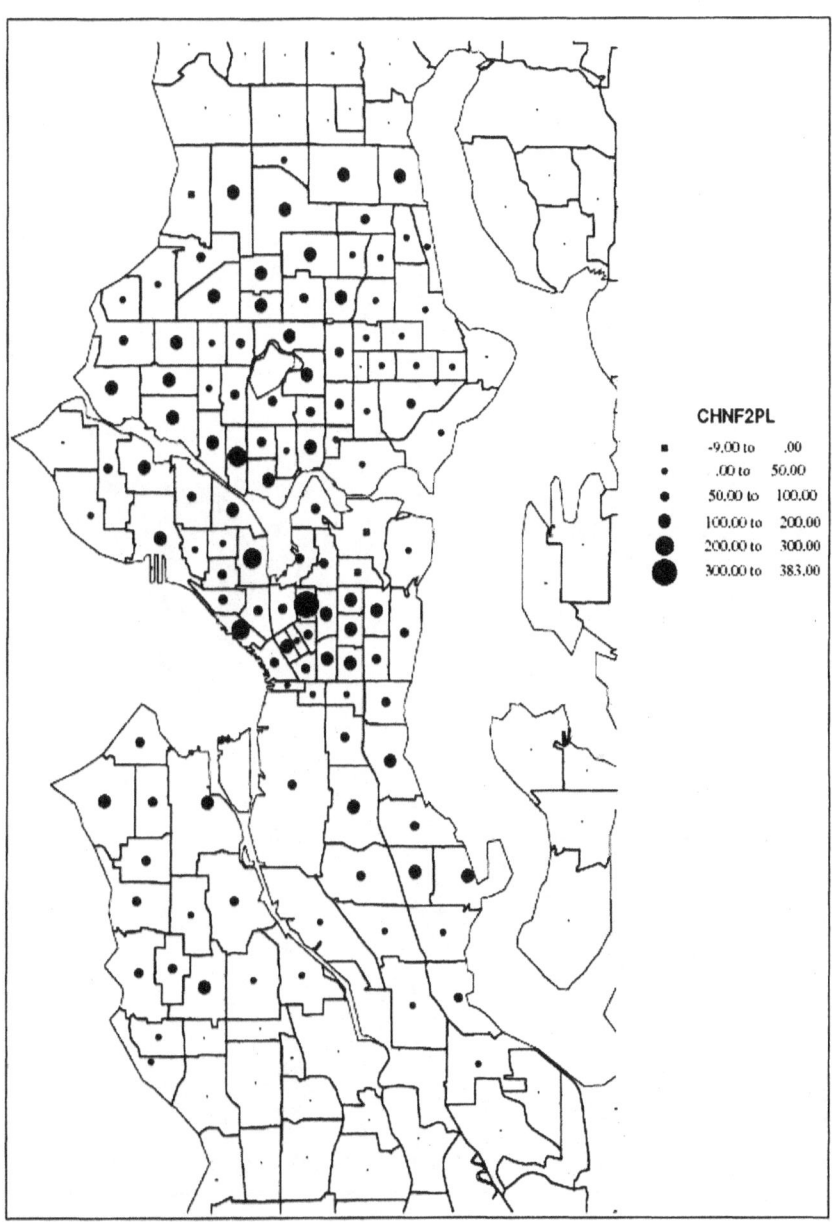

Figure 3-5
Change in Non-Family Households, 1990-2000: Two or More Persons

Richard Morrill

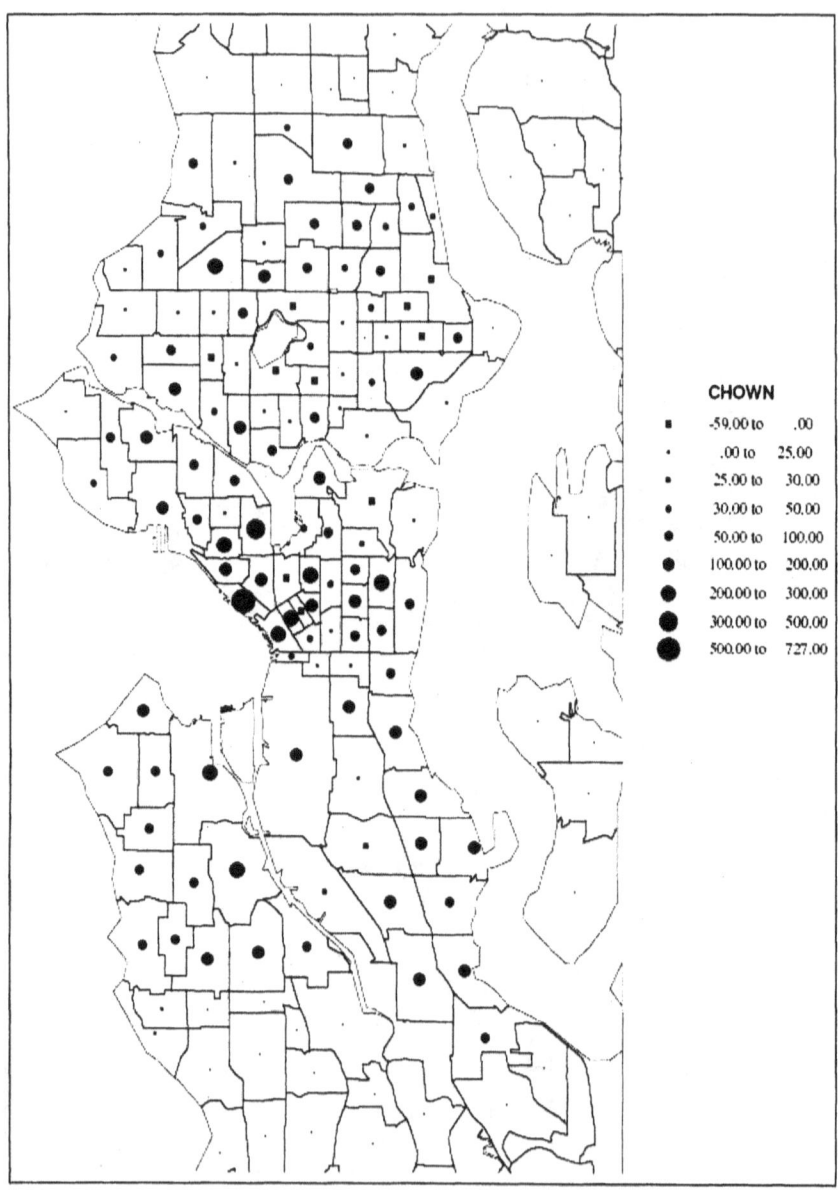

CHOWN

-59.00 to	.00
.00 to	25.00
25.00 to	30.00
30.00 to	50.00
50.00 to	100.00
100.00 to	200.00
200.00 to	300.00
300.00 to	500.00
500.00 to	727.00

Figure 3-6
Change in Home Ownership, including Condominiums

corridors), the University district-Wallingford and Lake City (far NE). Large complexes were prevalent in most of the main areas of gentrification, but smaller structures were common in a few areas of change such as the Greenlake area.

Housing Values and Rents

Change in housing values and rents (Figure 3-7) may be the single best indicator of gentrification, especially in those areas with over 100 percent appreciation during the decade. It is important to realize how different the map is from the corresponding map of median housing values, since in most of the wealthy areas percent changes were relatively modest (50 to 100%). Four areas of gentrification stood out: 1. part of downtown Seattle and Capitol Hill, from low to moderately low; 2. Beacon Hill and Rainier Valley (to the SE), from quite low levels up to moderate levels; 3. the northern part of West Seattle and 4. the Fremont-Green Lake area west of the University of Washington. The highest values reflect access to downtown and the university, coupled with high levels of professional employment, and often, views! Change in median rent was quite parallel to change in home values, with gentrification in the same four areas, but relatively more pronounced downtown and on Capitol Hill. In downtown and Capitol Hill, rents inflated but from relatively moderate levels, while in the University to Wallingford areas, rents inflated less, but from already high levels.

Education

Change in shares with college degrees (BA/BS or professional degrees) is also a good indicator of gentrification, since the 1990s continued the trend from the 1980s of greater income returns to education. Increased shares of the college educated (Figure 3-8) prevailed in most areas of gentrification, in the areas west of the university (including far to the west, from low to moderate levels), in the Green Lake and Queen Anne areas (near the university and downtown respectively), from already high levels, in the near downtown from moderate levels, and in West Seattle and Rainier Valley, from low to moderate levels.

Occupations

Because the structure of occupations was totally redesigned for the 2000 census, it is unwise to try to compare the mismatched categories of 1990 and 2000 censuses. With that caution in mind, I will compare only the professional-managerial category (more inclusive in 2000) in order to see the pattern of relative change (Figure 3-9). Tracts with highest shares of professional and managerial occupations almost perfectly correspond with areas of gentrification (downtown, Capitol Hill, south along Lake Washington, West Seattle, Queen Anne, Fremont, Wallingford and Green Lake). Areas of relative decline are

Richard Morrill

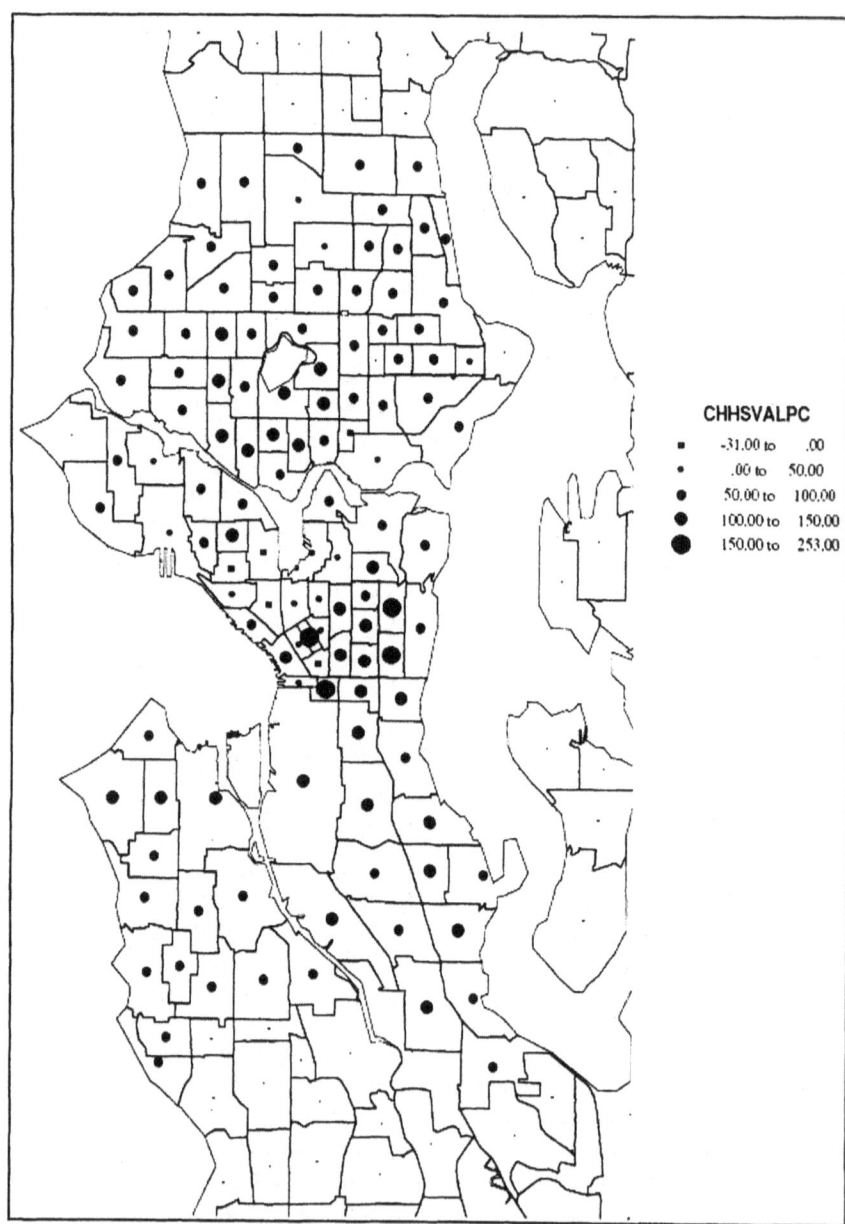

Figure 3-7
Percent Change in Housing Values, 1990-2000

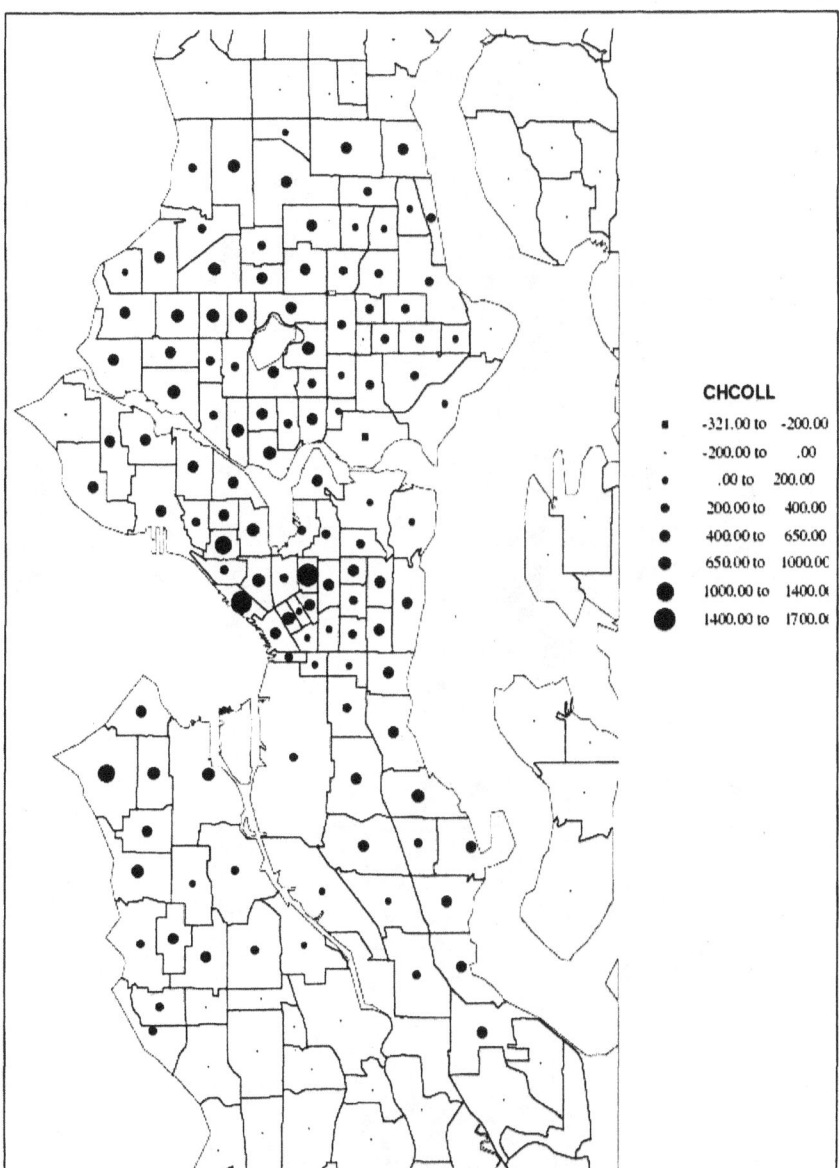

Figure 3-8
Change in Percent with College Degrees, 1990-2000

Richard Morrill

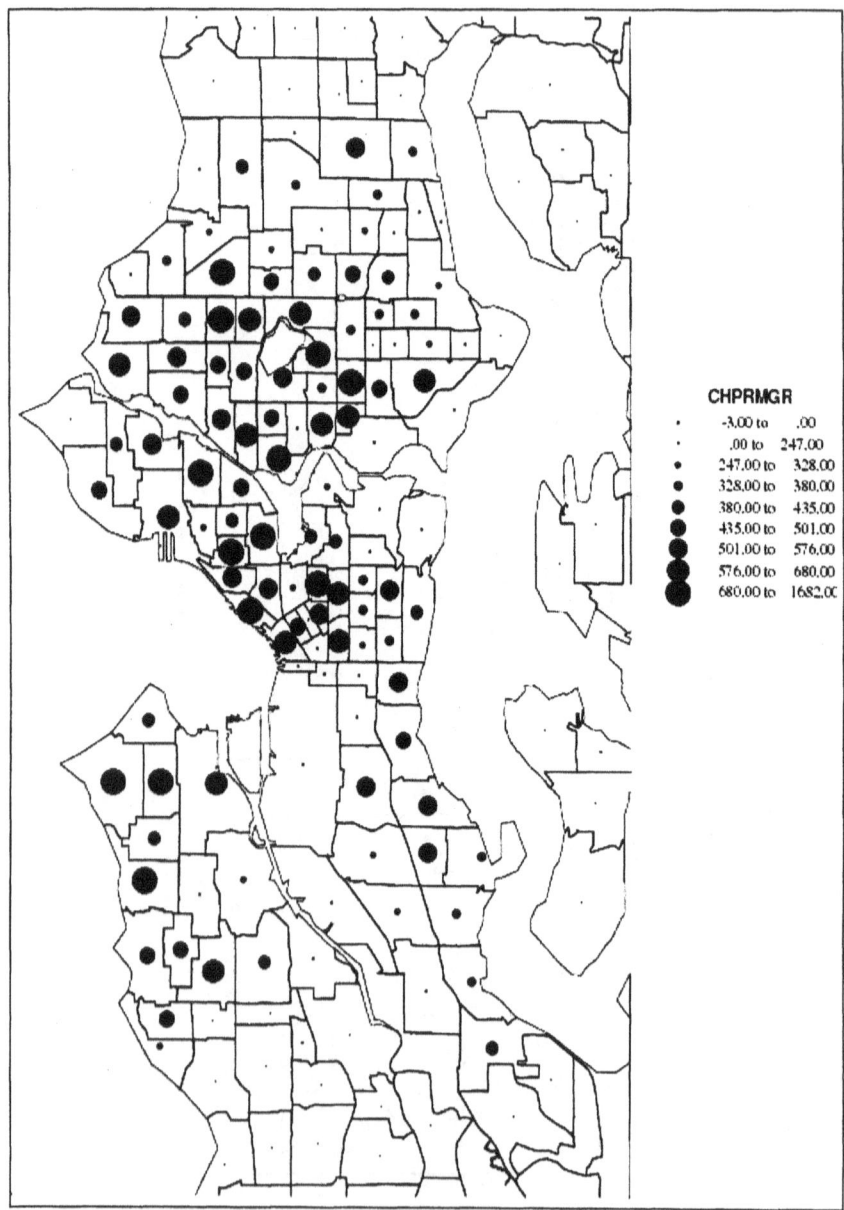

Figure 3-9
Change in Professional / Managerial Share of Employment, 1990-2000

either affluent areas already high in professionals, or at the northern and southern edges of the city, areas with increased shares of minorities and immigrants, with lower levels of education.

The distribution of clerical, sales and office workers does not relate to the areas of gentrification, but shares are high in one area of rapid growth, immediately northeast from downtown. Not surprisingly, service worker shares declined in most areas of gentrification and increased in the northern and southern edges of the city, the areas of growing minority and foreign born shares. Clearly, gentrification is primarily related to professional occupations and secondarily to some part of service and sales-office occupations. The displacement of many service and clerical workers to the edges of the city and beyond is a major effect of higher class resettlement of the city core.

Income, Poverty and Inequality

By now the reader will not be surprised that the areas of greatest gain in median household (Figure 3-10) income were for the most part the areas of gentrification downtown and near downtown to the north and east, the Fremont-Green Lake area west of the University, part of West Seattle and down the shore of Lake Washington to the southeast, plus a few areas with very high professional occupations. Areas of least income growth were the northern and southern edges of the city, with many new immigrants, and a few already affluent, but less professional parts of the city, for example, Magnolia and far southwest Seattle.

Change in the percent of poor persons (not mapped) is not quite the mirror image of change in income—most areas of gentrification did experience reduction in the percent poor, especially in the downtown to university corridor, and in areas of minority displacement in the south end. Increased shares of poverty occurred in the areas of recent immigration and where non-professional employment prevailed, as in the far north of Seattle. However, despite increased income and reduced poverty, the levels of poverty are still high in downtown Seattle, where several shelters are located, the University district (students, temporarily) and in minority areas to the south and southeast.

Income Inequality

Again it is not surprising that as inequality is highest in metropolitan areas with high shares of professional and managerial occupations, so is inequality highest in the parts of Seattle dominated by professionals—downtown, greater Capitol Hill, and near the university. Income inequality is relatively low in middle and upper class areas of families and owned homes and, intriguingly, in the low income minority areas of southeast Seattle.

The geographic concentration of domestic migrants (*migration;* not mapped) is very concentrated, and indeed, a powerful indicator of gentrification in the area broadly surrounding Lake Union. Note that these are not people

Richard Morrill

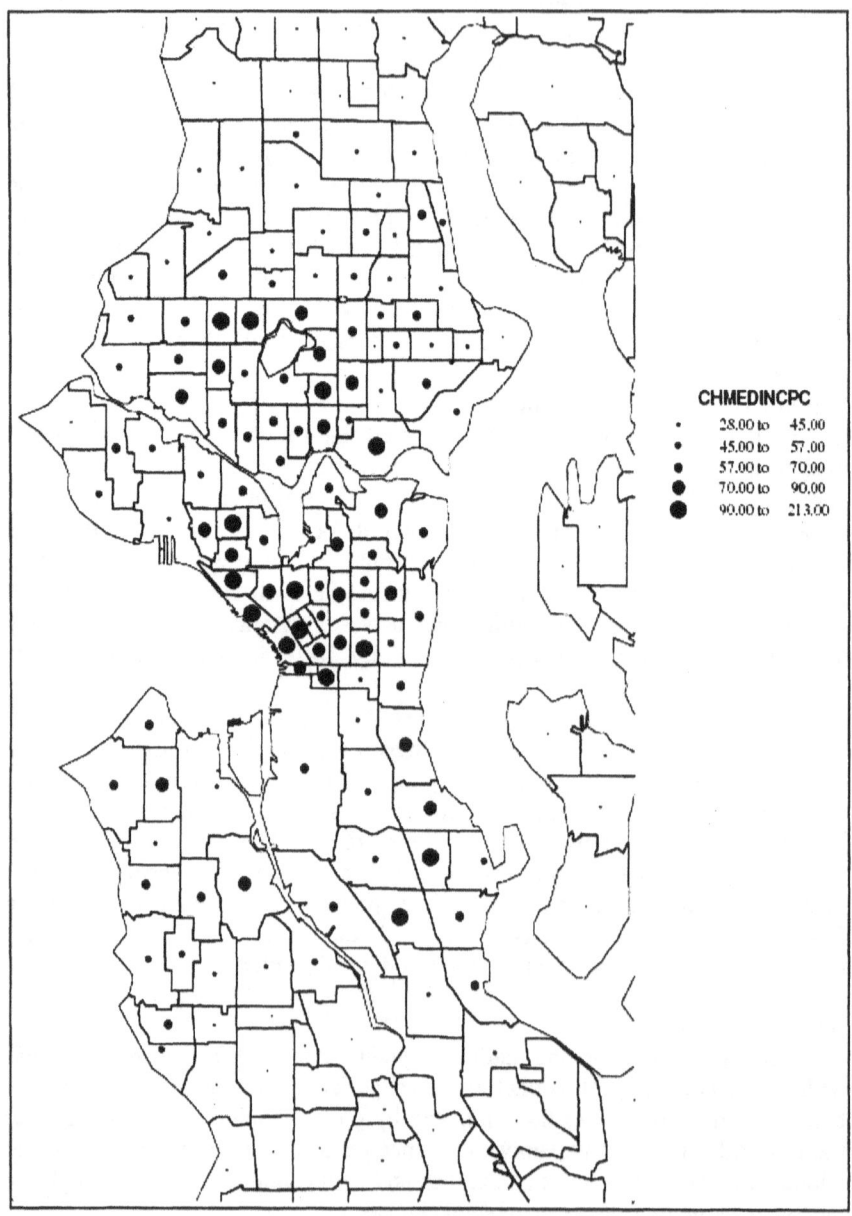

Figure 3-10
Percent Change in Median Household Income, 1990-2000

moving within the county—those values are far higher in the suburbs. In rather fairly large numbers, these agents of social change are migrants from other counties and other states, attending the universities, and filling high tech and professional jobs in the central gentrifying area. Increases in the migrant share were primarily downtown, on Queen Anne and west of the university (Florida 2002, 291).

Place of Work / Means of Transportation to Work or Study
    With these elements (not mapped), it is no surprise that the zone with the highest proportion working in the city (over 80%) is precisely the zone of professionals and high levels of education, the belt across the city from downtown to Green Lake, and the areas of gentrification—while the lowest levels are in poorer areas and at the edge of the city. The map of change in the share working in the city is more complex; downtown shares rose in some newly gentrifying areas of Queen Anne, Ballard and Green Lake, while shares working in the suburbs rose significantly in the singles, non-family areas encircling downtown; many of these work in the high-tech 520 corridor on the eastside but prefer the excitement of inner Seattle living.

DIMENSIONS OF GENTRIFICATION

These maps of 1990-2000 change in a number of variables paint a convincing descriptive picture of components of social change-cum-gentrification. The picture is quite complex and multivariate; there is unlikely any single construct to be derived. Rather this is precisely the kind of complex process for which data reduction/factor analysis was designed. How are the many variables interrelated, and which help measure the various possible forms of gentrification discussed earlier?
    After a number of experiments with varying combinations of variables, the following parsimonious set resulted in three simple dimensions of social-demographic change, 1990-2000 (Table 3-2)
    The ordering of the three dimensions does not imply their relative importance to social change in the city, only different forms of a complex process. They do support both the economic and cultural interpretations of gentrification discussed earlier. Dimension 1 captures the form of gentrification in which downtown landowners, developers and the city successfully reclaim the downtown core for middle and upper class residence as well as high-rise offices. Some poor are displaced. Dimension 2 recognizes the more direct displacement form of gentrification in residential areas, of lower class by higher class households, and often of Blacks by whites. Dimension 3 reflects the significance of both lifestyle and job and school related demand for inner-city living by the young.

Richard Morrill

Table 3-2
Factor Analysis Results

Variable	Dimension One: Redevelopment	Dimension Two: Displacement	Dimension Three: Replacement
Income Change	.85		
Percentage Poor, Change in	-.68		
Median Rent, Change	.68		
Ownership Percentage, Change in	.66		
Population Change, Percentage	.48	-.47	
Percentage Black, Change in		-.88	
Percentage white, Change in		.77	.41
House Value, Change in		.76	
Percentage Migrants			.72
Percentage College Educated, Change in			.71
Percentage Non-Family 2 Persons or More		.34	.56
Change in Percentage Professional	.35		.55
Percentage Aged 25 to 34, Change in	.43		.48

Dimension 1: Redevelopment
"Rich and poor" relative change in income, rent and ownership and population growth, mainly via downtown core high-rise development

Dimension 2: Gentrification-Displacement
"White and Black" class displacement of poorer by richer and/or Blacks by whites; little population change, but housing price inflation

Dimension 3: Gentrification: Replacement
"Lifestyle" concerns lifestyle and class: the young, educated, professional and mobile—and often unmarried versus the more traditional lower and middle class families.

The ordering of the three dimensions does not imply their relative importance to social change in the city, only different forms of a complex process. They do support both the economic and cultural interpretations of gentrification discussed earlier. Dimension 1 captures the form of gentrification in which downtown landowners, developers and the city successfully reclaim the downtown core for middle and upper class residence as well as high-rise offices. Some poor are displaced. Dimension 2 recognizes the more direct displacement form of gentrification in residential areas, of lower class by higher class households, and often of Blacks by whites. Dimension 3 reflects the significance of both lifestyle and job and school related demand for inner-city living by the young.

CLUSTER ANALYSIS

The map discussion revealed that patterns across the above variables had specific geographic patterns, suggesting that high and low levels of scores on each of the three factors ought to exhibit distinctive spatial distributions. A reasonable way to uncover such patterns is to use cluster analysis to group tracts with similar values in the three dimensions. Cluster analysis does not yield a clear unambiguous number of sets of clusters, but hierarchical clustering (Ward's Method) with varying numbers of clusters led to selection of an 11-region solution, a compromise between greater precision and desired simplicity. The regions are profiled in Table 2, with mean factor scores and mean values on 12 component variables; the clusters are mapped in Figure 3-11. We can characterize the eleven clusters or subregions as follows:

1 General decline in status—moderate, increasing minorities;
2. General decline in status – small;
3. Gentrification "c"—displacement, but little change in status (see 10)
4. Gentrification "c"—rejuvenation by young, educated, income decline
5. Gentrification "c"—small status change, but shift to young, educated, non-families
6. Transition -- Population, income and whites gain, but not young and educated
7. Transition -- Same, but strong planning influence
8. Gentrification "a" Core redevelopment – moderate
9. Gentrification "a" Core redevelopment – high
10. Gentrification "b" Displacement – moderate displacement and housing inflation
11. Gentrification "b" Displacement – high displacement and housing inflation

Richard Morrill

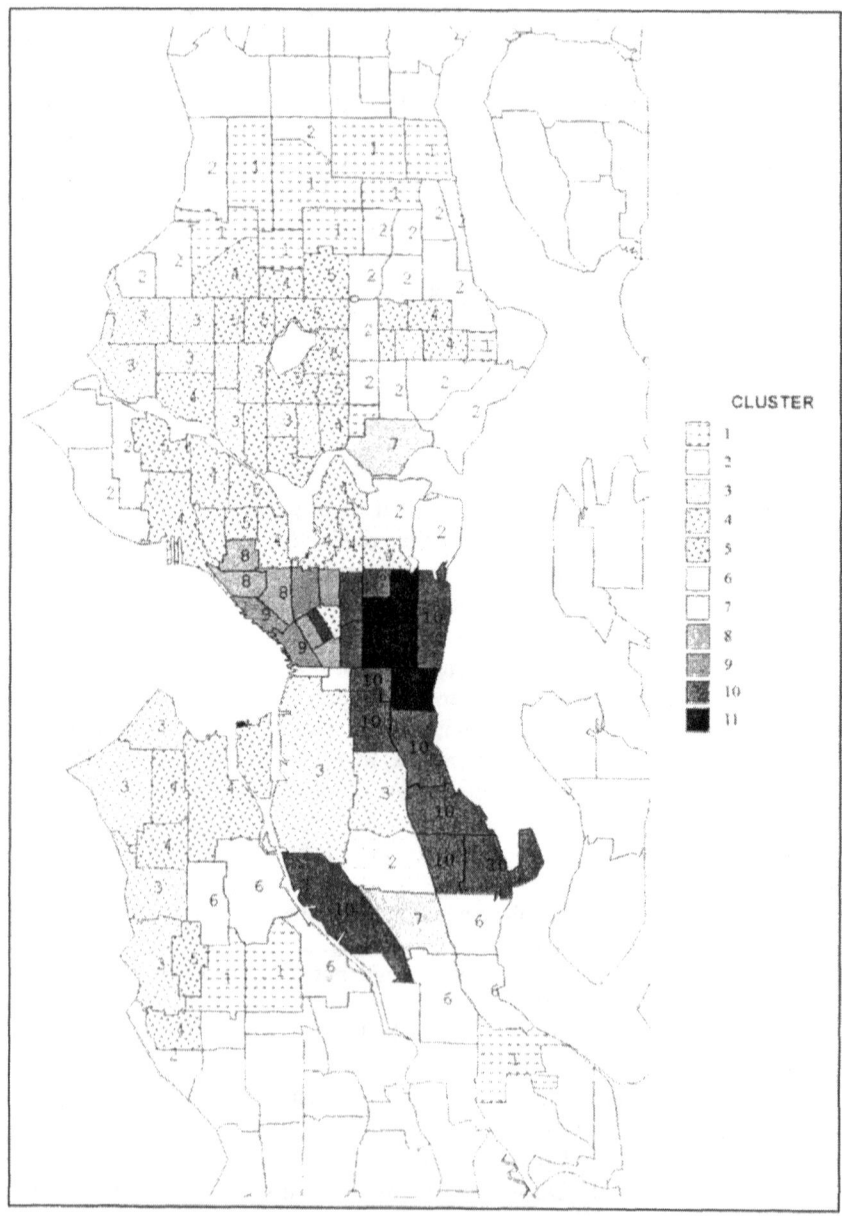

Figure 3-11
Clusters

Discussion of Clusters

The pattern of clusters reveals a distinct zonation or sectorization with respect to downtown Seattle, thus rather beautifully supporting the expectations discussed earlier. That is, a core of gentrification in areas of highest access to downtown and to the University of Washington, transitioning to areas of actual decline at the periphery of the city. Further, because of the variety of agents contributing to gentrification and renewal, different forms of gentrification predominate in different sectors.

Clusters 1 and 2 experienced moderate to small absolute and relative declines in status—income, rents, home values, home ownership, education and occupation. These clusters occupy the far northern and far southern fringes of the city, mainly early postwar settled areas, as well as more affluent view and waterfront edges of the central core; these are the primary single-family home areas of Seattle. Cluster 2 tracts are, for the most part, historically wealthy and white, while cluster 1 tracts, away from Puget Sound and Lake Washington, experienced significant apartment construction, white loss, minority population growth (the only cluster to gain Black households). These latter areas have the lowest rents and least housing price inflation and are thus attractive to less affluent families, often working downtown, but who are outbid for more central locations. These areas had below average income growth, and an increase in poverty rates.

Clusters 3 and 4 exhibit smaller declines or stability in overall status, but did experience social change—a transition or succession suggesting a potential next wave of gentrification. These clusters, too, show a below-average rise in income or rents, but above average gains in the college educated, often 35-54 year old population, and losses in the elderly. Cluster 3 (Ballard, West Seattle, Fremont) experienced well-above average housing value inflation and cluster 4 (Queen Anne, Eastlake) above average gains in professional managerial workers. These clusters are intermediate in location, in a roughly concentric zone inward from the relatively declining zones 1 and 2 but beyond the core more gentrifying zones 6 to 11. Both clusters are dominated by smaller houses/bungalows from the 1920s to 1950s—usually industrial worker housing in the 1940s and 1950s, but now gaining population of the more affluent students and 'new economy' professionals, working around or between downtown Seattle and the University of Washington. These new residents are replacing an aging population. This aging population is one that is either dying in place or moving out of the city to more affordable and safer far suburban and exurban communities—that is, they *may be* willingly displaced. From the location and from commuting patterns, the cluster 3 and 4 tracts are north and west, or immediately south of the university, areas directly in the influence zone of the university and associated biotech and high-tech activities around Lake Union, while the tracts in Queen Anne attract replacing and rejuvenating downtown workers; and tracts in West Seattle, traditionally blue collar, are being transformed by a wave of downtown-commuting professionals.

Cluster 5 is similar to the preceding clusters 3 and 4, but comprise areas more fully gentrifying, or at least with a more dramatic degree of social change. These tracts are in the same intermediate zone, often intermingled with cluster 3 and four tracts. Almost all are in the Queen Anne- Ballard-Fremont-Wallingford and Greenlake areas north and west of downtown and the university, and often tracts of significant recent apartment construction (urban "villagization") as well as housing reinvestment, and townhouse infill development. These areas have above average gains in income, rent, housing values, professionals and the college-educated, and young non-family households, including many partnerships, typically opposite sex. The share of persons over 25 with BA degrees rose by an amazingly high sixteen percent. These changes were abetted by growth management policies of densification and infill, by the city and state encouraged location of high tech jobs, but they also represent the logical zone of expansion of these activities and these populations, and the transition was made easier by the aging of pre-existing populations and declines in small businesses.

Clusters 6 and 7 are somewhat anomalous, and probably not gentrifying in the expected sense. Cluster 6 consists of six south Seattle tracts historically Asian and mixed-industrial and lower class. The tracts grew in population, families and home ownership, and in income and median rents, but education and occupation levels fell, because the growth was entirely Asian and Hispanic, or racially mixed and often immigrant. The cluster might just qualify as an area of community revitalization of a non-elite population. Cluster 7 includes two tracts, one containing the University of Washington itself, where the rise in status is a consequence of very small numbers of non-dormitory university housing. The other tract contains the "New Holly Park" public housing project, with deliberate displacement of poor, mainly Black households, via the inclusion of "market rate" housing, filled by liberal professional households, often public-sector employees.

The remaining two sets of clusters are the more traditional downtown resurgence (clusters 8 and 9) and whites-displacing-blacks character (clusters 10 and 11). Cluster 9 includes the four core downtown tracts of extreme change in population (100%), income (140%), and rent (99%), home ownership (new condominiums), and above average gains in the college-educated, in professionals, and even gains in Blacks and Asians, often immigrant professionals. The growth is entirely in the form of high-rise mixed use apartments and condominiums. This resulted in the displacement of many older SRO buildings and hundreds of the poor, although a number of downtown shelters remain. Cluster 8 includes the surrounding (and intermingled) downtown and edge-of-downtown tracts, including the First Hill hospital district, and with the next highest population gains, high income and rent gains, by far the highest gains in 25-34 year olds, and the second-highest gains in the college-educated and professionals. The most remarkable attribute of this downtown ring cluster is the extremely high share of migrants – from outside the county, and usually from outside the state.

Clusters 10 and 11 lie entirely on Capitol Hill, the oldest Seattle residential community (1860-1910) just east of downtown, and to the east in Madrona and Leschi and in the historical Black community extending southeastward (known as the CD or "central area," down through Rainier Valley). Capitol Hill (the northern edge) has always been relatively "liberal", educated and professional; the large Jewish population in the 1940s and 1950s was tolerant, and the area became the main locus of gay settlement and consciousness, at least since the 1970s. Finally just east and south of Capitol Hill, the "CD" was the actual core of Black settlement, not in the industrial lowlands adjacent to downtown, but by historical accident, in an inherently accessible and fairly desirable area. Constrained from expansion west and north from around 1970 by strong white demand (cluster 4 areas near downtown and the university), the Black community grew southward in the 1970s and 1980s, right down to the city limits, displacing lower and middle class white families to the southeastern suburbs. Cluster 11 consists of tracts with exceptionally high Black population loss (-25%) and white reentry (share up 12.5%), and with by far the highest housing price inflation (145%), as well as of non-family households (and as much as two-thirds gay and lesbian), and also with above average gains in income, rent, college education, professionals and young adults 25-34 years of age. These areas are as low as 10-15 minutes by excellent transit from downtown and First Hill jobs, often with large historic homes, and were thus probably inevitably at risk of reinvestment and displacement—almost entirely the result of individual decisions, with little or no public intervention. The surrounding set of tracts, cluster 10, extends far down the area of historic Black settlement, but is most prevalent in the more affluent, more desirable tracts along Lake Washington, some of which never lost a white majority, even if locally segregated, and which are now experiencing losses of Blacks, moderate gains in whites, high housing value inflation, and above average gains in young professionals and non-family households.

This is the point at which it is customary to answer the 'why' question with an appropriate statistical model. I do not do so for two reasons: first, there is no satisfactory dependent variable encompassing enough of gentrification, although I could have treated change in median income, in share of Blacks or whites, change in median housing values (or rents), or change in non-family households, or change in professionals; second, most of the available predictor variables are hopelessly ambiguous as to endogeneity or exogeneity; all are at least partly outcomes. Other plausible variables, which could be obtained, like the location and types of employment change, are also simultaneously determined; or like distance from downtown or the university, true but totally obvious. Thus I rely on the above recounting of the varying context and situation of social change across the city and cluster types.

DISCUSSION AND CONCLUSION

From the tabular comparisons of change in the city of Seattle with change in the rest of King county, from the maps of decadal change in a number of characteristics, and from the factor and cluster analyses, the fact of gentrification in the city is certain. The city experienced substantial increases in population, in income, in house values and rents, in levels of education and of professional employment in different forms in different parts of the city. The city, as a result, experienced decreases in the Black population, in poor persons, and, relative to the rest of the county, even in single parent households. There is no other word for it—a massive shift in the class structure and degree of inequality—and not a case of the tide raising all boats. The city indeed rose in median as well as mean income, but because of the in-migration of higher-class households, not because of a rise in status of the lower class households already here. Indeed inequality deepened, and there was a net out-migration of the less affluent.

The agents of gentrification were overwhelmingly educated professionals—white, Asian and some foreign born—primarily young singles, families and unmarried partnerships, but also many empty nesters and even some traditional families!

The geography of this gentrification was decidedly central, in the core area dominated by downtown and the University of Washington, and between them. Indeed the census tracts with highest rent and housing inflation were those with good access to both. Within this gentrifying core, occurred some interesting variation in the agents: in and around downtown, families, and single professionals and service workers were prevalent. To the east, on Capitol Hill and into the Central Area ("CD") area of reinvestment, where Black families were displaced, young singles and same sex partners were common. In West Seattle and Queen Anne, young singles and both young and empty nester families were significant. And in Wallingford, Fremont and Green Lake, west of the University, students, young families, and many unmarried male-female partners were common.

Since the city grew substantially in population, the displacement and replacement forms of gentrification were less important numerically than the redevelopment form, because of the sheer large additions to the housing stock. Possibly, for example, the magnitude of downtown growth relieved what would otherwise have been a far greater degree of displacement in the surrounding areas. Also, while the displacement of Blacks from the core area of gentrification can be interpreted as a victory of more powerful whites over weaker Blacks, it is possible that some of the displaced may turn out to have become fairly satisfied new suburban residents, not viewing themselves as victims. This is somewhat similar to the experience in Washington DC (Glick, 2003). While the "Plan" is intended to bring middle class whites back to the city, those displaced include winners as well as losers in terms of housing.

In the face of higher rents and housing costs, and in addition to declines in real average wages relative to the educated professional elite, the majority of the population, who fill all those lesser jobs, dealing with stuff and people rather than ideas, either had to double up in existing housing or shift from their own houses to far less desirable apartments, or move to the far edge of the city or far beyond, Thus, enduring a longer and longer commute –or at the extreme, falling into homelessness. Yet the liberal elite is astoundingly indifferent to the plight of this hapless, disempowered majority, who are not only told that they must accept inferior housing and give up the wasteful "American dream" of their own homes, but should also give up their selfish cars and enjoy a long bus commute perhaps to those core service jobs they cannot hope to live near.

Why did this occur? The economic context was industrial restructuring and globalization, the burgeoning high-tech and information economy, which attracted young professionals from the rest of the US and from abroad. The environmental context was the Seattle region's glowing reputation as a mecca for outdoor recreation. But why the city of Seattle and the central core of the city in particular? Certainly the city experienced a large increase in high tech and information jobs in precisely the greater Lake Union area, around which gentrification occurred. In addition, the social-environmental context proved to be critical, and in at least three ways—the high tolerance for and visibility of unmarried partners, both same and opposite sex, the re-creation of a vibrant, fairly exciting downtown and near downtown street and night life—which had been absent from 1955 to 1985, and now immensely attractive to singles, young couples/partners, and many empty nesters, and third, the absence of a sizeable minority underclass. Because Seattle did not have a sizeable inner blighted area, because the 1890-1940 housing stock of the core was basically sound, because the micro-natural environment, the hills, views and lakes and waterfront, was so attractive, and because of the global position of Seattle and the competitiveness of its industrial and professional sectors, the core really did constitute a huge potential for profitable redevelopment and, ideally, a source of municipal revenues to assist the less competitive. The high degree of social tolerance and the high quality of the regional natural environment helped attract exceptionally high numbers of the intellectual elite who most strongly support the forms of gentrification that have occurred, and the 'smart growth' philosophy and lifestyle that sustain it. Obviously the city government, as well as liberal city voters are sensitive to critiques of the negative displacement effects. As a result, the city has maintained a sizeable program of public housing, supported by a series of large housing levies. There are also church and other non-profit housing programs, but on balance the reality is a large net shift of poorer households and lower quality housing to the suburbs.

Finally there is the planning context, the role of a decade of growth management. Growth management did not cause gentrification directly, but it encouraged and enabled it. Growth management, via urban growth boundaries, upzoning, and designation of urban centers and urban villages, made infilling and redevelopment highly attractive and even necessary to builders of both offices and of housing. But the degree of change was certainly enhanced by both economic and demographic change, the attractiveness of the region to the young, driven in part by the growth of high tech sectors, and of households seeking an urban as opposed to a suburban lifestyle. Essentially the city itself is highly attractive physically and culturally to liberal, educated, urbanist parts of the population, and these people are the ultimate forces for gentrification.

Social change in Seattle in the 1990s certainly echoed the experiences of many other cities in the US, Canada and Europe, as both local governments and capital took advantage of demographic and economic and post-suburban cultural change to reclaim core areas of cities. While the Seattle example tends to support a predominance of gentrification and a class shift in well-being, over a more positive revitalization interpretation, the story is very complex, with some recognition of the social costs.

BIBLIOGRAPHY

Badcock, B. (1995). "Building Upon the Foundations of Gentrification: Inner City Housing Development in Australia in the 1990s." *Urban Geography.* 16:70-90.

Beauregard, R. (1990). "Trajectories of Neighborhood: The case of Gentrification." *Environment and Planning A*, 22:855-874.

Bourne, L. (1993). "The Demise of Gentrification." *Urban Geography*, 14:95-107.

Central Puget Sound Real Estate Research Committee. (2001). *Central Puget Sound Real Estate Research Report, 2001.* 52(1). Pullman, WA: Central Puget Sound Real Estate Research Committee.

Central Puget Sound Real Estate Research Committee. (2003). *Central Puget Sound Real Estate Research Report, 2003.* 54(1). Pullman, WA: Central Puget Sound Real Estate Research Committee.

Clark, E. (1994). "Toward a Comparative Interpretation of Gentrification." *Urban Studies*, 3:1033-1042.

Clark, E. (1991) "The Rent Gap Reexamined." *Urban Studies*, 32:1489-1503.

Florida, Richard. (2002). *The Rise of the Creative Class: and How It's Transformed Work, Leisure, Community and Everyday Life.* New York: Basic Books.

Glick, Jonathan. (2003). *Neighborhood Catch-22? Considering the Place(s) of Revitalization in the Gentrification of Washington, DC*. MA Thesis, University of Washington.

Hodge, D. (1979). *The Seattle Displacement Study*. Seattle: City of Seattle Office of Planning.

Hodge, D. (1981). "Residential Revitalization in a Growth Region." *Geographical Review*, 71:188-200.

Hodge, D and Lee, B. (1981). "Spatial Differences in Displacement Rates in US cities." *Urban Studies*, 21:219-231.

Knopp, L. (1990). "Some Theoretical Implications of Gay Involvement in an Urban Land Market." *Political Geography*, 9:337-352.

Lees, L. (1994). "Rethinking Gentrification: Beyond the Positions of Economics or Culture." *Progress in Human Geography*, 18:2:137-150.

Ley, D. (1986). "Alternative Explanations for Inner-City Gentrification." *Annals, Association of American Geographers*, 76:521-535.

Ley, D. (1996). *The New Middle Class and the Remaking of the Central City*. New York: Oxford University Press.

Smith, N. (1992). "Gentrification and Uneven Development." *Economic Geography*, 58:139-155.

Smith, N. (1996). *The New Urban Frontier: Gentrification and the Revanchist City*. New York: Routledge.

4 Who Pays for Education? The Urban – Suburban Conflict in Summit County, Ohio

Allen G. Noble, Deborah P. King, and Frederick Boateng

Funding of the educational system in the state of Ohio is in turmoil. Democrats joust with Republicans; the Republican controlled state legislature is in conflict with the Republican governor over the budget; the state Supreme Court takes the legislature to task for not adequately funding public education, which violates the state constitution; the National Tax Foundation ranks Ohio 35th in the nation in taxes per capita and 37th in taxes per $1000 of personal income; and the League of Women Voters reports that on February 5, 2002, 11 out of 15 school funding issues were defeated (League of Women Voters 2003, 3).

This chapter places the defeat of an innovative, but flawed, education tax proposal in the context of the larger education funding tumult. In a larger purview, it analyzes why one recent issue failure serves as an example of a central city-suburban conflict that typifies many American urban scenarios.

URBAN POPULATION STEREOTYPES

Helping to explain the dynamics of the issue we offer several loosely-drawn stereotypes which apply to citizens in both the city and suburbs. Although these are generalizations they help to clarify the positions of many voters in the election.

Suburban communities usually have two principal population components. First, there are the life-long residents of the community, or those who have moved from other, but similar, suburban places. While not ethnically homogeneous, they have only loose ties to specific ethnic groups and backgrounds. Having spent their lives in the suburbs, they identify with suburban culture and have a basic discomfort with the lifestyle of the central city, and in some instances even distrust.

A second population component is made up of those individuals who are more recent migrants to the suburbs. They often are seeking a haven from congestion, noise, crime, and declining facilities and infrastructure of the central city. They have a basic uneasiness that the conditions from which they are escaping, and which characterize the central city in their minds, may ultimately spread into their new location. It is a variation of the "not in my backyard" view.

Central city residents also have differing groups. Those residents of the inner city, unable to afford many aspects of modern life, may view suburbanites as affluent persons who siphon off the wealth of the city. They often have an innate inferiority complex which surfaces at times in open hostility. Even everyday life can be a struggle for them and publicly funded schools should be viewed as an asset.

Another population segment finds itself trapped between the inner city group, who they feel are given favorable treatment which they have not earned, and the suburbanites, who they view as increasingly the leisure class and who certainly do not work as hard as they do. Fundamentalist religious orientation often reinforces these views.

All of these basic orientations are modified by an individual's age, level of income, education and other socio-economic factors that cause their reactions to issues to vary from place to place and from person to person. Two such positions are attitudes toward taxation and their perception of the value of education. Finally, a certain *laissez faire* attitude affects all components of society, but with different impacts.

OPPOSITION TO NEW TAXES

Ohio like other states faces serious financial difficulties. The governor and the Republican majority of the legislature are in conflict over the raising of taxes and the necessity of providing support to vital services, education included. The governor threatens to drastically cut services (education funding) unless the legislature votes for higher taxes. While the governor's position appeals to many, the legislators have correctly read the will of the people. A columnist in Akron, Ohio's *Beacon Journal* (Hoffman 2003) commenting on a recent survey notes "more people are upset with him (the governor) over taxes than cuts. While 17 percent cited opposition to proposed tax increases in their disapproval, only 5 percent named budget cuts". The survey also "revealed the general anti-tax bias that runs through the state electorate like the proverbial third rail" (Hoffman 2003). Much of this attitude derives from the educational level of citizens in Ohio where 83 percent of the citizens have attained a high school diploma or higher (Bureau of the Census 2000) but only 21 percent have earned a Bachelor's degree or higher. This compares to national values of 80 percent for high school degrees and higher, and 24 percent for Bachelor's degrees or higher.

To a large extent, these figures reflect the orientation of Ohio's economy and the philosophy of many political and education leaders in the state. An economy primarily oriented to manufacturing, as Ohio's has been, needs a trained work force which a high school level education provides. The critical need for a college-trained population has not been so apparent. Hence, thinking and policy have not caught up with necessity. As the state seeks to meet the challenges of a post-industrial economy with its lowered needs for manufacturing support, the compelling necessity to advance education has not been effectively communicated to the citizens of the state, nor to enough political leaders. The situation even impacts elementary and secondary schools which the Ohio Supreme Court has judged to be inadequately funded. Perhaps the greatest obstacle to educational advancement at all levels is the certainty that such a gain requires additional financial commitment and support. Such support must, of course, come from state revenue.

Contrary to widespread popular opinion in Ohio, state taxes are not high when measured against those of other states. In fiscal year 1999, Ohio ranked 35th in taxes per capita and 37th in taxes on personal income (League of Women Voters 2003). In Ohio, public education is now financed principally by property taxes. Recently, however, this resource has been declared to be inadequate by the Ohio Supreme Court, who call upon the legislature to design an adequate system to fund state public education as mandated by the state's constitution. Total reliance upon property taxes in an age of tax abatements to attract development, and an aging population base is not only unwise—it is not meeting the financial requirements.

With respect specifically to education issues, one aspect of the opposition to taxes relates to basic mistrust of government officials to deliver on funding approved in the past. The *Akron Beacon Journal* reported (2002f), that "every state tax increase since the 1930s has been enacted as new money for schools. . . . After each tax was enacted, however, the new money was redirected." One especially blatant example involves the state lottery profits in Ohio. Admittedly, revenues from the state lottery are declining because of the poor state of the economy, but although the lottery was sold to Ohio voters as a painless way to finance public education, the legislature regularly and routinely diverts profits away from education and into the general fund where it goes into other programs. Compounding the problem is the conduct of the legislature. When profits do go to school districts and various educational facilities, then the general educational appropriations are reduced by a similar amount. Thus education rarely receives the entire amount of additional funding promised as a result of voter approval of the lottery.

Redirection of revenue from tobacco fund settlements represents a similar instance. Education was trumpeted as the beneficiary only to find once again, that the proceeds are redirected to the state's general operating fund.

As a consequence of such misdirection, local schools have had to resort to bond issues and local property tax levies. Further complicating the education funding situation is the issue of private enterprise or charter schools and their support by state revenue. It is argued by many that this diversion reduces support to public schools without much reduction of work responsibilities. The number of students in private schools is not large enough to affect the workloads in public schools. Thus, state financial support which is based upon total school enrollment removes resources without reducing work.

CURRENT FUNDING SCENARIO

In most school districts tax increases (bonds) must be approved by voters in a referendum. Tedin,et al (2001) found that approval has been more and more difficult to get in recent years. Conducting a survey of the National Association of School Boards, they found that one-fourth of school districts had recently experienced the rejection of a bond proposal. In Ohio, public education is currently financed principally by property taxes. Reliance on property taxes is inadequate and hence the state is not meeting its constitutional responsibility. In the state of Ohio, the funding reform conflict has been tied up legally since 1988 when the basic unfairness of the way public schools were funded was realized and court challenges were instituted.

The citizens of Ohio have seen property taxes routinely increased at a time when the population who are homeowners, is steadily aging. Many are already retired with fixed incomes and slowly declining purchasing power and support for school funding wanes as different personal budget items take priority. The population of Summit County is aging. In contrast, the national figure for median age was 32.9 years in 1990. By 2000, the country's median age was the highest it has ever been, 35.3 years. Nationally, the number of people over the age of 85 continues to rise. This cohort equaled 1.2 percent in 1990 and in 2000 equaled 1.5 percent of the total population. Examining the cohorts over age 65 years of age, the percentages were 12.5 in 1990 and 12.4 in 2000. Data for the state of Ohio and Summit County are presented in Table 4-1 below. Ohio and Summit County show median ages for 1990 and 2000 that are higher than the national figures. As well, the percentage of population over 65 is greater than for the United States as a whole, and the population cohort over 85 years is on the rise. This trend is guaranteed to continue with the aging of the baby-boom generation and aging property owners are an unreliable source of school funding. It is well documented that senior citizens are more likely to vote than younger adults, and their attitudes toward politicians and issues while often self-directed, cannot be neglected.

Table 4-1
Age Characteristics

variable	United States		Ohio		Summit County	
	1990	*2000*	*1990*	*2000*	*1990*	*2000*
Median Age (in years)	32.9	35.3	33.3	36.2	34.3	37.2
Percentage Aged 65 Years or Above	12.5	12.4	13.0	13.3	13.8	14.1
Percentage Aged 85 Years or Above	1.2	1.5	1.3	1.6	1.3	1.6

Source: Bureau of the Census 1990, 2000

STUDY AREA

Summit County is located in northeastern Ohio. Akron, the largest city in Summit County is located approximately 35 miles southeast of its largest neighbor, Cleveland (Figure 4-1). The city of Canton is to the south and Youngstown is directly east. By Bureau of the Census definition, Akron is included in the Cleveland-Akron Consolidated Metropolitan Statistical Area. The region, urban in nature, has a population over one million. General population characteristics for the county and the City of Akron for 1990 and 2000 are shown in Table 4-2. However, for school funding purposes it is the county level that matters.

Within Summit County there are seventeen whole school districts, but school district boundaries do not necessarily coincide with county boundaries (Figure 4-2). There are four peripherally located districts which cross the county boundary with Summit County voters. Reminderville located in the extreme northeast corner of the county falls within the Aurora school district in adjoining Portage County. As well, students in Clinton and Franklin in the southwest corner of the county are part of the Northwest School District in Wayne County. The City of Green in the southeast has a few families that attend the Jackson Schools in Stark County, and finally, a section of the Highland School District is located within Copley Township along the western edge of the county. For the most part, these enclaves are small in both geographic area and population,

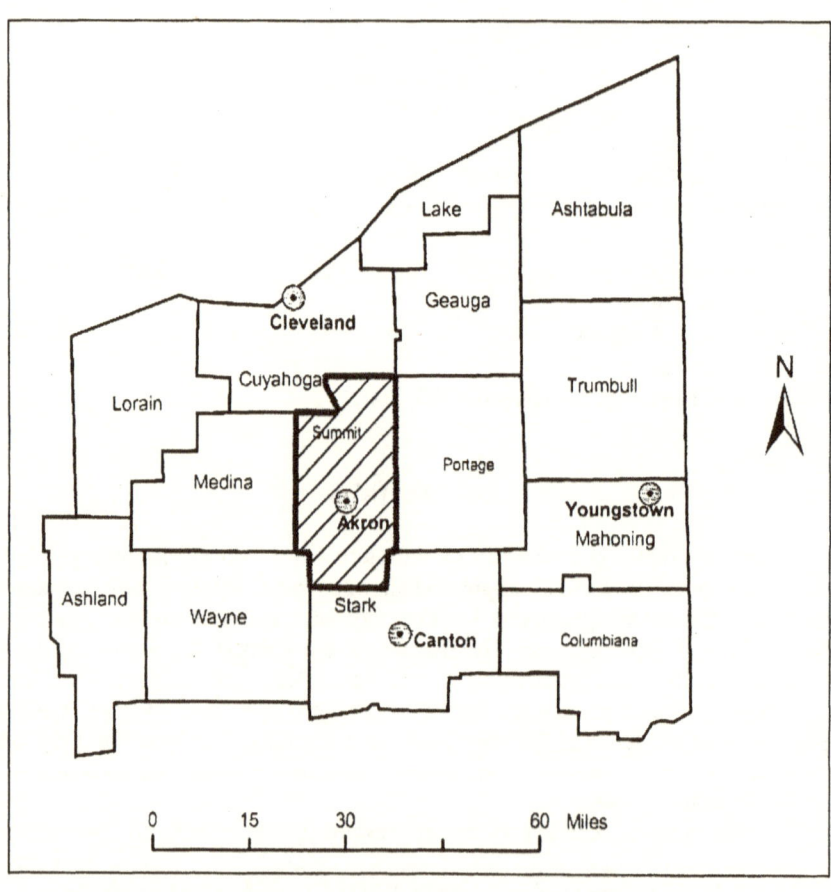

Figure 4-1
Location of Summit County in Northeastern Ohio

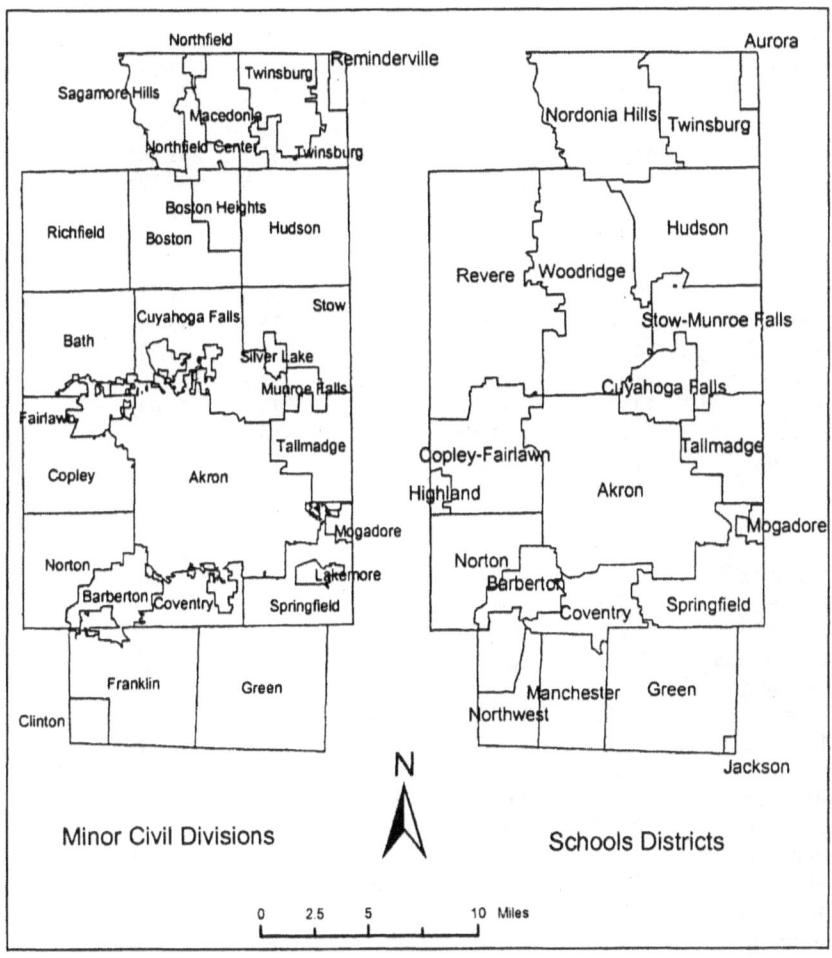

Figure 4-2
Census and School District Boundaries, Summit County, Ohio

Table 4-2
Population Characteristics by Minor Civil Division

Minor Civil Division	Population 1990	Population 2000	% Change from 1990	Median Age (Years), 2000	Median Hshld. Income (Dollars), 2000	College Graduates (%), 2000
Akron	223,019	217,074	-2.67	36.6	21,835	18
Cuyahoga Falls	48,950	49,374	0.87	31.8	42,263	26
Stow	27,998	32,139	14.76	32.8	57,525	36
Barberton	27,623	27,899	1.00	22.0	32,178	11
Green	19,179	22,817	18.97	36.5	54,133	26
Hudson	17,128	22,439	31.01	33.8	99,156	67
Twinsburg	9,606	17,006	77.04	38.3	61,638	39
Tallmadge	14,870	16,390	10.22	35.3	49,294	24
Springfield	14,773	15,168	2.67	34.6	41,226	10
Copley	11,130	13,641	22.56	34.2	55,195	40
Franklin	14,910	12,339	-17.24	34.0	51,082	20
Norton	11,475	11,523	0.42	30.6	47,085	17
Coventry	11,295	10,900	-3.50	39.8	41,276	17
Bath	9,015	9,632	6.84	30.4	88,899	54
Sagamore Hills	6,503	9,340	43.63	35.6	67,401	37
Macedonia	7,509	9,224	22.84	29.1	68,908	32
Fairlawn	5,779	7,307	26.44	33.6	62,180	46
Richfield	5,010	5,424	8.26	39.6	71,336	32
Munroe Falls	5,,359	5,314	-0.84	40.2	61,169	34
Northfield Center	3,982	4,931	23.83	40.5	59,213	24
Mogadore	2,967	3,893	31.21	36.4	51,540	18
Northfield	3,624	3,827	5.60	36.2	41,028	13
Silver Lake	2,756	3,019	9.54	34.0	70,875	51
Lakemore	2,684	2,561	-4.58	48.2	34,129	8
Reminder-ville	2,163	2,347	8.51	33.9	56,964	30
Twinsburg Township	1,896	2,153	13.55	38.1	54,659	29
Clinton	1,175	1,337	13.79	430	49,353	18
Boston Heights	733	1,186	61.80	37.5	80,884	41
Boston	1879	1,062	-43.48	31.4	51,146	30

Source: Bureau of the Census, 1990, 2000.

but allegiance toward a county-based tax initiative for school improvements, of which they are not a part, can be logically questioned.

Geographically speaking, the myriad of boundaries within the county makes analysis challenging. School funding issues are most often placed on the ballot at the local school district level. Demographic data are available by census enumeration units such as minor civil divisions, tracts or block groups and election results are available based upon city, township or village wards, and precincts. For Summit County there are 32 minor civil divisions according to the Census, as well as hundreds of precincts, all of which contribute to the larger voting behavior scenario. Historically, the seventeen school districts are larger, in many cases, than the minor civil divisions. As population dynamics shift within a county, school district boundaries remain unchanged with suburban districts feeling more and more of the brunt of population increases.

Four school districts in Summit County have average enrollments over 5,000 students: Akron, Hudson, Stow-Munroe Falls and Cuyahoga Falls. With the City of Akron, these three suburban districts with large enrollments represent well the differing pressures placed upon school districts as population changes. Between 1990 and 2000 population growth for these areas varied. Cuyahoga Falls experienced "baby boom" growth earlier as the suburb just to the north of Akron, and between 1990 and 2000 population growth slowed to just one percent, while the city of Akron lost three percent of its population. Timing for growth was later for Hudson and Stow-Munroe Falls and populations increased 31 percent and thirteen percent respectively between 1990 and 2000. *The Plain Dealer* (Davis 2003), reporting on population change from 2000 to 2002, highlighted the following Summit County communities with population gains greater than five percent: Peninsula (8.5%), Macedonia (6.9%), Richfield (6.1%) and Stow (5.5%). The City of Akron (-1.3%) and Lakemore (-1.7%) registered the highest population losses in the county. The shift in population from city center to suburbs continues in Summit County, yet the schools need to be maintained. The question becomes "Who Pays for Education?" Demographically, can the location of support be identified? What is the most logical way for citizens to pay for school facilities, curriculum, programs, supplies and personnel needed regardless of whether the city/district is in a stage of population growth, stability or decline?

THE FALL 2002 PROPOSAL

The general election in November of 2002 gave Summit County voters a chance to supplement school funding by supporting a 0.5 percent sales tax increase. The county sales tax would increase from 5.75 percent to 6.25 percent. Monies raised over 30 years would be shared throughout the county for permanent school improvements. The Proposed Sales and Use Tax for the

---

OFFICIAL QUESTIONS AND ISSUES BALLOT   9(12)
GENERAL ELECTION — NOVEMBER 5, 2002
SUMMIT COUNTY

12   **PROPOSED SALES AND USE TAX**
                COUNTY OF SUMMIT

A majority affirmative vote is necessary for passage.

The County Council of Summit County proposes to levy a sales and use tax in the amount of one-half of one percent (1/2%) for the purpose of providing additional revenue for permanent improvements within the County, to be distributed by the community improvements board established by Ordinance 2002-374 for school districts, for a period of 30 years, effective January 1, 2003, or the earliest time permitted by law.

Shall the resolution of County Council of Summit County proposing a 1/2 of one percent sales and use tax, be approved?

| YES | 165 ➡ |
| NO | 166 ➡ |

Source: Summit County Board of Elections, 2002.

Figure 4-3
Summit County Ballot

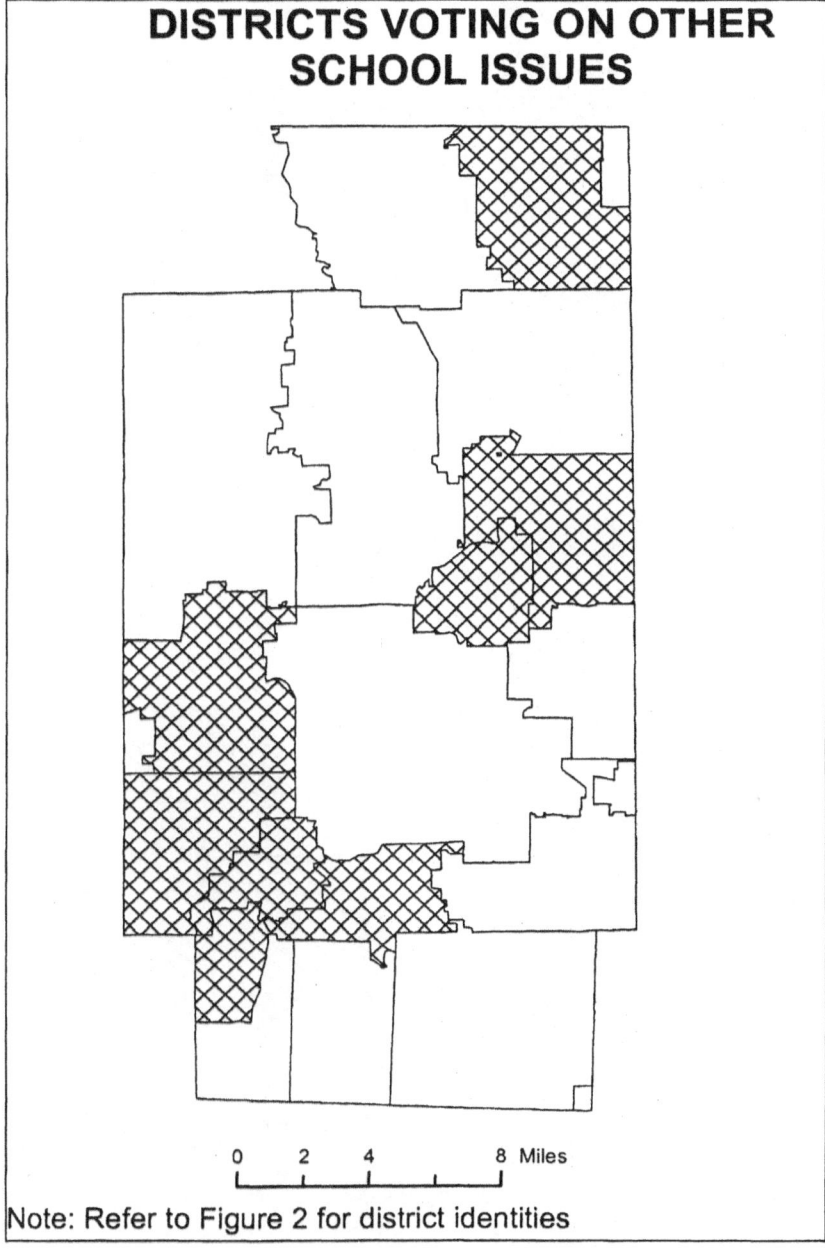

Figure 4-4
Districts Voting on Other School Issues

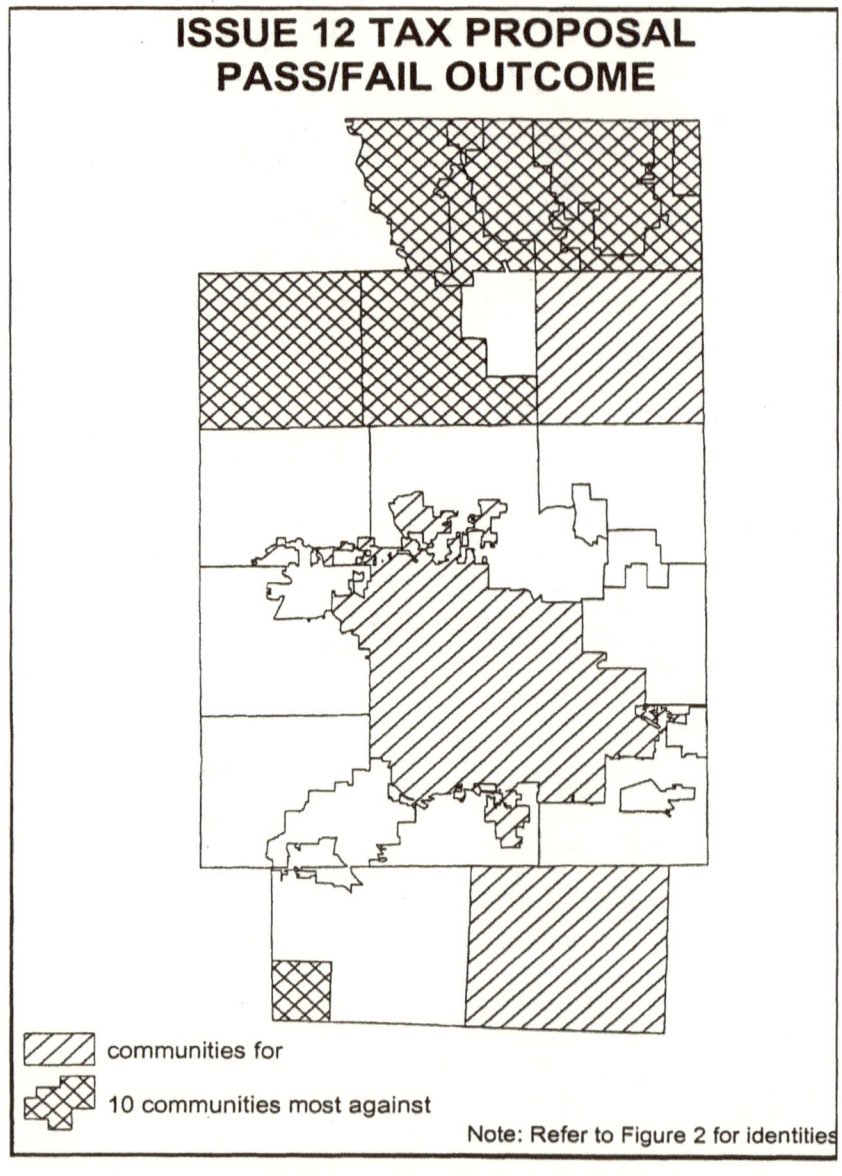

Figure 4-5
November 2002 Pass / Fail Outcome

County of Summit appeared on the ballot as shown in Figure 4-3.

School financing issues, like this sales tax increase, are appearing more often on ballots in both primary and general elections as districts wrestle with increasing costs and decreasing funding from the state. In November 2002, 31 districts in northeast Ohio out of a total of 97 districts (about one-third) voted on funding issues. In Summit County, seven school districts placed issues on the general election ballot: two tax renewals, one tax replacement and four tax increases (Figure 4-4). Citizens in these districts were voting on the county sales tax proposal at the same time they were weighing local increases.

By examining the sources of support as reflected by "for" votes, and lack thereof, for a county-based tax initiative to support public schools, the central-city/suburban conflict becomes apparent. What areas in Summit County, Ohio supported the tax and what areas did not? Can the pass/fail election results, entwined with differing social and economic parameters, support the premise that indeed an urban/suburban split exists?

ISSUE 12: THE VOTE

Were Summit County voters willing to support a sales tax to fund school improvements for the next 30 years? The outcome was:

For the sales tax: 74,947 (46%)
Against the sales tax: 86,922 (54%)

The sales tax proposal was defeated by an eight percent margin and countywide, Issue 12 passed only in three places: the cities of Akron, Green and Hudson (see Figure 4-5). Based on census boundaries, the map clearly indicates the strong negative position of the northern tier of suburbs. Of the top ten communities casting the most votes against the sales tax issue, nine are in the northern part of Summit County. As previously mentioned and displayed in Figure 4-4, Twinsburg was working to pass their local school funding issues and the sales request was most likely perceived by voters as just too much at one time.

Reminderville students are included in the adjoining Portage county school district and voters there could not view the sales tax as a benefit to their community schools. Clinton in the southwest corner of the county was a similar situation to Reminderville. Clinton voters cast three negative votes for every yes vote for the proposal. Clinton students are not part of a Summit County system.

The urban-suburban argument could certainly be made that voters in the northern part of Summit county have more orientation, hence allegiance, to Cuyahoga County (Cleveland) for employment and shopping and could not be convinced to support the sales tax proposal. Perhaps these people live in Summit County to avoid the typically higher sales tax of Cuyahoga County in the first place. Did the perceived distance of, and benefit primarily to, the Akron Public Schools sway the voters in the northern suburbs? Does a bias exist within the county? After all, Akron had a lot to gain if the issue passed. The mayor backed the proposal and campaigners from Akron were diligent. Many aging schools in the city would receive long overdue repairs and in some cases buildings would be replaced altogether.

As shown in Figure 4-6, The City of Hudson has a consistent history of passing school related issues. *The Plain Dealer* (October 27, 2002) states, "Districts that routinely passed school taxes had commonalities – businesses to share the tax burden, educated voters, high income levels, high property values and good state report card scores". The cities of Hudson and Green are socially and economically similar and well matched with these parameters. Also important, Akron, Hudson and Green were not voting on their own local school issues in November 2002, as were seven other districts in Summit County. Suburban voters in districts with other school issues were deciding not just how much they could afford to pay, but also were controlling, more protectively, the destination of their future contributions. Of these suburban issues, five of the seven passed in November 2002.The Green local school district also had an issue on the November 5 ballot to require use of the revenue from the proposed sales tax increase for construction. This displayed at least one community's attempt to ensure that sales tax receipts would in fact be directed to school repair and new construction. It passed with an approval of almost two-thirds of those voting (64.19%). That the issue received such a high approval may confirm the idea that misdirection of approved funding has become an issue for voters. In the event, however, the issue became moot with the defeat of the sales tax issue.

The two districts, Copley and Norton, which had failing issues on the November ballot, continued to have a lack of success in presenting property tax issues. In May 2003, both districts saw their proposals fail again. Coventry voters have the poorest record of support for school funding in the county. Norton is not much better (Figure 4-6).

Table 4-3 shows voter registration statistics for the city and the county. Interestingly, the percentage of eligible voters (18 years and over) for the county as a whole and the city of Akron are the same. Both the county and the city show a sizeable increase in the percentage registered from 1990 to 2000. According to the local Board of Elections, this is due in large part to the fact that the voter registration files are now purged less often. If voters move away, or die, they now remain on the rolls for a period of time, creating artificially high numbers in 2000. Additionally, 2000 was a presidential election year and registrations and turnout are typically higher for these elections.

It is one thing to register to vote, and quite another thing to actually go out and vote once or twice a year. When it comes to voting behavior, city-county disparities are apparent. Voter turnout for this issue ranged from a high of 70

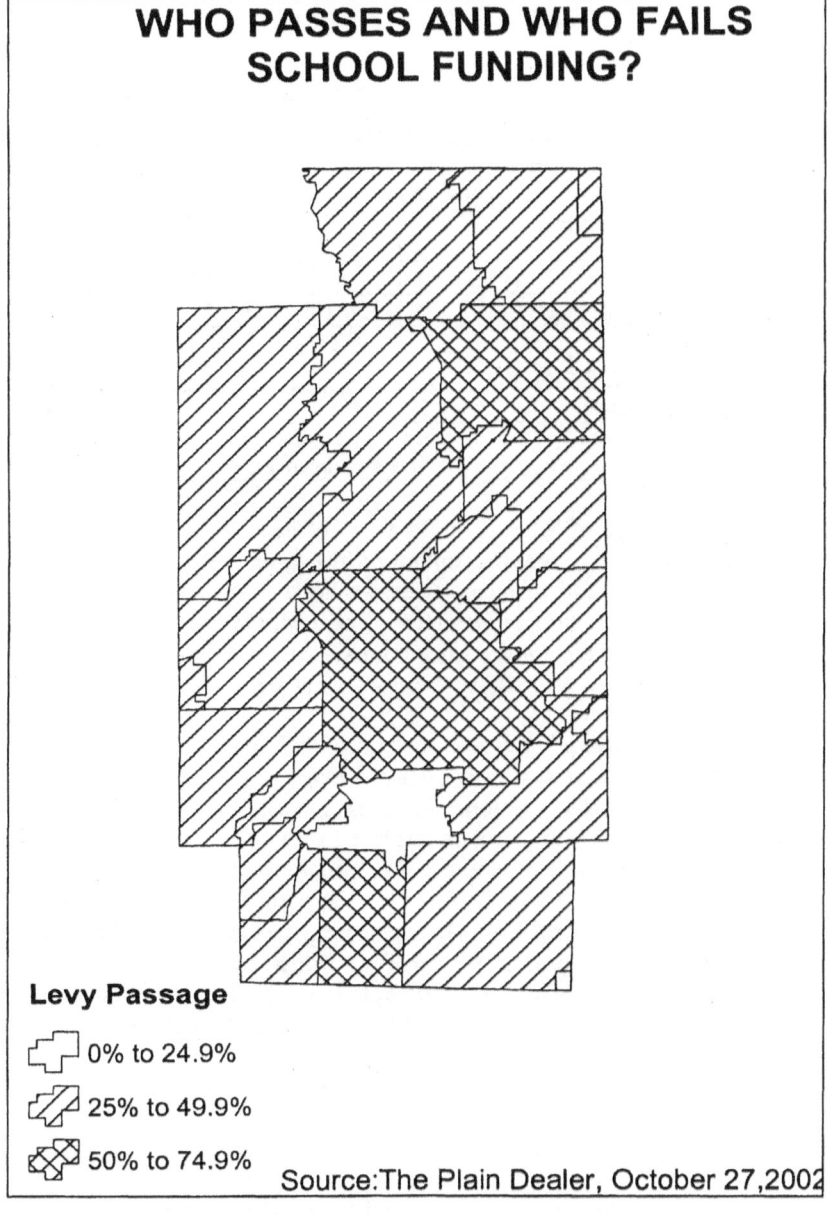

Figure 4-6
Who Passes and Fails School Funding?

Table 4-3
Eligible Voters

| | Summit County | | City of Akron | |
	1990	2000	1990	2000
Total Population	514,990	542,899	223,019	217,074
Population 18 Years and Above	389,201	406,913	168,468	162,108
Percentage of Total	75%	75%	76%	75%
Registered Voters	282,655	354,189	109,239	127,427
Percentage of Eligible Voters Actually Registered	73%	87%	65%	79%
Sources: Source: Bureau of the Census, 1990, 2000.				
Note: Between 1990 and 2000 the law changed regarding how long voter registration records are to be maintained. Currently, files are purged less often.				

percent in the Village of Silver Lake to a low of just 36 percent in Northfield Village. In the City of Akron, the turnout for the general election in November 2000 was 43 percent and there the sales tax issue passed. For the remaining areas of the county, the turnout averaged 53 percent. On average, three percent of the voters did not vote for the sales tax issue at all. Button (1993) refers to behavior not to vote on an issue as "roll-off", and states that Blacks "roll-off" more often than Whites.

Twinsburg Township had a five percent roll-off, representing the high, and just one percent of the voters from Clinton Village skipped the sales tax issue. As mentioned previously, Clinton Village is not part of the Summit County Public Schools. In Twinsburg, voters displayed strong feelings against the sales tax proposal and the roll-off was four percent. Citizens of the Twinsburg School District had two of their own school related issues on the ballot: a 6.9 mill tax renewal and 2.75 mill tax renewal. Both of these issues in the Twinsburg district passed. As noted, voter turnout ranged from 70 percent to 36 percent for the proposed sales tax. Approximately 3,000 voters or 3 percent did not address the issue with their vote. Highest and lowest turnout percentages are given in Table 4-4

FINDING COMMON GROUND

Based on just one general election, and a non-presidential election at that, can an explanation be found for the sales tax defeat by comparing voter turnout, age, median income and education attainment? Closer examination, however, shows little correlation with data provided by the Census.

Figure 4-7 gives the median age pattern for civil divisions in Summit County. No clear relationship seems to be provable between age and voting behavior on the sales tax issue. The three districts (Akron, Hudson, Green) all fall within the middle category of median age (Figure 4-7), but so too do many

Table 4-4
Voter Turnout by Rank for November 5, 2002, by Municipality

Highest 10 Turnout		%		*Lowest 10 Turnout*		%
1.	Silver Lake	70		1.	Northfield Village	36
2.	Munroe Falls*	64		2.	Lakemore	42
3.	Stow*	58		3.	**City of Akron**	**43**
	Norton*	58		4.	Reminderville	44
	Bath	58		5.	Barberton*	47
	Richfield Twp.	58			Boston Twp.	47
7.	**Green**	**57**		7.	Twinsburg City*	48
	New Franklin Village	57			Twinsburg Twp.*	48
	Fairlawn*	57			Clinton Village	48
	Franklin Twp.	57		10.	Springfield	49

* Voted on local school-related issues on November 5, 2002. **Green** and **Akron** passed the sales tax proposal.

districts opposed to the issue, and some of them strongly (compare Figures 4-5 and 4-7).

Age also does not seem to be related to voter turnout. Green ranked among the top ten highest districts in voter turnout (Table 4-4), Akron ranked among the lowest, and Hudson was in the center. Perhaps the widely held view that senior citizens come out to vote in higher proportions and that they do not favor tax increase issues has limited viability. Another socio-economic factor frequently cited in discussion of voting behavior is educational level. Again, the results from these three districts supporting the levy are not instructive (Figure 4-8). Hudson falls within the highest category of college graduates, Akron in the lowest, and Green in the center. There appears to be little correlation between education attainment and approval or rejection of the sales tax issue.

However, it should be remembered that we did not have any information on how individuals voted. We simply cannot know if individuals with higher education or lower education voted or how they voted. Hence, it cannot be determined with certainty that higher education affected the vote positively and lower education negatively, as is widely thought to be the case.

A final socio-economic indicator often advanced is income. Figure 4-9 gives median household income for civil divisions in Summit County. Not surprisingly, the pattern of income in districts which favored the sales tax is the same as that of education—Hudson high, Akron low, Green in the center, and the same caveats apply.

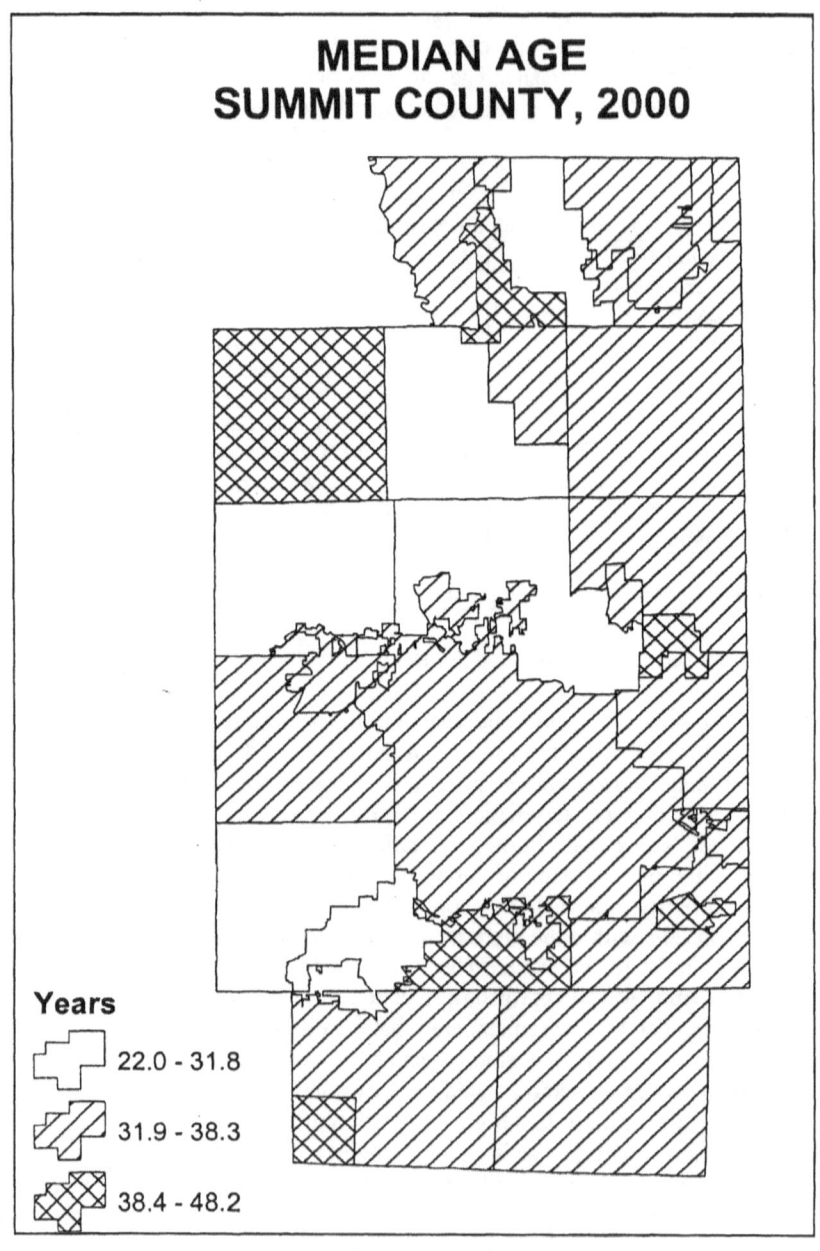

Figure 4-7
Median Age in Summit County, 2000

THE VOTERS WRITE

Perhaps the clearest answer as to why some people and districts favored the sales tax and others did not, is to be found in the opinions expressed by writers of "Letters to the Editor" in the *Akron Beacon Journal* (2000a through f, 2003) the local daily newspaper. Letters reflecting positive reactions and attitudes (and presumably favorable votes) in addition to hand wringing and depreciation of voter attitudes and performance generally dwelt upon three themes. There was a common plea to support education, remarks on the value of "good education", and the practicality of approving local funding in order to secure matching funds from state sources which otherwise would not be forthcoming. Negative letters were more revealing. They gave several specific reasons for not voting in favor of the sales tax issue. One important consideration expressed in many letters was the attitude that voters had been misled in the past and felt they would be in the future. One letter (*Beacon Journal* 2002e) asked the question, "Who would be sure that in, say, 15 to 20 years money would not be redirected elsewhere? We have seen this happen in other matters." Another letter (*Beacon Journal* 2002d) observed that "there would be no accountability of the powers that be". The writer further noted that "Most people also felt they had been 'had' by the promise that creating the Ohio lottery would help schools. This new appeal for funding seemed to be another case of someone trying to pull the wool over the eyes of the public". Other letters sounded the same theme of unhappiness over monies approved by voters for education being diverted to other purposes.

The often referred to lottery theme emerged after the 1973 passage of State Issue 1 by Ohio voters by better than a 2 – 1 margin. The Ohio Legislature earmarked profits to education in 1983 (Ohio Lottery Commission 2003) However, from time to time, some funds have been diverted to support other needs. Even more significant, however, has been the subterfuge engaged in by the members of the legislature who reduce other funding previously earmarked for education by amounts approximating the lottery proceeds. In effect, this results in a zero sum game for Ohio public education and is one of the most critical reasons for the problems of education funding in the state.

Clearly associated with the issue of basic mistrust of government officials is the question of the length of life for the proposed sales tax. For many voters, both in Akron and the suburbs, the long period seemed to offer unusually favorable opportunities for diversion and misuse. The 30-year life of the tax was determined by the estimated time needed to raise sufficient funds to meet the matching requirement to secure state funds.

Nevertheless, beneath these often expressed reasons for the defeat of the issue, a few other undercurrents surfaced. Some voters felt that the sales tax proposal offered no relief for "overburdened property owners" but merely added more tax. Others felt that the sales tax would be inadequate to cover the

Allen G. Noble, Deborah P. King, and Frederick Boateng

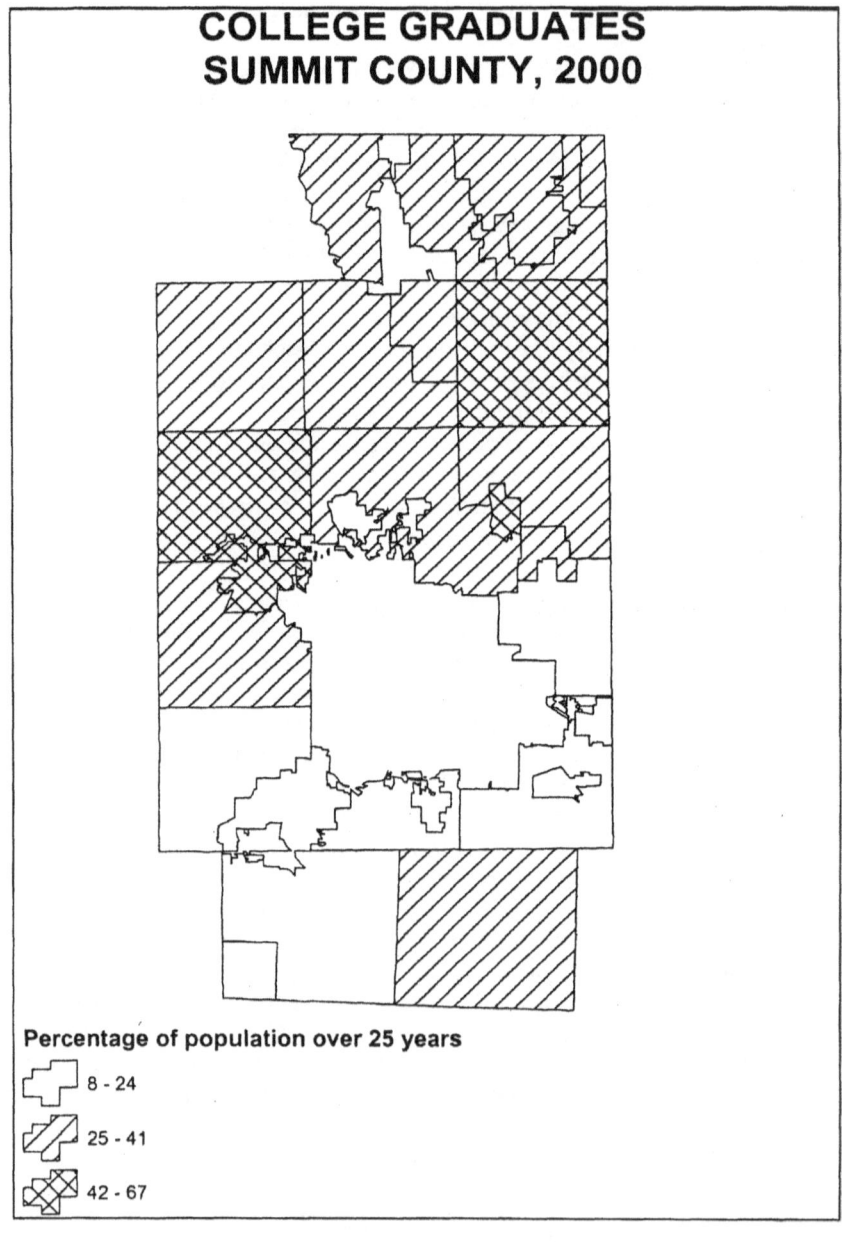

Figure 4-8
College Graduates, Summit County, 2000

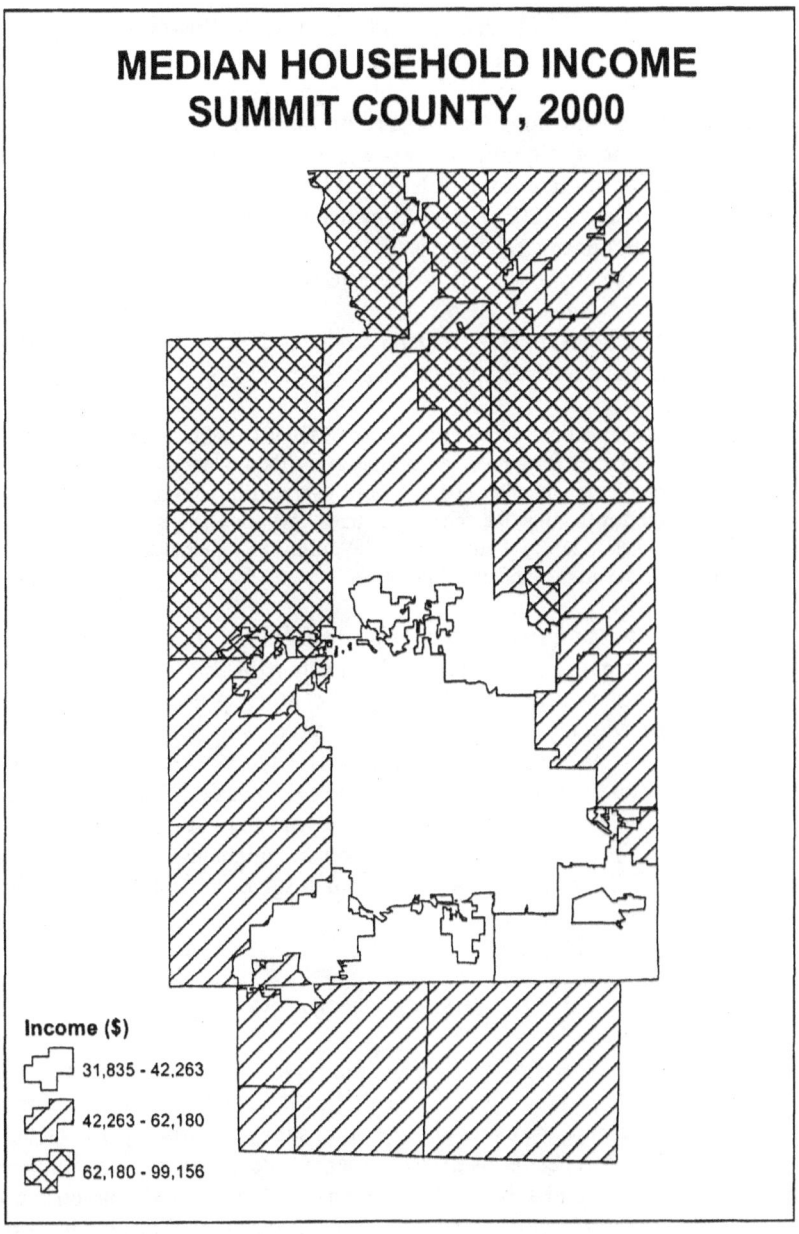

Figure 4-9
Median Household Income, Summit County, 2000

inevitable cost overruns. The idea of a sales tax was the first-ever attempt by an Ohio county to fund education in an alternative fashion. Many voters were skeptical and numerous letters to the editor found fault with the promoters for not publicizing and explaining the logistics of the issue. "No one ever laid out a clear plan as to who was going to oversee the disbursement of funds and how foreseeable problems, such as possible illegal uses of money would be handled" (*Akron Beacon Journal* 2002e) Barberton mayor, Randy Hart agreed, "voters didn't completely understand the issue . . . . Barberton voters approved a renewal levy for the city's schools, while rejecting the sales tax (*Akron Beacon Journal* 2002a).

A November letter (*Akron Beacon Journal* 2002b) listed many of the unanswered questions on the minds of voters.

> What concerned me was that the Akron Mayor Don Plusquellic and Summit County Executive James McCarthy [both Democrats] were to appoint a nine member board. I wasn't sure what the board was to do. Would it monitor the release of funds? What decisions would it make, what authority would it have? Would it be required to adhere to a per-student disbursement formula?

Many of the questions and objections embedded in letters to the editor have their root in the strongly held distrust which suburban and rural residents have for the City of Akron officials. The mayor, a strong personality who led the campaign for the sales tax, is not noted for his diplomatic skills and antagonisms between city and suburbs have grown during his mayoral tenure. On the evening of the sales tax issue's defeat, the mayor on television said, "there are people in suburbia who would rather cut off their right arm than help Akron." A letter writer observed, "A more humble public servant might have stressed how to come together in the spirit of cooperation to resolve our collective problem" (*Akron Beacon Journal* 2002c).

THE SOLUTION

The problem of raising matching funds for school construction was ultimately solved for Akron by the passage in May 2003 of an increase in the city income tax. Perhaps the cycle of depending solely on property taxes, at least in Summit County, has been broken. At the same time the success only increases the gulf between city and suburbs. Only voters in Akron could vote on the tax increase, but estimates are that about 60 percent of the tax will be paid by people who work in Akron but live elsewhere (*Akron Beacon Journal* 2003). One can only wonder how many citizens in the suburbs that did not have a chance to vote on the income tax change are aware that a change has indeed been approved.

REFERENCES

Akron Beacon Journal (2002a). Letter. "Outlying voters doom issue 12", 7 November.

Akron Beacon Journal. (2002b). Letter. "A fine idea...", 13 November.

Akron Beacon Journal. (2002c). Letter. "Smelled like fried pork", 13 November.

Akron Beacon Journal. (2002d). Letter. "Accountability is the key", 13 November.

Akron Beacon Journal. (2002e). Letter. "Issue 12 failure is no surprise", 13 November.

Akron Beacon Journal. (2002f). Letter. "Tax issues ahead", 12 December.

Akron Beacon Journal. (2003). Letter. "Akron schools win", 7 May.

Bureau of the Census (1990). 1990 Decennial Census of Population. http://factfinder.census.gov

Bureau of the Census (2000). 2000 Decennial Census of Population. http://factfinder.census.gov

Button, James 1993. "Racial Cleavage in Local Voting: The Case of School and Tax Issue Referendums." *Journal of Black Studies,* 24:29-41.

Davis, Dave. (2003). "Cleveland Still Losing Residents to Suburbs; Cuyahoga Only County that Drops in Numbers." *The Plain Dealer.* 10 July.

Gonzales, Jennifer and Ebony Reed. (2002). "The ABCs of Passing School Issues Successful Districts have Similar Qualities." *The Plain Dealer,* 27 October

Hoffman, Steve. (2003). "Paying attention, paying taxes," *Akron Beacon Journal,* 6 March.

League of Women Voters of the Akron Area. (2003). *The Voter* (January) 1-9.

Ohio Lottery Commission (2003). www.ohiolottery.com/about/history/html

Summit County Board of Elections (2002).

Tedin, Kent, Matland, Richard and Weiher, Gregory. (2001). Public Schools Through Referenda. *The Journal of Politics,* 63: 270-294.

5 A Major Challenge for Romanian Towns: The "Large Habitats"

Ioan Ianos

Romania was one of the most highly centralized countries of the former communist system. Its contradictory evolutions were the result of increasingly incoherent voluntary interventions. In 1948, the country was largely rural, with less than one quarter of the population living in urban areas. Over the next four decades, though, the total urban population approached 55 percent. That increase was not sustained by a new town-building program, however. Instead, it was the result of the overpopulation of the existing urban centres.

The growth of the urban population came from extensive industrialization, a process that was generalized in the 1980s, and proved very appealing to the rural workforce. Simultaneous with the industrialisation drive, a house-building programme to accommodate the newcomers and their families was put into place (Ianos, 1993). As a rule, compact clusters of new buildings began extending in some parts of the towns or on their outskirts where no constructions existed. There were instances when whole new towns would be raised on vacant land.

At the end of the totalitarian period, the new urban pattern was marked by the appreciable share of these structures, particularly in the county-capitals that rose to these ranks after the year 1968. These compact urban aggregates, formed of multifamily apartment-blocks, were the property of the state (95%). The specialist literature designates them as "large habitats." As long as the state was the owner, it oversaw the maintenance functioning of utilities. In the wake of the massive privatization of the housing sector after 1990, this task devolved on the dwellers' association set up in each apartment block.

The impact of economic restructuring and moreover the slump in people's real incomes is also seen in the steady degradation of these habitats and the depreciation of the urban image, in general. The process of social homogenisation promoted by the past regime materialized in the haphazard location of the workforce in these large residential districts. After 1990, an obvious process of segregation started to occur, with residential districts becoming better individualized, revealing the presence of an upper class.

The large area occupied by the apartment blocks, the abundant population of residential districts and the limited financial means of the local communities make it extremely difficult to integrate these structures into modern urban ensembles capable to offer better comfort and a more attractive urban image. These large habitats are a challenge for urban planners when trying to find adequate solutions to ameliorate their artificiality and make them compatible with the other town structures, as vulnerable themselves and subjected to an ample restructuring process (the case of industrial estates, in particular).

GENERAL CHARACTERISTICS OF ROMANIA'S TOWNS IMPACTING THE LARGE HABITATS

Explosive Urban Growth

The highest urban population growth in Romania took place after 1966. Growth was prompted by a pro-natal policy promoted by the totalitarian regime after 1967 and by the imbalances caused by the uneven development of the urban and the rural areas (Cucu, 1970). The mass transfer of the rural population to towns called for a sustained house-building programme, of a collective type (four to ten story structures) nearly throughout. At the national level, one is struck by the almost perfect relationship (very high correlation coefficient: $r = 0.986$) between the increase of town-dwellers and the housing stock over 1977-1992, for example.

In the 1966 – 1998 period, the urban population increase across the country exceeded six million inhabitants. Their distribution (excepting Bucharest) represented 42.8 percent of the total urban population growth. With a growth of 700,000 inhabitants, Bucharest held only 11.2 percent. Considering that 11.9 percent (an additional 740,000 inhabitants) were contributed by the new settlements given a town status, it follows that all the other middle and small towns registered a population growth of only 34.1 percent. Noteworthy, more than one-third of this volume represented the contribution of middle towns, that is, of the county capitals.

It is this last category of towns that registered explosive changes with spectacular population growth rates. Also some small towns acquired an important urban status within the national settlement network, the number of their inhabitants soaring, for example. Slobozia (by 5.56 times), Ramnicu

Valcea (by 4.79 times), Zalau (by 4.65 times), Slatina (by 4.52 times), and Vaslui (by 4.47 times), due to the very fast pace of industrialization which attracted the rural population. In the range of big cities—former regional capitals, Suceava and Pitesti alone (both middle towns in 1966) more than tripled their populations (by 3.11 and 3.06 times, respectively). Similar explosive rates of growth recorded a few small and middle towns specialized in one or two industrial sectors (Mangalia, Colibasi, Navodari, Rovinari, etc).

Dominance of Industrial Activities

The fundamental changes suffered by the structure of urban activities were the outcome of the policy that equated towns with industry (Candea, 1981). It was mirrored by the direction in which functions evolved and tended to specialize. The nationalization of the large industrial manufacturing firms in 1948 and the subsequent development of industry, in general, and within heavy industry in particular, have changed the ratio between the main economic sectors in almost every town. The new socialist relations established in the economy in social and cultural life, reduced the towns' traditional territorial functions by simplifying and restructuring them. The tertiary functions, which had played a major urban polarization role in the interwar period, gave way to the industrial function (Manescu, 1999).

Three major stages marked the process of urban industrialization, generating the large habitats: 1) the priority development of regional centres and of new industrial branch-specialized towns (1950-1970); 2) the planting of large industrial units in the county capitals and in middle towns (1970-1980); and 3) the industrialization of small towns and of some rural settlements scheduled to become agro-industrial centres (1980-1989) (Figure 5-1).

Since 1989, the industrial function has considerably waned, and its importance is expected to continue to diminish as the tertiary sector is being revitalized. A more complicated situation faces the industrial branch-specialised small and middle towns having one single enterprise in their territory and a large habitat. The drastic slowdown of that enterprise's activity, or even the halt of its production, when other mass services cannot be put in place, has a direct impact on the physiognomy of the large habitat and on the local community's capacity to adapt it to the new conditions.

Disturbed Intra-Urban Structure

The demographic explosion in the upper and median sector of the urban hierarchy was made possible only when the internal town-structure suddenly grew more complicated as industries were being planted therein or elsewhere in the neighborhood (Ungureanu, 1980). On the other hand, the new workforce, originating from the countryside, had to be accommodated, so the construction of big residential districts began.

Ioan Ianos

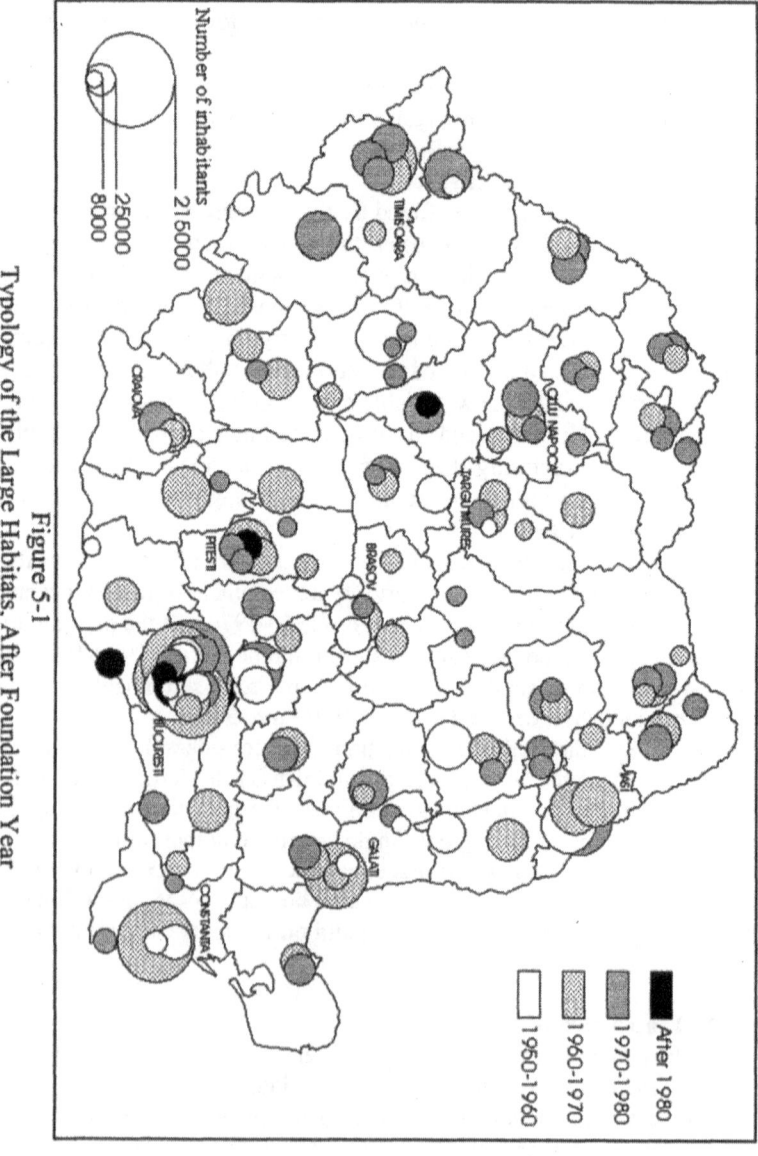

Figure 5-1
Typology of the Large Habitats, After Foundation Year

With the passing of a highly restrictive law passed in 1974, the urban structure was deprived of flexibility. In addition to this, it was often corseted by bizarre rules. So, the large cities and the middle towns would progressively lose their personality and begin to look very much alike. According to urban planning schemes, central zones were to be demolished and "civic centres" built in their stead and equipped with administrative palaces, culture houses for trade-unions and youth organisations, as well as other constructions with a less typical architecture. These dominated the urban landscape. The absence of car parks, of playgrounds for children, and the great density of apartment blocks left only small verdure islands. An unhealthy intimacy between streets, pedestrians and the blocks-of-flats developed.

The often brutal intervention into the internal town structure caused functional disruptions, visible in the urban morphology to this day. In terms of the magnitude of disruptions, one can distinguish the following types: fundamental disruptions, major disruptions, minor disruptions and no functional disruptions.

The first category groups the small and middle towns whose originally simple structure (a central commercial-administrative and residential area and a peripheral zone) was completely disturbed by the construction of industrial zones, residential zones, and by the reconstruction of the dominantly administrative and commercial zone. This category includes mainly the county-capitals, whose inhabitants more than tripled after 1966.

The second category lists the large cities, most of them discharging regional functions (Bucharest, Craiova, Iasi, Baia Mare, etc), in which the massive demolitions affected partly the central areas, but the periphery too. In parallel, a second industrial ring would be built, closing in the external residential districts (Talanga, 1989).

The third category includes most of the small and middle towns, whose population increased by some 1.2-1.8 times after 1966. Their central zone, largely demolished to make room for the "civic centres," but also the outskirts where industrial estates or new residential districts were built, were seriously disrupted.

The fourth category of urban centres, represented by small agricultural towns or spas and health resorts, escaped functional disruptions. The small changes made to the central zone physiognomy did not alter their largely traditional particularities.

The rigid dwelling quarters, with plenty of discomfort for their inhabitants, and an internal macrostructure stamped by significant industrial locations, makes it difficult to plan out the future development of towns. Prospective integration of these residential and industrial structures into the urban environment means mitigating functional disruptions by creating microstructures with specific functions and finding architectural solutions to restore the original look of a town.

THE LARGE HABITAT: CONCEPT AND GENESIS

Placed against this very contradictory background, the "large habitat" is the brainchild of an egalitarian, voluntary policy which tried to cope with industrialization—induced disruptions to an urban system. That type of voluntarism emanated from two sources: the utopian ideology depicting the socialist town as "industry and blocks-of-flats," and the dictator's providential ability to ensure urban development by personal decision-making. The idea was that town evolution could be imposed and controlled from the outside.

There are some towns in Romania in which the dismal reality of the presence of big residential districts (a kind of "urban tumor" grown in the urban organism as a result of a certain urban policy) cannot be ignored. Their genesis and configuration, as well as some other particularities could very well lie at the basis of the "large habitat" concept. This concept features large surface-areas with compact construction, totaling over 2,500 apartments of the multi-family block-type; most of them built by the state and let to persons.

The origin of these large habitats may be traced to the industrialization policy which set up big units frequently employing over 2,000 people. This industrial infrastructure had a great technical concentration within a single site (Oancea,1973). Hence the necessity to develop a large residential area in the immediate vicinity to accommodate the workforce and their families. A deficient peri-urban infrastructure limited commutation in favor of immigration, with people moving definitively to town. The gap between town incomes, mainly from industrial work, and the trifle revenues obtained by villagers from agriculture, lead cohorts of people to leave the countryside for the big industrial centres ready to take in the labor surplus (Ianos, 1987). What added to the rural pressure on the town was almost total collectivization of the land, thereby releasing huge labour excesses in the countryside (Sandu, 1980). This situation, together with a radical town-planning policy, resulted in the appearance and expansion of large habitats which, in some cases, used to dominate the entire urban landscape.

Depending on the nature of the built-in space the large urban habitats occupied three categories of areas: terrain cleared by massive demolitions; terrain situated at the periphery of the built-in area but closely linked to it, and empty terrain lying far from other built-in areas, in which case new towns would emerge.

THE LARGE HABITATS AND THEIR PLACE IN TOWN

Out of the 265 towns in Romania only 78 include large habitats as elements of the townscape structure. Their geographical location is relatively even given that large and medium-large towns have a similar geographical distribution. The second category lists mainly the administrative seats, county capitals, as well as other towns highly industrialized after 1970. There is an obvious relationship between the number of large habitats and town-size (Figure 5-2). Bucharest, Romania's biggest city, has twenty large habitats, next in line stand the regional capitals: Timisoara (5); Cluj-Napoca, Iasi, Craiova and Brasov with four each. Among the 78 towns, 49 have one large habitat alone, however this does not mean that it is of lesser importance within the respective town structure.

In order to appraise the place held by the large habitats in the life of Romania's towns it should be recalled that they concentrate an extremely numerous population, from less than one percent of the total population to nearly 100 percent in the case of new towns. The smallest percentage is recorded by some of Bucharest's large habitats like Vatra Luminoasa, Baneasa, or Ion Mihalache (under 1% each). The highest percentages include the all-out "socialist" towns built either between 1952-1970 (Campia Turzii, Victoria, Onesti, Moldova Noua, Plopeni, Motru, etc), or after 1980 (Rovinari). It is only over the past few years that the proportion of large habitats has somewhat diminished through the illegal urban overflow outside the initial perimeter, visible in the individual constructions cropping up close to town.

The share of large habitats in towns with over 200,000 inhabitants varies between 90.1 percent in Iasi, where new buildings were erected right after 1950, an ongoing process up to the very end of the totalitarian period, and 26.4 percent in Braila, marked by stagnation. In Bucharest, 63.7 percent of the population lives in these habitats, with significant increases after the year 1970, precisely at the time when the city was closed to migrants from other parts of the country.

The *housing stock* of these large habitats is vital for the urban population. The proportion of dwellings in these habitats is somewhat lower than the percentage of their inhabitants, because the average number of persons there is higher than that of individual residences. The reason for these figures is that apartments in blocks were let to young families, mainly workers, who adjusted to the state's pro-natal policy adopting the many-children model. In contradistinction, the families living in individual houses had one child or none at all.

The share of large habitats within the overall housing stock oscillates in broad lines within the same limits (Figure 5-3); topping the table are the new towns, some big cities having the lowest record. The middle towns, especially the strictly specialized ones, developed at a very fast pace in the 1970s and 1980s and now register a great proportion of large habitats/total housing stock (Navodari, 97%; Slobozia, 76.4%; Slatina, 69.2%; Zalau, 62.1%, etc).

For a long time now, the function of large habitats has been to accommodate the workforce, fluxes of people streaming between them and the industrial zones in public transport means, deficient as a rule. Passengers had often to cross the central town zones or use a direct connection between the two types of functional zones.

Ioan Ianos

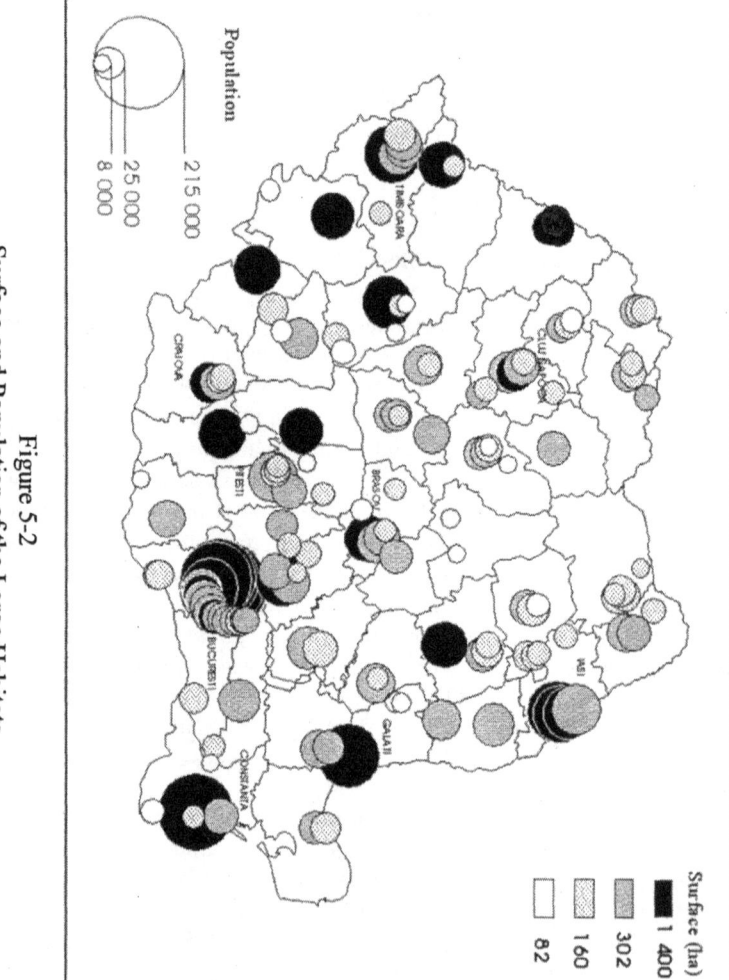

Figure 5-2
Surface and Population of the Large Habitats

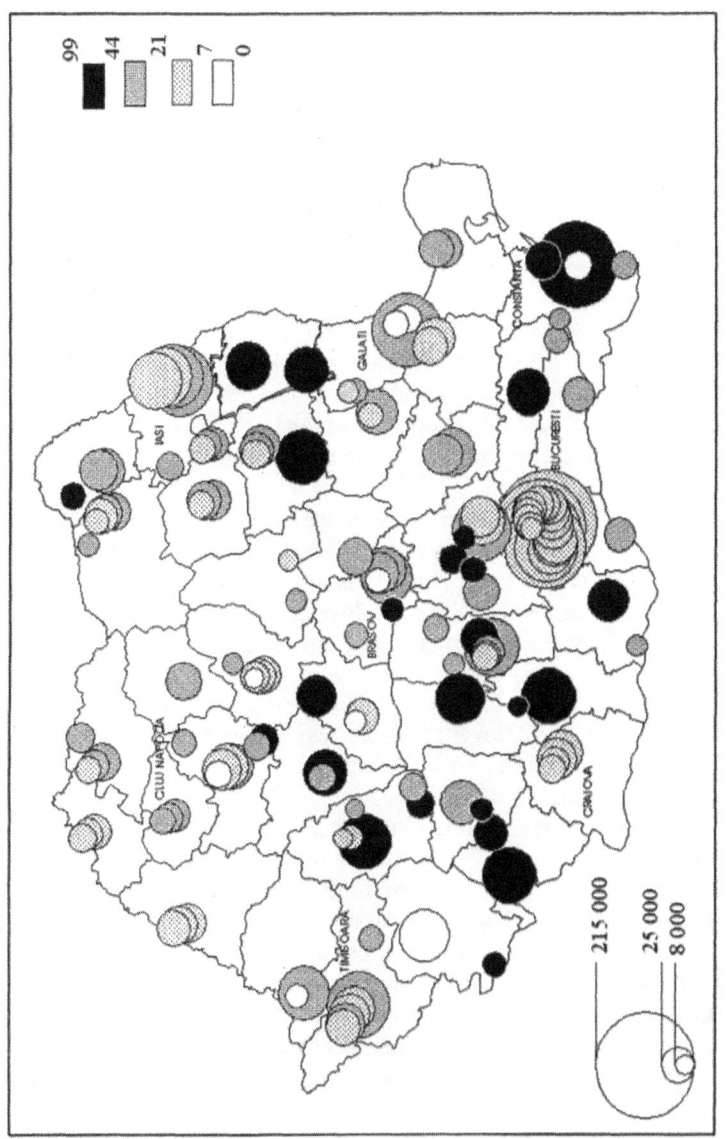

Figure 5-3

The Share of Large Habitat Population in Total Population, as a Percentage

The gravest problem in the large habitats during the socialist period was the shortage of services which more often than not failed to meet even a minimum demand (Ianos, 2002). So, their inhabitants had to undertake regular trips to the central zone for trivial errands. The only services available in these habitats were related to schooling—primary and secondary grades. All the others, especially commercial services, fell far short from the offer of the central zone.

THE LARGE HABITATS IN THE POST-1990 PERIOD

Although apparently stable, large habitats have been strongly affected by the downfall of the totalitarian regime through privatization, new relations with other urban functional zones, explosive growth of ordinary services, and the urban image they create.

The privatization of the housing stock was a legislative initiative (Law No 6/1990 and Government Decision No 88/1991) stipulating that tenants could buy the residences they occupied. It was an attractive offer because the price charged by the owner—the state, was quite low: 3-5 annual salaries (depending on the number of rooms and comfort level). The money could be paid immediately or by installments.

While before 1990 privatization in the large habitats barely reached a few percentage points, at present it comes close to 100 percent, the difference to the hundred coming from the fact that some flats are still in the administration of enterprises which had let them to their employees. Privatization values (Figure 5-4) are the lowest in some highly specialized towns, in which the proportion of apartments held by industrial units is fairly high, for example, Cernavoda (Nuclear Power Station, about 30 percent of the total housing stock), Plopeni (a big mechanical factory) and Mioveni ("Dacia" car manufacture). In the last two cases only 75 percent of the housing stock is private ownership.

In the Bucharest districts of Drumul Taberei, Parcul Tineretului, Baneasa, Stefan cel Mare, Mihai Bravu-Muncii, almost all dwellings are private. Some districts with negative images (Giurgiului, Berceni, Rahova-Alexandria) have been 96 percent privatized. In the central zone (Libertatii Blrd.) where part of the flats belong to some central-state institutions, the percentage is 95.

In regard of the functional integration of large habitats, two aspects should be recalled: first, their links with the big industrial estates are loosening; second, public transport to the central zones has improved. Large habitats are becoming increasingly more independent of the near-by industrial units given that the latter have drastically slowed down their activity so that these habitats no longer have to supply them with labor.

This isolation in relation to the other functional zones was augmented by the *explosive development of services* in each and every district. In the beginning, ordinary services were provided in a chaotic manner, by boutiques

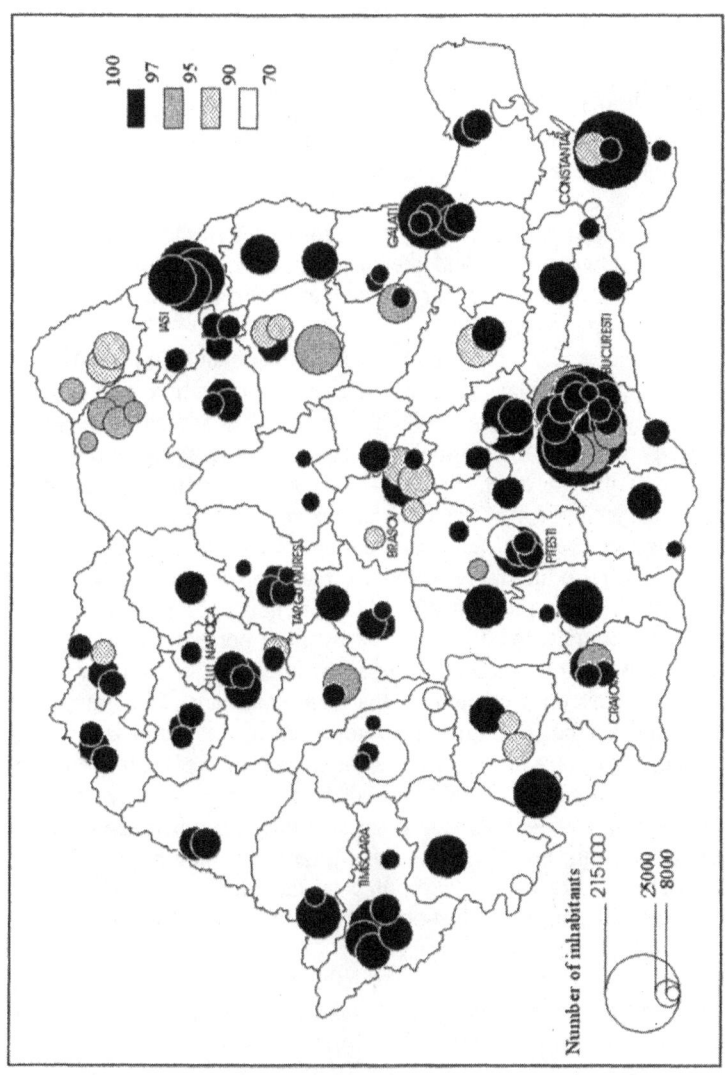

Figure 5-4

The Privatisation Degree by Large Habitats - 1998 (%)

placed at the main crossings or along major arteries, filling in the void felt by the large habitats. In time however, a process of self-selection took place mirrored by the numerical decrease of these boutiques; on the other hand, shops specialized in selling only certain types of commodities began to open.

The establishment of shop or restaurant chains by Romanian entrepreneurs, providing lower prices, in the vicinity of some big stores of the "Billa," "Carrefour," "Metro," or "Mega-image" type, dislodged the boutiques from the main arteries. They would move in-between the block-of-flats close to their customers. Their space pocket is now relatively stable, and is expected to last at least ten more years.

The urban image of large habitats is steadily deteriorating as family incomes are dropping dramatically and the local community cannot afford to provide the necessary urban facilities, nor can they maintain a decent standard of collective behavior and life in common.

Extensive privatization did little to improve the urban image, in general, and of apartment-blocks, in particular. The very high cost of running water, heat, natural gas, electricity, and telephone, which in most cases surpasses people's incomes, makes any initiative for capital repairs or for equipping doors with alarm systems out of the question. These habitats hide deep poverty pockets which also accounts for the lack of personal and property security. Besides, the new owners are slow in changing their mentalities, which has negative effects on the way the areas surrounding these blocks are managed and kept.

The massive demolitions pursued by the totalitarian regime have in some instances reduced the number of buildings by over 30 percent (Ianos, 1996). Every family used to have at least one dog about the house. After the terrain was cleared, dogs used to stay on protected by the local community. In time, they would proliferate and so the first stray dogs appeared in the urban landscape, creating a real plague in some towns. In Bucharest, for example, statistics put their number at approximately 250,000-300,000, no control measures having been taken over the past few years to stop them breeding. They have come to be a threat for people at night, but also in the day-time when they might become extremely aggressive. The measures taken now by the Municipality meet with the staunch resistance of animal protection organizations, or of simple citizens who are accustomed to living in their company.

Aggression on the green areas of large habitats is a basic urban image problem. Since large habitats were designed to host a great density of apartment blocks (to meet the demand of a relatively poor population), playgrounds for children and car parks are very scarce. After 1990, despite the general living standard slumping, the number of cars doubled quite rapidly. In order to park the cars, verdant areas were destroyed and as a result, the concrete structures overheated in summer, increasing the discomfort of their inhabitants. Another type of aggression on green areas was the siting of restaurants and amusement equipment in public parks. In this way, the verdant area per inhabitant shrank far below the normal limits.

THE REINTEGRATION OF LARGE HABITATS INTO THE URBAN AREAS

The most difficult problem urban planners have to cope with is to integrate these large habitats into the urban space. Present trends appear to postpone the attainment of this goal indefinitely. The high unemployment rates - over 30% in some Moldavian towns or in mining zones – (Figure 5-5), inertia of mentality and individual behaviors, together with the population's low incomes make urban remodeling a very difficult task.

One must bear in mind two basic aspects: in the first place, these large habitats, which occupy vast areas, shall continue to exist for a very long time as physical structures; in the second place, there are no available funds to move the population living in these concrete mammoths. Even though their population appears to be decreasing for the moment, they are still supposed to outlive one more generation at least. The decrease is due to people moving away to the countryside – an attractive destination; others build themselves houses in better residential districts, and others still are simply aging, and many more fall into this category.

The waning interest for flats in large habitats is reflected in a much lower selling price (by about 30%) compared to 1992 levels. So, urban planners must have in view clear-cut, but also flexible, projects. Unfortunately, general urban planning schemes entailing coherent intervention to space out these habitats in the country's big cities, Bucharest included, do not exist as yet. On the contrary, the Municipality's initiatives suggest greater construction density to use the areas' facilities in the most profitable way. Costs to connect to water, sewerage, gas and other networks are minimal, but the impact of the new structures on urban functionality and landscape is catastrophic (playgrounds, parking areas and verdure spots are reduced dramatically).

The decentralization of services concentrated in the town center and the development of intra-urban poles implies a new town planning approach and a new attempt at using the spaces occupied by large habitats. The restructuring of the industrial estates in the neighborhood of large habitats and their available space may be used to create new residential buffer zones to ameliorate the disruptions in the urban landscape.

The restructuring of the large urban habitats should be intertwined with plans to reintegrate towns into their geographical space. Creating adequate links to neighboring areas and enlarging towns along the main access roads to the peri-urban space may diminish the negative effects caused by the steady degradation of life in the large urban habitats.

Ioan Ianos

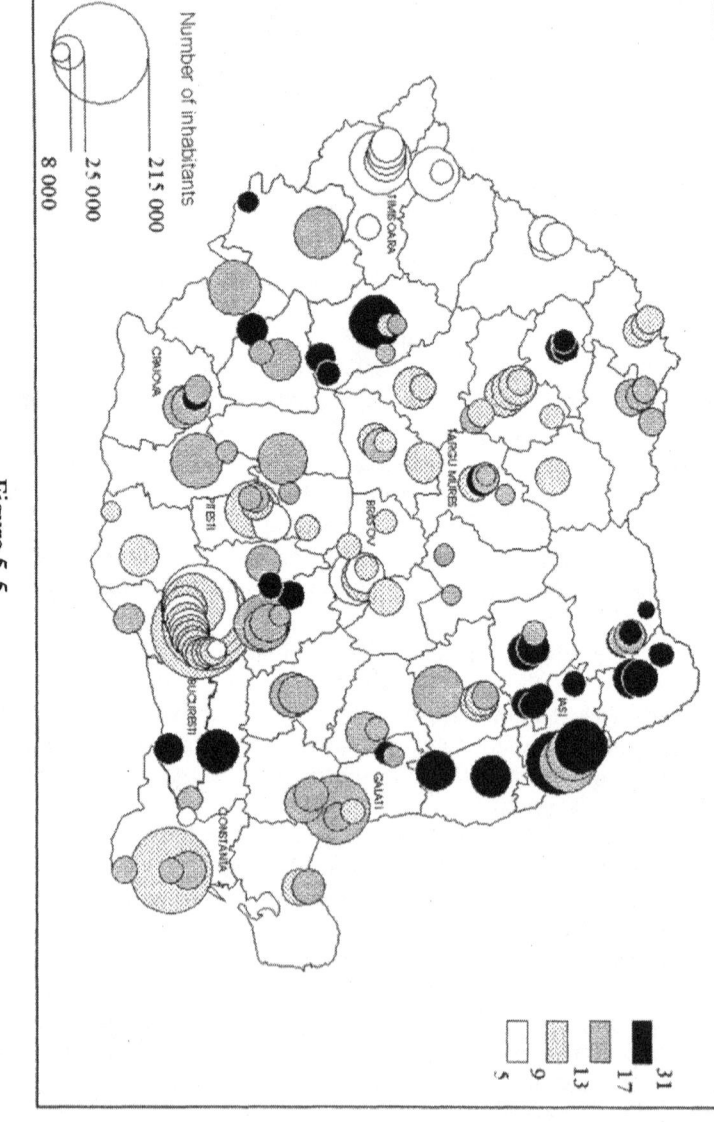

Figure 5-5
Unemployment Rate by Large Habitats (%)

CONCLUSIONS

The problems facing the large habitats are very complex indeed. The present study is intended essentially as a preliminary approach. So far now, other urban elements have come into the focus of our attention, for example, industrial restructuring, the reinvigoration of historical centres, the development of business centres and of services centres. However, we firmly believe that the greatest challenge for urban planners and for the local communities is the large habitat.

The question is to make a correct diagnosis of each and every urban center, and prescribe the adequate treatments. Diagnosing does not raise very special problems, but treatment implies costs and at this stage funds are lacking. Therefore, tasks must be specific for short-, medium- and long-term goals in order to enhance the positive effects of punctual interventions.

The elaboration of adequate urban planning schemes to facilitate the functional integration of these large habitats is urgent in every case. The first step is to have them remodeled. A second step is to select those elements capable of insuring substantial restructuring. Any urban restructuring act must observe the town's local and regional assets and the place it is likely to occupy within the urban systems.

REFERENCES

Candea, M., Erdeli, G. (1981). Consideratii Geografice Asupra Spatiului Urban din Romania, *Studii si Cercetari de Geologie, Geofizica si Geografie, seria Geografie*, XXVIII.

Cucu, V. (ed.) (1970). *Orasele Romaniei*. Bucuresti: Stiintifica.

Ianos, I. (ed.) (1987). *Orasele si Organizarea Spatiului Geografic: Studiu de Geografie eEonomica Asupra Teritoriului Romaniei*. Bucuresti: Academiei.

Ianos, I. (1993). A Comparative Analysis Between Urban and Industrial Hierarchy of the Romanian Towns. *GeoJournal*, 29:1.

Ianos, I. (1996). Functional Disruptions in the Internal Structure of Romania's Towns, in Davies, R.J. (ed.). *Contemporary City Structuring, International Geographical Insight*. Cape Town: Society of South African Geographers. pp.405-417.

Ianos, I. (2002). "The Maturing of the Romanian Urban System." in Geyer. H.S. (ed.). *International handbook of urban systems: Studies of urbanization and migration in Advanced and Developing Countries*. Edward Elgar: Cheltenham. pp.295-327.

Manescu, L. (ed.) (1999). *Orasul Buzau si zona sa de influenta*. Bucuresti: Universitatii din Bucuresti.

Oancea, D. (ed.) (1973). *Gruparea Urbana Galati-Braila.* Bucuresti: Academiei.

Sandu, D. (ed.) (1980). *Fluxurile de Migratie in Romania.* Bucuresti: Academiei.

Talanga, Cr. (1989). "Repere Geografice in Dezvoltarea Industriala a Municipiului Bucuresti." *Terra*, 2.

Ungureanu, Al. (ed.) (1980). *Orasele din Moldova. Studiu de Geografie Economica.* Bucuresti: Academiei.

6 Brownfields Redevelopment and Pennsylvania's "Growing Greener" Initiatives: The Case of Letterkenny Army Depot

John Benhart, Sr. and Rebecca S. Hawthorne

A wide range of businesses including agricultural products, manufacturing, trucking, and offices have located in the Cumberland Valley Business Park (CVBP), which was previously part of the Letterkenny Army Depot (LEAD). The CVBP has three of the key criteria for a business park: transportation access, existing infrastructure, and lots of land. In 1995, the army base was realigned, and 1,450 acres in the southeastern portion were given to Franklin County for reuse. The Franklin County Commissioners created the Letterkenny Industrial Development Authority (LIDA) to redevelop and manage the land for the CVBP. The park can be considered a major brownfield redevelopment project. Brownfields are sites contaminated by past uses that have potential for reuse. Due to the contamination from military activities on the base, the southeastern portion of LEAD where the CVBP is located was listed on the U.S. National Priorities List. However, nearly 800 acres were redeveloped for industrial and commercial uses, and 250 acres were given to the community for recreational use. In the end, a total of 1,450 acres will be redeveloped as part of the business park or community space.

Federal regulations, such as CERCLA, RCRA, and NEPA and state regulations, such as Act II 1995: Land Recycling and Environmental Remediation Standards Act and the Keystone Opportunity Zone, set standards for the clean up and redevelopment at LEAD. Federal and state programs and funds provided incentives and initiated clean up and redevelopment. In addition, for LEAD, unique solutions, such as institutional controls, were used to make land available for transfer and the disposition of utilities to the LIDA helped to fund remediation and development.

LITERATURE REVIEW

The majority of information for this research was obtained from the Letterkenny Industrial Development Authority's library. These sources included the *Environmental Baseline Survey for Letterkenny Army Depot BRAC 95* and its addendum (Roy F. Weston, Inc. 1995a, 1995b), *Action, Environmental Assessment for BRAC 95 Disposal and Reuse of Letterkenny Army Depot, Chambersburg, Pennsylvania* (U.S. Army Corps of Engineers Mobile District 1997), and other related planning documents (Roy F. Weston 1995c, 1995d) that were prepared for the 1995 Letterkenny Army Depot realignment. These documents described the environmental and economic conditions of the property and the actions taken to clean up, transfer, and redevelop the property. The Cumberland Valley Business Park website, www.letterkenny-business.com, provided information on the business park, its tenants, utilities, incentives, permitted uses, and location. An overview of the entire redevelopment process and BRAC was obtained from an interview with John Van Horn (2003) of LIDA and a meeting headed by Mr. Lynn Ramsey (2003), the Acting Deputy Commander at LEAD. Local newspapers online provided information regarding recent events at Letterkenny. The EPA website (U.S. EPA 2003) and Environmental Law Handbook (Sullivan 2001) provided information on national regulations for brownfields. Barr Engineering is a company specializing in brownfield development that also had a website with information concerning brownfield redevelopment processes.

Brownfields

A brownfield is a contaminated property that has potential for redevelopment or reuse for social and economic purposes (US EPA 2003). These sites are often abandoned "eye sores" in a community that present environmental hazards. They are expensive to redevelop, in comparison to clean, undeveloped real estate referred to as greenfields. Redevelopment is especially important for communities in which the industries have left or where the parties responsible for the contamination are hard to find. However, the government and private agencies are seeking brownfield development more in recent years with aid from federal, state, and local funding and programs that encourage cleanup and redevelopment of contaminated real estate (Barr Engineering Company 2003). Brownfield redevelopment has social, economic, and environmental benefits that include increasing the local tax base, revitalizing the economy, eliminating urban sprawl, conserving land, and cleaning up unsightly hazards. On the other hand, brownfield development is complex. Because of the environmental hazards and liability issues, development generally takes longer, costs more, and requires the involvement of more agencies and people, and there is always the risk of failure. Every brownfield site is different with its own unique liability issues, contamination, and reuse plans. Developers must consider the contamination present, the future use and target market, regulations, zoning, time schedule, financing, and most importantly the location. Letterkenny Army Depot is an exceptional case for brownfield redevelopment because it has two listings on the National Priorities List (NPL). According to the EPA, the definition of a brownfield excludes facilities listed on the NPL (US EPA, 2003). However, the Army has realigned the base and transferred excess areas, including the NPL sites, for redevelopment with stipulations after the proper remedial actions were taken. LEAD was a contaminated property with potential for reuse that was redeveloped, and therefore LEAD can be called a brownfield.

ENVIRONMENTAL CONDITIONS AT LETTERKENNY: A BACKGROUND AND HISTORY

In 1942, LEAD acquired 19,423 acres of land from farms and residences to establish an ammunition storage facility. It was one of the U.S. Army's largest bases. Over 16,000 acres are still devoted to ammunition storage. The industrial and maintenance areas were located in the southeast corner of LEAD. Base facilities included warehousing, vehicle storage, industrial, maintenance, offices, military housing, and recreation. It also has a 300 million-gallon reservoir located offsite near Roxbury, sanitary sewage treatment facility, roads, and utilities. Over the years, missions have included storage, repair and maintenance of military vehicles and munitions consisting of cleaning, stripping, painting, lubrication, and plating activities. Many of these practices used solvents, blast media, paints, chemicals, petroleum products, and metal have lead to contamination of soil, groundwater, and surface water ((U.S. Army Corps of Engineers Mobile District 1997). Today, LEAD is the top air defense and tactile mission provider for the U.S. Army. LEAD maintains systems that are crucial to wartime. These systems include the Patriot, Avenger, Sparrow, Sidewinder, and Phoenix (Ramsey, 2003).

REDEVELOPMENT OF LETTERKENNY ARMY DEPOT AND CREATION OF A BUSINESS PARK

Location

Located 5 miles north of Chambersburg in Greene and Letterkenny townships in Franklin County, South-central Pennsylvania, Letterkenny Army Depot has a strategic location for economic growth shown in Figure 6-1 on the following page. The depot is within a few miles of Interstate 81, US Route 11, and 14 miles from the PA Turnpike. Letterkenny is 90 miles north of Washington D.C. and 50 miles south of Harrisburg. Most eastern cities can be reached by interstate highways within a day's travel. Farmland, scattered residences, and state forest surround LEAD and create an attractive quality of life for businesses and their employees. Several large corporate firms, such as Ingraham Books, Target, and Food Lion have already taken advantage of the accessible location and amenities Franklin County has to offer.

Federal Regulations

The Resource Conservation & Recovery Act (RCRA), Comprehensive Environmental Response, Compensation, & Liability Act (CERCLA), Community Environmental Response Facilitation Act (CERFA), and the National Environmental Policy Act (NEPA) are the main federal regulations involving brownfield sites . These statutes involve hazardous waste disposal, environmental protection, and the reuse of contaminated properties. The Army spent over $100 million to clean up the NPL sites in the 1990s to comply with CERCLA and RCRA (Ramsey 2003). Two groundwater treatment plants and a groundwater interception system were added. Soils were remediated with low temperature thermal treatment or excavated to bedrock and disposed off-site. The industrial sewer lines were repaired after contaminated soils were removed from sewers. Surrounding residences were connected to public water to prevent contact with contamination off-site (Roy F. Weston, Inc. 1995a).

CERCLA is a broad environmental statute that covers the cleanup of past hazardous waste and funding for cleanup when the responsible party cannot. It is called the Superfund. In 1986, amendments to CERCLA included the regulation of Federal facilities under the statute and remediation procedures for hazardous waste sites. Under CERCLA criteria, sites are placed on the National Priorities List. Due to spills and releases of hazardous waste related to the military practices, Letterkenny is subject to CERCLA and has two sites on the National Priorities List (Environmental Assessment, 1997).

Under RCRA, the EPA has the authority to regulate all processes concerning the hazardous waste from "cradle to grave". It also includes standards for solid waste, and underground storage tank facilities with a permit system. Hazardous waste at LEAD is regulated by RCRA. RCRA required the closure of two industrial wastewater lagoons in the early 1990s and monitoring

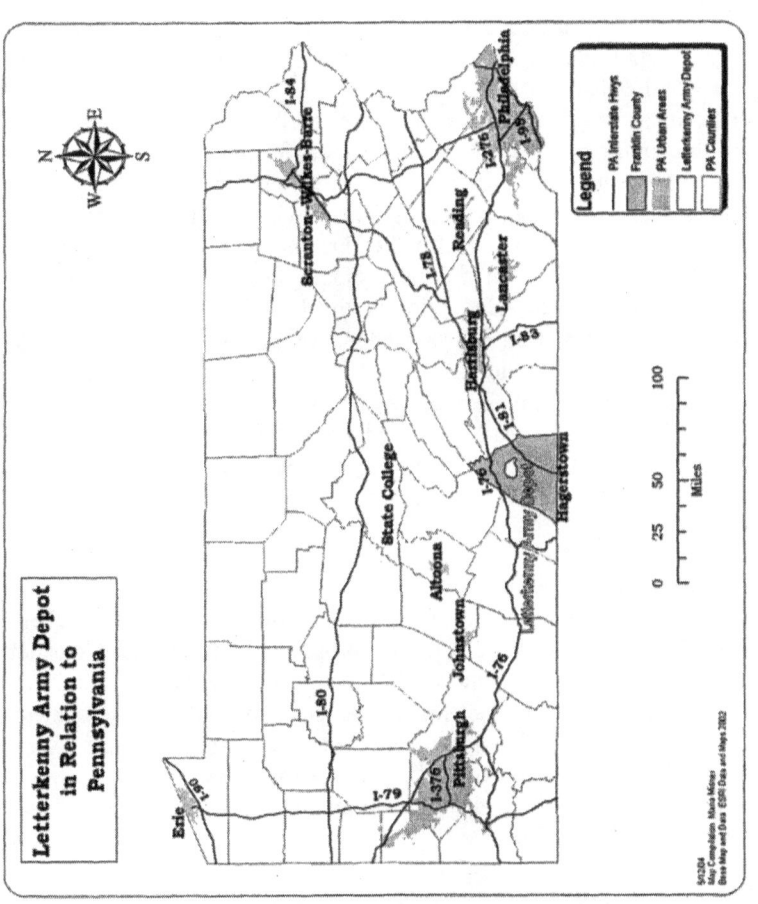

Figure 6-1

of 63 Solid Waste Management Units (SMWUs) in LEAD. Hazardous waste generated at LEAD is sent to a RCRA permitted off-site area (Final Addendum, 1995).

CERFA is an amendment from Section 120(h) of CERCLA concerning contamination assessment, cleanup, and federal agency involvement for transferring federal property. Petroleum products and CERCLA hazardous substances of the parcels must be evaluated before land is transferred. Since LEAD is part of the National Priorities List, parcels may not be considered for transfer until approved by the EPA Administrator (U.S. Army Corps of Engineers Mobile District 1997).

The National Environmental Policy Act (NEPA) requires federal agencies to study the environmental effects of major federal actions and consider alternative approaches. The goal of NEPA is to include environmental factors along with social and economic issues. The Environmental Impact Statement (EIS) is the main component of NEPA that documents the environmental effects and alternative approaches for federal projects. Federal agencies conduct an Environmental Assessment (EA) prior to the EIS. The EA is a preliminary analysis that determines if an EIS is needed. An EIS is not required if the EA ends with a finding of no significant impacts (FONSI) (Sullivan 2001). The environmental impacts and alternatives for property disposal at Letterkenny Army Depot (LEAD) followed NEPA guidelines. A FONSI was the result of the final environmental assessment for the disposal and reuse of the base's excess area in the southeastern corner of the base. So, an EIS was not necessary (Roy F. Weston, Inc. 1995c).

Federal Incentives

The Taxpayer Relief Act (TRA) and Small Business Liability Relief and Brownfield Revitalization Act are federal programs that encourage cleanup of environmental hazards. President Bill Clinton signed the TRA in 1997, which contains a brownfield tax incentive for cleanup and redevelopment of brownfields that allows businesses to deduct cleanup costs from their taxes. The 2002 Small Business Liability Relief and Brownfields Revitalization Act provide a revolving loan fund and cleanup grants and seeks to protect innocent stakeholders (U.S. EPA 2003).

State Regulations and Incentive Program

Act II 1995: Land Recycling and Environmental Remediation Standards Act and the Keystone Opportunity Zone (KOZ) are two of the main regulations that encourage remediation and redevelopment of brownfields in Pennsylvania and are relevant regarding land transfer at LEAD (Department of Community and Economic Development 2003). These statutes promote reuse of contaminated sites, protect greenfields, and release landowners from liability if certain standards are met. Governor Tom Ridge passed Act II in 1995 as a cleanup standard and liability protection for the buyer. The seller cleans up the site, an environmental audit is conducted, and the new owner cannot be held liable for past contamination.

Another recent state law that provides incentives for redeveloping land is the 1999 Keystone Opportunity Zone program (KOZ). Over 37,000 acres of developable land in Pennsylvania are enrolled in these zones of opportunity where state and local taxes are reduced or eliminated (Pennsylvania Come...able, 2003). The program creates zones of opportunity for businesses to locate and create jobs and promote community development. Michigan is the only other state to pass similar legislation. When the bill was sent to Governor Tom Ridge, he stated, "Keystone Opportunity Zones offer promise and hope to some of Pennsylvania's most desperate and hopeless neighborhoods by using a very powerful tool—no taxes" (*DCED News* 1998). The CVBP is one of 12 KOZs in Pennsylvania (Letterkenny Industrial Authority 2002).

Geology

LEAD is situated in Great Valley, which is part of the Valley and Ridge Province. This section of the Great Valley, which runs northeast to southwest, is called the Cumberland Valley. The limestone ridges and valleys dominate and bear southwest in the valley. The western part of the valley is made of shales, siltstones, and sandstones in the rolling hills, while less resistant limestone lies in the broad, flat lowland of the eastern valley with sinkholes and caverns beneath the surface. LEAD is mostly underlain by Martinsburg shale except for the carbonate rocks along the eastern and western borders. The elevations of LEAD are mostly between 600 and 750 feet. However, the elevation is much higher in the northwest, 2300 feet where Broad Mountain is. Elevation in 1,450 acres given to Franklin County varies between 765 feet in the north, 680 feet in the southeast, and 650 feet in the southwest. From the north towards the center of the excess area, the land slopes downhill and then rises to an elevation of 772 feet. Less weather resistant limestone underlies the lower elevations and more resistant shale lies beneath the higher elevation in the center (U.S. Army Corps of Engineers Mobile District 1997).

Surface and Groundwater

Intermittent streams flow through the limestone and broad valleys. Streams in shale tend to meander through smaller steeper valleys. Surface drainage flows into either the Susquehanna River to the northeast or the Potomac River to the southwest. In each case, the surface waters wind up in the Cheasapeake Bay. Rowe Run receives the surface runoff from the eastern part of the BRAC realignment. Rowe Run discharges into Muddy Run, then the Conodoguinet Creek and then into the Susquehanna River. The western and southern portion of the 1,450 acres given to Franklin County for reuse drain into Rocky Spring where wetlands have been delineated. Rocky Spring flows into the Back Creek, then the Conococheague Creek, and the Potomac River. In addition, storm water in this area drains into the one of the two storm water drainage systems and flows toward the Conococheague. The area north of Coffey Avenue enters one of the drainage systems and discharges into an outfall ditch near the Industrial Wastewater Treatment Plant and ends up in Rowe Run. Storm water in the southeast warehouse excess area flows into a drain outfall and discharges southward to the Conococheague Creek (U.S. Army Corps of Engineers Mobile District 1997). It was important to address contamination on LEAD not only for the reuse of the base, but for the environmental quality of the entire Chesapeake Bay watershed.

The groundwater within LEAD flows to two basins. The complex geology and topography of LEAD influences the groundwater flow within the depot. The topography variances that create rolling hills coincide with changing groundwater levels. Overall, the groundwater in the western excess area flows southwest to the Rocky Spring Lake. Since the Martinsburg shale in the southeastern section of the excess area is slightly elevated, the groundwater flows northeast, east, and southeast. As expected, the water table is shallow near streams and lower elevations and deeper where the topography rises (U.S. Army Corps of Engineers Mobile District 1997).

Contamination and Cleanup

The Army has spent over $100 million to cleanup the NPL sites in the 1990s (Ramsey 2003) in compliance with CERCLA and RCRA. Two groundwater treatment plants and a groundwater interception system were added. The lagoons closed. Soils were remediated with low temperature thermal treatment or excavated to bedrock and disposed off-site. The industrial sewer lines were repaired after contaminated soils were removed from sewers. Surrounding residences were connected to public water to prevent contact with contamination off-site.

With the remnants of previous generation's pollution over, LEAD is nastier than traditional brownfields sites. LEAD has two sites included on CERCLA's National Priority List (Van Horn 2003). These sites are the Property Disposal Office (PDO) and the Southeastern Industrial Area (SIA), which are the areas of interest for redevelopment. Environmental testing between 1980 and 1989 revealed the contamination in the soil and the groundwater at LEAD. In 1986, the EPA placed the PDO and SIA areas under the Uncontrolled Hazardous Waste Site Ranking System and recommended it be placed on the National Priorities List. Investigations in 1900 acres of the southern portion of LEAD revealed soil, groundwater, and surface water contamination with chlorinated solvents from degreasing and cleaning practices at LEAD. The 978 acres of the SIA were added to the NPL in July 1987, and the 1900 acres of the PDO were added in March 1989. According to the EPA, NPL properties are excluded from the definition of a brownfield site (US EPA 2003). However, LEAD can be considered a brownfield because it was a contaminated property redeveloped for economic and social benefit of the local community.

The waste sites associated with contamination in the PDO include the scrap yard, sinkholes, quarry landfill, ammunition and drum storage areas, pesticide storage areas, oil burn pits, paint can shedding, vehicle storage, above ground storage tanks, and open trench landfills. The soil, surface water, and groundwater of the PDO area was contaminated with chlorinated solvents from activities on the base. The groundwater from the PDO discharges at Rocky Spring where it becomes surface water that flows into the Rocky Spring Branch of the Conococheague Creek and part of the Potomac River watershed. The contaminated surface water usually leaves the depot below health standards. Oil burn pits and drum storage revetments were the main sources of groundwater contamination. Contaminants seeped through the soils down to the bedrock and groundwater. The Army originally proposed a groundwater treatment system to clean the groundwater and surface water before it entered the Rocky Spring Branch, but the diffused bubble aeration treatment suspended the sediment, which could increase the amount of PCBs flowing into the spring. As a result, the Army, EPA, and PA DEP changed the remedy to institutional controls and monitoring. Volatile organic compounds (VOCs) levels are below state standards by the time the water reaches the property line (Roy F. Weston, Inc., 1995b).

The SIA area was contaminated by storage areas, test tracks, open vehicle storage, breaks in industrial wastewater sewage lines, underground storage tanks, polychlorinated biphenyls (PCBs) transformers, storm drainage system, battery acid disposal pit, and landfills. VOC contaminated soils were excavated to bedrock, treated, and placed back on the site with a geotextile membrane and cap over top. A groundwater treatment system cleans VOC contaminated groundwater in the Northern SIA. In 1993, the Army identified leaks in the industrial wastewater sewage lines that allowed VOCs to leak into soils and bedrock. Emergency repairs began in October 1994, and emergency removal of the contaminated soils occurred in 1997. Emergency removal of sediments was also used where wastewater was previously discharged into the sewer system.

LEAD began RCRA programs in 1987. The Army identified 63 solid waste management units (SWMUs) in LEAD and 53 in the excess area. Most of these SWMUs are located in the NPL sites and were evaluated under CERCLA. The former industrial wastewater treatment plant lagoons, discharge of untreated wastewater to storm sewers, faulty industrial wastewater sewer lines, disposal lagoons, oil burn pits, and disposal trenches contributed to the majority of the VOCs in the groundwater at LEAD. Two industrial wastewater lagoons existed in LEAD. The first industrial wastewater lagoon constructed in 1954 was an unlined hole in the ground used as a settling basin. A sinkhole formed beneath the lagoon and VOCs leaked into the subsurface. In 1967, a second lagoon was built. It had a double wall concrete liner, but subsidence eventually caused the lagoon to leak into the subsurface also. RCRA regulations required the Army to close these two lagoons in the early 1990s. LEAD placed 6 monitoring wells around the lagoons that are checked periodically and developed a PADEP approved Groundwater Assessment and Abatement Plan to treat groundwater at Rowe Spring (Roy F. Weston 1995a).

BRAC 1995

The commission for the Base Realignment and Closure Act (BRAC) selected over 100 Army facilities for closure or realignment in the 1990s (Global Security 2002). In 1995, the Base Realignment and Closure Act hit LEAD. The BRAC Commission recommended realignment of the depot instead of closure. Realignment for LEAD meant disposing of property excess to the base's main missions, which were ammunition storage and tactical missile disassembly and storage (Department of the Army Base Realignment and Closure 1995). The President and Congress agreed on the realignment in September 1995 (Roy F. Weston 1995d). The realignment meant dispersion of other missions at LEAD and the disposal of excess facilities and 1,450 acres of property in the southeastern portion to the community for redevelopment (U.S. Army Corps of Engineers Mobile District 1997). Prior to realignment, the Army conducted extensive environmental studies documented in the Letterkenny Army Depot Environmental Baseline Survey (EBS), and an Environmental Assessment was prepared to examine the impacts of disposal and reuse of the surplus area. The EBS recommended the southeastern area of the base for disposal and reuse. (Roy F. Weston 1995c).

After BRAC: LIDA and CVBP

As a result of BRAC, the Cumberland Valley Business Park (CVBP) was created. In 1997, the Franklin County Commissioners created a local authority, the Letterkenny Industrial Development Authority (LIDA), to manage redevelopment of the CVBP as a business and industrial center. The U.S. Army conveys property to LIDA first. LIDA sells or leases the property as its Board of Directors sees fit. LIDA also owns the electrical utilities and relies on Allegheny Power to operate and maintain the system. CVBP has several features that attract new industries. The park includes community spaces, green spaces, offices, and factories. The location of the park has accessible transportation and is within a few hours of several metropolitan areas. The CVBP offers 1,200 acres of land, facilities, and infrastructures and buildings that are already in place for businesses to use. Franklin County and surrounding counties also offer a skilled workforce and good quality of life for employees (Letterkenny Industrial Authority 2002).

The CVBP operates similarly to a township. It has a Board of Directors and each property holder obtains membership and voting rights in the CVBP Association. The CVBP Association and LIDA developed a Declaration of

Covenants, Conditions, and Restrictions for properties within the CVBP to protect property values and to ensure that properties are held, sold, and conveyed properly. Property in the CVBP may not be subdivided without approval from LIDA and the CVBP Association. Each owner is responsible for maintenance of their property concerning trash, waste, lawn mowing, tree and shrub pruning, parking, loading areas, exterior lighting, and safety standards. Properties are subject to reasonable inspections. The following are listed as Prohibited Uses to prevent human exposure to contaminants: residential uses, vehicle and mobile home sales, mobile home parks, and recreational campgrounds. Oil drilling and refining, water drilling, quarrying or mining, junkyards, landfills, paper mills, recycling facilities, and garbage disposal or processing are prohibited. In addition, food production uses, such as animal farms, milk processing, livestock production, stockyard, vineyards, orchards, gardens, and commercial fruit production are not allowed in the CVBP either. Permitted uses include a list of commercial, business, professional, and light industrial uses, like automobile shops, business services, carpentry shop, commercial printing, equipment sales and service, food processing and packaging, manufacturing, restaurants, truck terminal, warehouses, etc. The declaration contains general use provisions for minimum building size, building occupancy, off-street parking and loading, landscaping, signs, architectural design and materials, outdoor storage, exterior lighting, nuisances, tree removal, antennas, drainage, waste, utility lines, etc. In addition, the Board of Directors may grant variances and waivers. These rules apply as long as they do not undermine the ordinances of Greene Township or Letterkenny Township. Like a township has parks and recreational facilities, the CVBP also has Common Property for use and enjoyment of its members (Benatec Associates, 1999).

Reuse Plan

The key components for reuse of the BRAC excess area deal with traffic circulation, open space, development districts, and land use. Military facilities have different circulation patterns compared to public and private areas. LEAD has restricted entrances. Roads are present at LEAD, but road network must be reworked so that each building or parcel is easily accessible to places outside of the former base. A main boulevard, "loop road" and primary and secondary roadways with trees along them were part of the Vehicular Circulation Plan. Coffey Ave. is the main boulevard that was added to connect two main entrances. The "loop road" includes improvements to California Ave., Texas Ave., Carbaugh Ave., Pennsylvania Ave., and Vehicle Road that connect parcels to Coffey Ave. Primary connector roads join the boulevard or loop road with the surrounding communities while secondary connector roads are constructed for specific parcels (U.S. Army Corps of Engineers Mobile District 1997).

The open space aspect of the plan coordinates with existing open space and the road network to make the area marketable and community friendly. It seeks to protect the farmland to the west of the excess property and the golf course in the center. Streams and drainage systems are also included in the open spaces. In addition, a green corridor of trees along Coffey Ave will supplement the open spaces. The plan also includes trails between open spaces and recreational facilities (U.S. Army Corps of Engineers Mobile District 1997).

The development districts plan divides the 1,450 acres given to Franklin County into districts based on land use. The 7 districts include industrial, office, administration, community/open space, warehouse/distribution, light industrial, and highway industrial/distribution. Community preference, future development, and potential for property were considered for these land uses (U.S. Army Corps of Engineers Mobile District 1997).

Incentives at the CVBP

Businesses can also benefit from special economic incentives. Employers may take advantage of the Military Partnership and use military services that include hydraulics, welding, painting, and electronic systems. Several funds are available to industries locating within the park. Franklin County Area Development Corporation distributes the Letterkenny Opportunity Fund to facilitate development. The Foreign Trade Zone reduces the cost of importing materials into the park. 300 acres of CVBP are designated to Pennsylvania's Keystone Opportunity Zone (KOZ), which reduces or eliminates the taxes for businesses. Other funding for the CVBP includes PA Capital Loan Fund, PA Industrial Development Authority, Machinery and Equipment Loan Funds, Ben Franklin Partnership, Industrial Resource Center, Customized Job Training, and Job Training Partnership Act. In CVBP, businesses can benefit from low taxes and the low cost of living, and services provided by the Army and LIDA (Letterkenny Industrial Authority 2002).

Disposition of Utilities

Utilities in CVBP are provided through LIDA at low rates for tenants. After BRAC 95, the Army conveyed its utilities to LIDA with an agreement that LIDA would continue to provide utility services to the Army as long as there are military operations at LEAD (U.S. Army Corps of Engineers Mobile District 1997). LIDA has contracts with Allegheny Power for electric, PPL for natural gas, and Sprint for telecommunications, which spent $1 million on a fiber optic network. The Army base is #1 customer for utilities. LIDA depends on the income obtained from the sale of utilities to the Army base to fund development in the CVBP (Van Horn, 2003). In addition, CVBP has onsite water and sewage treatment facilities. The Franklin County General Authority provides water, wastewater, and rail in the CVBP (Letterkenny Industrial Authority 2002).

Land Transfers with Institutional Controls

The Environmental Baseline Survey (EBS) is used to determine if parcels are suitable for transfer. It follows the standards set in CERFA and an amendment to CERCLA in 1992 for contamination assessment, clean up, notification, and approval by regulatory agency for closure or realignment of federal facilities. Under CERFA, parcels at LEAD were classified into 7 categories based on the level of contamination from least to most. As a result, parcels ranking in lower contamination categories were available for immediate transfer to spur reuse and redevelopment (Roy F. Weston 1995b).

The Army transferred the excess property in phases as parcels were identified for no further remedial action under CERCLA (Environmental Assessment, 1997). This allows the Army to convey parcels to LIDA without waiting for the remediation of the entire excess area. The Army designated Phase I and II parcels as suitable for transfer based on the Phase I EBS in August 1996 and the Phase II EBS in July 1997 (Roy F. Weston, Inc. 1998).

Phase I Parcels

No significant impacts were identified in the Phase I parcels except the VOC groundwater contamination, which can be attributed to the high water table beneath the parcels. The Army declared the parcels suitable, and LIDA identified the buildings and parcels that were the best candidates for reuse. Although several areas of contamination were identified, Phase I parcels do not contain any areas that require remediation. However, a final remedy that protects human health and the environment must be implemented to comply with federal and state standards (Roy F. Weston, Inc. 1998).

Institutional controls were placed on the Phase I parcels as the final remedy for soil contamination and temporary solution for groundwater contamination. In this case, institutional controls are restrictions on soil excavation and groundwater as a result of the Army's past uses and contamination. However, the soil did not exceed EPA's soil and ambient air contamination standards, but the groundwater did based on the EBS. As a result, the use of groundwater is prohibited and soil excavation and subsurface construction is restricted unless a waiver is obtained from the Army, DEP, and EPA. In addition, residential use is prohibited. Only industrial or commercial activities may take place on the property (Proposed Plan..., 1995). The institutional controls become deed restrictions once the property transfer takes place. The controls prevent human contact with contaminated groundwater, are easy to implement, and facilitate the property's availability for reuse. LIDA insures that tenants follow the institutional controls, but the Army remains responsible for the remediation of the groundwater. The transfer of 233 acres of Phase I parcels occurred in 1998 (U.S. Army Corps of Engineers Mobile District 1998).

Phase II Parcels

Institutional controls were also placed on Phase II parcels. Similarly, the Army found these parcels suitable for transfer based on the industrial, commercial, or agricultural future use of the property. Again, LIDA identified the buildings and property for reuse (Roy F. Weston 1995c).

The soil was remediated, but deed provisions still restricted soil excavation. Deed restrictions designated the certain properties for industrial or commercial use only. The use of groundwater is prohibited, but there is another institutional control preventing exposure to the contaminated groundwater. Limited depth transfer is an institutional control for Phase II parcels. According to the EBS, releases or disposal of hazardous substances on many of the Phase II parcels have never occurred. However, volatile organic compounds drained through porous limestone beneath the parcels and contaminated the groundwater. These pollutants did not originate in the Phase II parcels. As a result, the entire property was not transferred. Buildings, structures, and soil from the surface to a depth of eight feet below the ground were part of the transfer. The transferred property remains above the seasonal high groundwater table to prevent contamination or exposure to humans (Roy F. Weston, Inc. 1995c). 327 acres of Phase II were transferred to LIDA in 2002 (Zarnowski, 2003).

Phase III

201 acres of land were transferred to LIDA in September 2003 as Phase III. The land was used for military vehicle storage since the 1940s, but only 35,000 tons of soil contained contaminants that leaked from the vehicles. The soil was removed, and the site was approved for transfer within a year of remediation (Zarnowski, 2003)

CLOUD OF BRAC 2005

Before BRAC 95, LEAD employed approximately 6,300 people. As a result of the base realignment, 4,500 jobs were lost and local communities degraded as residents left to find employment elsewhere. The local schools lost money because the federal government had given the schools funding for each child whose parents worked at LEAD. The economic impact was not just local. Many people that commuted to LEAD from Juniata, Somerset, Cumberland, and surrounding counties lost their jobs. However, by transferring and redeveloping the land for CVBP, the area was able to recover from the downsizing of the base. Unfortunately, LEAD is vulnerable to another round of BRAC in 2005. However, the base has a convenient location and lots of land to accommodate the Army's needs without encroaching upon other properties (Ramsey, 2003).

CONCLUSION

In early 2004, LIDA received a "clean" deed for 300 acres that were formerly limited depth transfers. Tests indicated that the soil and groundwater do not contain any contaminants. The "clean" land will be easier to lease or sell even though the CVBP offered incentives and protection to buyers (Hook, 2004).

The Cumberland Valley Business Park was a successful BRAC realignment and brownfield redevelopment as a business park because it was an accessible site with established infrastructure and 1200 acres of land for development. The reuse of LEAD provides an example for other military bases and large scale contaminated properties as well as development of business parks. It is possible to reuse contaminated properties like LEAD with the innovative use of federal and state funding and programs, marketing, and environmental liability insurance, incentives, and institutional controls on land transfer. In addition, it is important to create a development authority, like LIDA, that can manage and set standards for the business park, provide utilities, facilitate development and reuse, and rehabilitate a declining economy.

REFERENCES

Barr Engineering Company (2003). Brownfield Discussion Page. [online]. Available: http://barr.com/brownfield.html [July 15, 2003]

Benatec Associates (1999). *Cumberland Valley Business Park Declaration of Covenants, Conditions, and Restrictions.* [online]. Available: http://www.cvbp.org [29 March 2004]

Department of the Army Base Realignment and Closure. (1995). *Manual for Compliance with the National Environmental Policy Act.* Washington D.C.: Department of the Army, 1995.

Global Security (2002). *Base Realignment and Closure (BRAC).* [online]. Available: http://www.globalsecurity.org/military/facility/brac.htm [Sept. 11, 2003]

DCED *News.* (1998). "Gov. Ridge Hails Unanimous House Passage of Keystone Opportunity Zones." 29 Sept. 20 Accessed via <http://www.dced.state.pa /PA_Exec/DCED/newevent/cd.html>July, 2003.

Hook, Jim. (2004). "LIDA Gets 'Clean' Deed to 300 + Acres." *Chambersburg Public Opinion.* February 7. Accessed via http://www. publicopiniononline.com/news/stories/20040207.

Letterkenny Industrial Authority (2002). Cumberland Valley Business Park. [online]. Available: http://letterkenny-business.com [July 20, 2003]

Department of Community and Economic Development. (2003). State of Pennsylvania Keystone Opportunity Zones. Accessed online July 1. Available at http://koz.inventpa.com/ [July 1, 2003]

Ramsey, Lynn (2003). *Command Overview*. Letterkenny Army Depot HQ Building 10, Chambersburg. 12 Sept.

Roy F. Weston, Inc. (1995a). *Environmental Baseline Survey for Letterkenny Army Depot BRAC 95 Action*. West Chester, PA: Roy F. Weston Inc.

Roy F. Weston, Inc. (1995b). *Final Addendum to the Environmental Baseline Survey for Letterkenny Army Depot BRAC 95 Action, Chambersburg, Pennsylvania*. West Chester, PA: Roy F. Weston., Inc.

Roy F. Weston, Inc. (1995c) *Finding of Suitability to Transfer for the Phase II BRAC Parcels, Letterkenny Army Depot*. West Chester, PA: Roy F. Weston Inc.

Roy F. Weston, Inc. (1995d). *Proposed Plan for BRAC Parcels, Letterkenny Army Depot*. West Chester, PA: Roy F. Weston Inc., 1995.

Roy F. Weston, Inc. (1998). *Record of Decision for Phase I Parcels, Letterkenny Army Depot*. West Chester, PA: Roy F. Weston Inc.

Sullivan, Thomas E.P., (ed.) (2001). *Environmental Law Handbook*. 16th ed. Rockville, MD: Government Institutes, ABS Group Inc.

U.S. Army Corps of Engineers Mobile District. (1997). *Environmental Assessment for BRAC 95: Disposal and Reuse of Letterkenny Army Depot, Chambersburg, Pennsylvania*. Chambersburg, PA: US Army Corp of Engineers Mobile District.

U.S. Army Corps of Engineers Mobile District. (1998). *Record of Decision for Letterkenny Army Depot Phase I Parcels*. Chambersburg, PA: US Army Corps of Engineers Mobile District, 1998.

U.S. EPA (2003). *Brownfields Cleanup and Redevelopment*. [online]. Available: http://www.epa.gov/brownfields [October 13, 2003].

Van Horn, John. (2003). Personal Interview, 15 Aug.

Zarnowski, Tatiana. (2003). "Depot Ready to Turn Over Land." *The Sentinel* 16 Aug. Accessed via http://www.cumblink.com/articles/2003/08/news/news03.

7 "Bow Wave" or "Development Flotsam"? Diffusion of Land Use Regulations in Pennsylvania

George M. Pomeroy and James Bennett

Controversies surrounding suburbanization, open space preservation, farmland protection, the provision of urban services, environmental concerns and a growing, central city-suburban divide, all drawn loosely under the umbrella of "urban sprawl," have appropriately attracted an attention that is chronologically sustained, grass-roots driven, and academically diffuse. Yet, given the controversies and issues that sprawl generates, there remains only a limited set of politically acceptable societal tools (Platt 1996)—the comprehensive plan, zoning, and subdivision regulation - that are used addressing issues of growth. Compounding the problem of having this rather limited toolbox has been a lack of attention to the spatial diffusion of land use regulations in relation to growth and also a poor understanding of what point or stage in the dynamic land use development process that these regulatory tools have most often been adopted. Even if additional controls are generated, it is not clear whether their timing is just in time or too late (Mookherjee and Pomeroy 1995).

Drawing the analogy to a "bow wave", John Fraser Hart (1991) in a well written and widely read journal article hypothesized that the urban-rural fringe was a zone of "intensively cultivated, high priced agricultural land that remains in front of the expanding urban edge" (36). This "zone of dissonance" and "jumble of contradictions" (36) is where an assortment of land use issues and controversies are most apparent and pressing, and where, most likely, regulatory tools might be most readily adopted.

What this research attempts to do is ascertain the degree of correspondence between the "bow wave" phenomena to the spatial diffusion of these traditional land use regulatory instruments. Are regulatory tools adopted preceding, coincident to, or subsequent to development? Does the adoption of regulatory tools even relate to the same spatial patterns? Or, is it perhaps reflective of state funding, administrative priorities, bureaucratic fashion, or other factors?

That is, is regulatory adoption part of the "bow wave"? Or, is it regulatory "flotsam" that arrives only subsequently and reactively to the wreckage of urban sprawl?

PATTERNS OF "SPRAWL" IN THE URBAN FRINGE: A DYNAMIC LAND USE DEVELOPMENT PROCESS

Variously labeled, identified, delineated and characterized by a wide assortment of researchers, what is referred to here as the urban-rural fringe is defined loosely, but usefully in this context, as a "continuum from the purely urban to the purely rural" (Bryant, 1982:2). Complementing this less stringent definition is Pryor's (1969) that this zone may be thought of as an area where "scattered urban expansion is taking place, rather an easily observable 'tidemark' around the outer edge of a growing city."

Those studying the urban fringe have long noted that the land use development process is one that is dynamic, even as our best efforts to delineate the fringe rely upon static data (as noted above). Several urban-rural fringe researchers have highlighted, outlined, described, and typified this dynamic process, most notably Furuseth and Pierce (1982), Russworm (1977), Hart (1991) Furuseth and Lapping (1999). Martin's (1975) conceptualization of this process into descriptive "stages of development" usefully captures an aspect of this development. This conceptualization is characterized in terms of decisions (to hold, sell, purchase or develop land), decision agents (farmer, developer, builder, etc.), price progression and elements of development (such as improvements) does well in articulating the processes of the land market (Sinclair 1967). Also, as changes in the fringe are for the most part, market-driven, then the model is wholly appropriate.

Missing in this is the when and how public intervention enters the process. As the "bow wave" of the sequential stages diffuse outward, is there a public planning related reaction or even pro-action? That is, as the market forces anticipate change, do public institutions, particularly municipalities capable of land use planning, also anticipate or react to change in any regular fashion? Asked another way, is there a "bow wave" of regulation?

CONTEXT, FRAMEWORK, AND DATA

While any number of settings would be likely useful to examine the diffusion of land use regulations, the metropolitan sphere of Philadelphia offers some particular advantages in analysis that are elaborated upon below. Falling in the context of Gottman's Megalopolis (1961), Philadelphia's suburban and rural hinterland offers a setting more or less representative of fringe settings general to both this super-metropolitan corridor and to metropolitan fringes nation-wide. "Sprawl" indeed may be thought of as a defining characteristic of the region as it is the glue that connects urban nuclei together.

Land Use in Southeastern Pennsylvania

In some ways Pennsylvania is several states in one. First, as a state located wholly within the traditional U.S. manufacturing belt, it has been subject to the same difficult economic transitions (including declining manufacturing employment) as other "rust-belt" states. Second, while parts of the state are Appalachian or even "mid-western," that portion of the state (the Southeast) within the study area shares many characteristics with the rest of Megalopolis and has weathered the economic transition better than the rest of the state. This southeast unit of the state has been characterized by a steadily growing population and rapidly changing land use. Third, despite having some of the larger metropolitan centers in the nation in Philadelphia and Pittsburgh, as well as other metropolitan centers (Allentown, Scranton, and Harrisburg among others), Pennsylvania is the "small town state" as it has the largest rural population of any state. Although much of Southeastern Pennsylvania is census-defined as metropolitan, it also exhibits a small town character that derives from earlier settlement patterns. The popular image of Amish buggies in Lancaster County is indicative of this character. Fourth, Pennsylvania in many ways (including economics) remains, especially in terms of land use, agriculturally oriented.

Land Use Controls in Pennsylvania

With over 2,500 municipalities (55 cities, 966 boroughs, and 1550 townships of various classifications), Pennsylvania, perhaps more so than any other state, has its politics, and by extension its land use controls, rooted in local government. Similar to New York state and in contrast to next-door Maryland, it is the townships and boroughs that choose (or choose not) to regulate land use. It is through Pennsylvania's Planning Code that the legal authority to plan is lodged in these local entities. Frequently criticized as too small in scale to appropriately deal with land use and environmental issues which are regional in scale, nonetheless it is these grassroots units which hold the power.

Furthermore, and despite recent planning activism at the state and selectively local level, Pennsylvania's planning climate has been rather conservative. This is changing, however, as illustrated by the increased activism of the Governor's Center for Local Government Services, the implementation of a "Growing Greener" program that mimics the "smart growth" programs of other states, and changes in the state's statutory code. While these innovations may seek to spark further planning innovation at the local level, it is still the traditional regulatory tools of zoning and subdivision regulation, along with the adoption of the comprehensive plan, that dominate the planning terrain in Pennsylvania (Governor's Center for Local Government Services 2001a).

Zoning, because of its frequent use (and misuse) is often referred to as the "wonder drug" of planning and for many zoning is planning. Although use of zoning, which "specifies the allowed uses of land and buildings, the intensity or density of such uses, and the bulk of buildings on the land" (So and Getzels 1988:251) dates to the early part of the 20th century, its use across the nation or even the state of Pennsylvania is far from universal. As of 2001, 60 percent of all Pennsylvania municipalities have enacted zoning and 90 percent of the state's population resides within these zoning-equipped municipalities (Governor's Center for Local Government Services 2001c). Some communities may defer to county-wide zoning, though this is the rare exception.

Subdivision regulations govern the processes of how a "tract of land is split into smaller parcels, lots, or building sites" (So and Getzels 1988:198) to insure proper development and construction standards are met and that infrastructure demands are adequate for future use. More specifically, these regulations are employed to insure the proper provision of transportation elements (both streets and pedestrian ways), adequate provision of sewer and water infrastructure, limit environmental impacts (for example, stormwater mitigation practices), and, increasingly and more controversially, address the community impacts of development through impact fees.

While innovative subdivision regulation has been more adventurous of late, most Pennsylvania municipalities practice a more garden-variety type of subdivision regulation. Subdivision regulations are even more prevalent than zoning ordinances both across the nation and within Pennsylvania. Within the state, 90 percent of all municipalities have some form of subdivision regulation, with over 1,250 relying upon their own ordinance and nearly another 1,000 defaulting to a county-wide ordinance.

Comprehensive plans, also known as general plans, are long-range (usually 10 to 25 years), topically comprehensive (addressing transportation, land use, capital facilities, etc.), and geographically whole (spatially referenced and involving the entire municipality) statements of vision, objectives, policy, and standards concerning the community, thereby serving as a "blueprint for future development in the community" (Center for Local Government Services. 2001b: 3) They often also serve as a "state of the community report." Plan formats vary substantially from place to place, depending on state-mandates, community preferences, municipal budgets, and planning fashion. While required in some states, especially those most urgently addressing growth management, comprehensive plans are generally voluntary efforts. This is the general case in Pennsylvania, where comprehensive plans are only required under the special and rare circumstances of adopting a transportation impact fee ordinance, participation in joint municipal zoning programs, or if the governing body is a county. Given its voluntary nature and the list of required elements for inclusion (Governor's Center for Local Government Services 2001b) in to these plans, many Pennsylvania communities have chosen not to develop and adopt a comprehensive plan.   Therefore, it is the least implemented of the three regulatory tools considered in this chapter. Currently, just over one-half of all Pennsylvania municipalities have a formal comprehensive plan.

The Data: Date of Regulatory Adoption
Via two complementary data sets, the adoption of comprehensive plans, subdivision regulations, and zoning ordinances was recorded across the study area. Both data sets were provided by the Governor's Center for Local Government Services, an arm of the Department of Community and Economic Development.
The first set of data was obtained from an online data base (an "e-library") of county and municipal land use documents. The data for the e-library was obtained via a May 2001 survey by the Center. Using the search features, database may be accessed to determine whether a municipality (or the county) has adopted zoning, subdivision regulations, or a comprehensive plan, along with the date of such adoption. In addition, even the actual text of a number of these ordinances, regulations, or plans may be accessed. For the purposes of this paper, simply the year of adoption was recorded. As a further cross-check on the first data set, each county planning commission office was called and asked to review the data relating to the municipalities within that county. However, the county planning commission office had no manner of verifying the dates provided in the e-library.
The second data set was used as a check on and complement to the first set. The second data set consisted of periodic surveys (1974, 1979, 1987, 1990 and 1992) of all municipalities in the state as to adoption of such planning practices. A flaw in this second statewide data set (particularly in those areas that are outside the area) is that, oftentimes, the survey instrument was incorrectly completed by a municipal official or a clerical worker not versed in the said municipality's planning activities. This second data set was generally consistent with the first data set, the flaws were problematic enough that this data was used simply as a complement to the first and not presented in the tables provided in the analysis below.

Study Area and Methodology
The methodology of this study is generally patterned after Hart (1991) for

reasons of practicality and comparability. Philadelphia's metropolitan region, while not of the size New York and its environs is as comparable as possible. Both cities are eastern port cities with diverse economic bases, possess similar economic histories, and share remotely similar demographic profiles. Further, both are part of the Gottman's Megalopolis (1961) and they are situated in similar physiographical fashion. Given these considerations, this facilitates comparability to the "bow wave" idea as illustrated by Hart.

There are also practical reasons for using Philadelphia. While certainly not an isotropic surface, these Pennsylvania portions of Philadelphia's hinterland used for the study are uniform or relatively so in terms of the legal landscape, land use characteristics, topography, and settlement pattern. The legal and administrative landscape discussed earlier is quite uniform (certainly more so than in Hart's New York case study), which is critical with this particular research question. Land use characteristics across the region are similar, too - small towns surrounded by farmland with a peppering of larger cities and an interstate network that interrupts the uniformity. This uniformity also holds topographically, as this is all coastal plain or highly eroded Appalachian Piedmont.

This fragmented nature of Pennsylvania's system of local government, while note above as a bane to regional planning efforts, is ideal for purposes of this study as this fragmentation offers a fine geographic scale of analysis than county-level units, which are problematic (Hart 1991). This remains true even as municipalities vary in size and in number per county.

The delineated study area consists of a seven county region that includes Berks, Bucks, Chester, Delaware, Lancaster, Lebanon and Montgomery counties (Figure 7-1). Counties not included in the study area are where larger cities (such as Allentown in Lehigh County), the Ridge and Valley system of the Appalachians, or state boundaries "interrupt" the landscape. Within the seven county region are 128 townships and 62 boroughs, for a total of 190 municipalities (Table 7-1).

The study, following Hart, has been further subdivided into four zones oriented concentrically to Philadelphia County. The zones, in distance from Philadelphia County, are Zone I (0 to 10 miles), Zone II (10 to 20 miles), Zone III (20 to 30 miles) and Zone IV (greater than 30 miles). A centroid was calculated for each municipal entity for the purpose of determining distance from Philadelphia County.

As noted earlier, the date of adoption for each respective regulatory tool (zoning, subdivision regulation, and a comprehensive plan) in each municipality was recorded. To compensate for local variability and to better measure the average diffusion effect the median date of adoption for each tool was calculated. In addition, the range of years in which 50 percent of communities adopted each respective tool was also noted. The second calculation adjusts for outliers, while the latter middle value does some of the same.

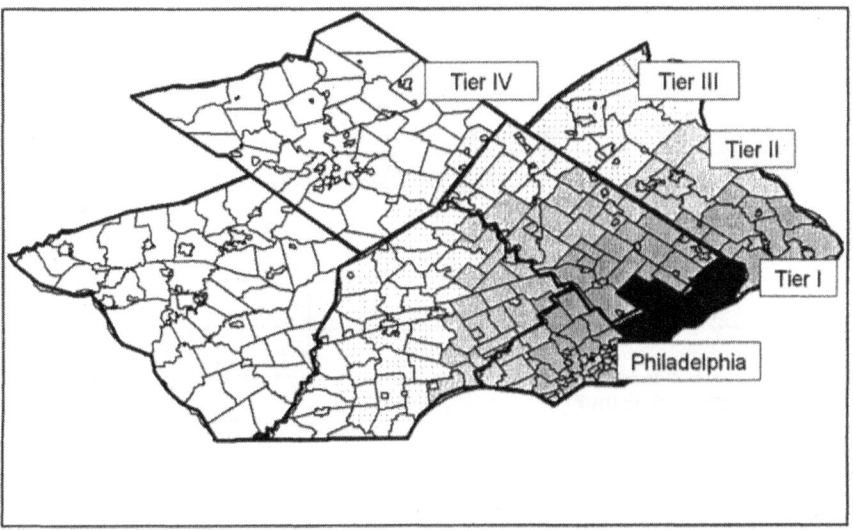

Figure 7-1
Study Area and Breakdown by Zones

Table 7-1
Study Area: Administrative Characteristics

Geographic Units/ Characteristic	Zone I	Zone II	Zone III	Zone IV
Total Municipalities	93	69	86	190
Boroughs	46	21	24	62
Townships	47	48	62	128

438 total municipalities.
Source: tabulated by authors.

FINDINGS

Reviewing the results, as presented in tables 7-2 and 7-3 below, one has difficulty ascertaining a bow-wave effect. However, when considerations are made for transportation linkages, historical development trends, and other local considerations, a case may be made that a bow wave effect may be made. Whether the bow wave arrives prior to, coincident, or subsequent to development is a different matter though.

Considering the adoption of comprehensive plans, examining the median year a comprehensive plan is adopted by zone, we find that the bow wave relationship exists generally. The effect is most notable for the boroughs. Median year of adoption for zone one (closest to Philadelphia) is 1975 and with each subsequent zone the median year of adoption climbs (1984, 1989, and 1991, respectively). For the townships, zone one has the earliest median year of adoption, though zones two and three upset the pattern somewhat. The median year for zone four is as expected—most recent. The range of years in which 50 percent of plans were adopted presents similar results, confirming a rough bow-wave effect for the comprehensive plans. Comprehensive plans are found in 79 percent of the municipalities within the study area.

After considering the role of interstate connections and the presence of other state roads, a bow wave effect may be even more easily discerned. With several federal interstate highways (I-76, I-78, I-80, and I-81) crossing the study area our "isotropic surface" becomes a bit interrupted. Municipalities in proximity to the interstate interchanges obviously feel the growth pressures a bit sooner and are likely to respond with regulatory action in a sequence that is not simply a function of geographic distance from Philadelphia.

Adoption of zoning, too, demonstrates a subtle bow-wave effect, though it is relatively muted if one considers median year of adoption (Table 7-3) alone. If one examines Table 7-3, Range of Years 50 Percent of Zoning Ordinances Adopted, the effect becomes much more obvious, especially with regard to the townships. The factors of transportation figure as largely here as they do with the adoption of comprehensive plans, as noted in the paragraph above.

While dates of adoption for zoning and comprehensive plans provided insight in whether there was a bow wave effect, subdivision regulation adoption dates proved problematic. The data for subdivision regulation was not consistent between data sources and officials at the Center for Local Government Services were skeptical at the dates provided by local communities. Given the inconsistencies, the subdivision data tables are not presented here. There was greater subjective confidence by officials in the data concerning zoning and comprehensive plan adoption. It can be said, however, that the subdivision regulation data was fairly consistent with the findings of the other two data sets. Two factors lie behind this conclusion. First, in a burst of regulatory zeal,

Table 7-2
Median Year Comprehensive Plan Adopted and Range of
Years 50 Percent of Comprehensive Plans Adopted

Geographic Units	Median Year Comprehensive Plan Adopted	Range Years 50% of Comprehensive Plans Adopted
Zone I		
All municipalities	1983	1972-91
Boroughs	1975	1970-85
Townships	1988	1974-94
Zone II		
All municipalities	1991	1984-94
Boroughs	1984	1973-94
Townships	1991	1987-94
Zone III		
All municipalities	1991	1982-94
Boroughs	1989	1970-93
Townships	1990	1987-93
Zone IV		
All municipalities	1992	1987-95
Boroughs	1991	1974-95
Townships	1992	1989-95

Table 7-3 Median Year Zoning Adopted and Range of Years 50 Percent of Zoning Codes Adopted		
Geographic Units	*Median Year Zoning Code Adopted*	*Range Years 50% of Zoning Codes Adopted*
Zone I		
All municipalities	1993	1985-96
Boroughs	1993	1985-95
Townships	1992	1973-96
Zone II		
All municipalities	1993	1985-97
Boroughs	1992	1985-94
Townships	1993	1986-98
Zone III		
All municipalities	1993	1990-97
Boroughs	1992	1984-96
Townships	1993	1990-97
Zone IV		
All municipalities	1994	1990-97
Boroughs	1992	1989-95
Townships	1994	1992-98

perhaps triggered by development trends, many communities adopted all three regulatory tools simultaneously or nearly so. Second, the effectiveness of each tool is often dependent on having the other adopted also. The adoption of all three has more than a simple additive effect.

SUMMARY, IMPLICATIONS, AND DIRECTIONS FOR FURTHER RESEARCH

Certainly a bow wave effect was demonstrated—but shouldn't this be expected? After all, if planning is simply a response to growth, and adoption of zoning, subdivision regulation, and comprehensive plans a simple indication of a societal response to social issues of growth, shouldn't we expect this pattern?

The quick response is yes; the more complete response is "not necessarily." The full answer is a bit more complicated. First, planning adoption is oftentimes a function of regulatory dictate from above. In a number of states (most notably and earlier, Florida and Oregon), adoption of planning tools comes as a requirement of state legislation. The pressure for regulatory action from above may be as a result of growth pressures in one part of the state (as in the case of western Washington for the state at large) or as a result of gubernatorial zeal. Maryland's SmartGrowth planning initiatives in the 1990s were prompted by growth issues certainly, but it was as much a function of Governor Parris Glendening's own push for planning innovation as anything else. Finally, planning associations in certain states may wield more or less influence on state and local government, also impact program implementation. What makes Pennsylvania a little distinctive, as discussed above, is the fragmented nature of its local government into over 2500 municipalities.

A second research question was also posed—is regulatory adoption part of the "bow wave" or is it regulatory "flotsam" that arrives only subsequently and reactively to the wreckage of urban sprawl? This question is much more difficult to answer given the findings. Perhaps further research linking measures of growth, such as population, building permits, and other indicators, could be studied with relation to date adopted. Anecdotal evidence offers little in trying to answer this question and if anything makes this question even tougher to answer.

The research questions are related and are appropriate, if not pressing. If local municipalities can better anticipate growth that comes in at least a muted bow wave fashion, then the need for planning initiative will become more obvious. Communities may see regulatory adoption as necessary and can act accordingly "before it's too late." In other words, for planning to be effective, it must be implemented prior to the arrival of growth. Two particular reasons or arguments for this stand out. First, planning at its simplest level implies orderly and cost effective arrangement of development on the landscape. The second argument is often of greater consequence and is what complicates most initial planning efforts. This second argument relates to the equity of the growth. If growth is perceived as imminent, speculation as to who are the winners (land owners or other parties who benefit) and losers (those whose land becomes restricted or who have their speculative opportunities foreclosed) complicates the process of planning. If planning initiative arrives soon enough, there is little to differentiate the potential winners and losers. All parties may be more likely to look at planning initiatives with the community's interest in mind at this point as they cannot reasonably or easily forecast how their own individual interests will be impacted. In other words, and to corrupt Garret Hardin's Tragedy of the Commons, the commons may be managed for the general community interest as no one is yet armed with the knowledge to best manage for the speculative interests in the community.

REFERENCES

Bryant, Chris. (1982). *The Rural Real Estate Market: Geographical Patterns of Structure and Change in an Urban Fringe Environment.* Dept. of Geography Publication Series No. 18. Waterloo, Canada: University of Waterloo.

Furuseth, Owen J. and John T. Pierce. (1982). *Agricultural Land in an Urban Society.* Association of American Geographers Resource Publications in Geography. Washington DC: Association of American Geographers.

Furuseth, Owen J. and Mark B. Lapping (eds.) (1999). *Contested Countryside: The Rural Urban Fringe in North America.* Aldershot: Ashgate.

Gottman, Jean. (1961) *Megalopolis: The Urbanized Northeastern Seaboard of the United States.* New York: Twentieth Century Fund.

Governor's Center for Local Government Services. (2001a). *Local Land Use Controls in Pennsylvania.* Planning Series #1. Department of Community and Economic Development. Harrisburg: Pennsylvania.

Governor's Center for Local Government Services. (2001b). *The Comprehensive Plan.* Planning Series #3. Department of Community and Economic Development. Harrisburg: Pennsylvania.

Governor's Center for Local Government Services. (2001c). *Zoning.* Planning Series #4. Department of Community and Economic Development. Harrisburg: Pennsylvania.

Hart, John Fraser. (1991). "The Perimetropolitan Bow Wave." *Geographical Review.* 81(1):35-51.

Martin, Larry R. G. (1975). *Map Folio No. 3: Land Use Dynamics on the Toronto Urban Fringe.* Lands Directorate, Environment Canada. Toronto: Information Canada.

Mookherjee, Debnath and George M. Pomeroy. (1995). "Perspectives on the

Urban Fringe and Growth Boundary of a Small Metropolitan City" in Rudolf Weiss and Thomas Schlotterback (eds.) *Festschrift for Vladimir Milicic*. Bellingham, Wa.: Western Washington University.

Platt, Rutherford. (1996). *Land Use and Society: Geography, Law, and Public Policy*. Covelo, Ca.: Island Press.

Pryor, Robin. (1969) "Delineating Outer Suburbs and the Urban Fringe." *Geografiska Annaler*. 51B(1):33-38.

Russworm, Lorne H. (1977). "The Urban Fringe as a Regional Environment." in Lorne H. Russworm, Richard Preston and Larry R.G. Martin (eds.) *Essays on Canadian Urban Process and Form*. Dept. of Geography Publication Series No. 10. Waterloo, Canada: University of Waterloo.

Sinclair, Robert. (1967). "Von Thunen and Urban Sprawl" *Annals, Association of American Geographers*. 57:72-87.

So, Frank S. and Judith Getzels; eds. (1988). *The Practice of Local Government Planning*, 2nd ed. Washington D.C.: International City Management Assoc.

8 Rich and Poor in Kolkata

Ashok K. Dutt and Animesh Halder

Like every city in the world, Kolkata (Calcutta) consists of both rich and poor. The contrast between the rich housing and better amenities provided to them from that of the poor is very evident. Many studies have been done on poor slum dwellers of individual Indian cities and for the country as a whole, analyzing their socio-economic characteristics, living conditions of sidewalk dwellers, and the culture of deprivation (Nangia, 1984; 1988, Planning Commission 1983; Wiebe, 1975; Rao and Rao 1984; Chakravarti and Halder 1991; Mukhopadhaya and Dutt 1993; Mukhopadhaya, Dutt and Halder, 1994; Dutt A. K., S. Tripathi, and A. Mukhopadhyay. 1994, Sheelin, 1996). A few studies relate to socio-economic profiles of cities such as Kolkata (Sen 1960) and Jamshedpur (Mishra 1959) and they state the conditions of both the rich and the poor. Few scholars have compared the rich and poor of any city. This chapter based on a *Socio Economic Survey of Calcutta Metropolitan Area, 1996/97* makes such a comparison.

CYCLES OF POVERTY AND AFFLUENCE

Poverty is painful. Poor people suffer physically because they have little food to eat and long working hours. Because they lack power and are dependent, they experience emotional pain from these daily humiliations. They have limited funds to save life when someone is sick in the family, although with whatever funds they have, they try to feed their children first (Narayan 2000). The rich, on the other hand, live a more relaxed life in which they have plenty to eat; their working hours are physically less strenuous; they do have 'power' because they have expendable money and 'connections' with those who can help them in need; also they have enough savings for a 'rainy day' or sickness in the family.

It is a fact that some people live better than others, but there are always some who live worse. Each person in each environment experiences the rich and poor differential in their own setting. A poor person in Kolkata cannot be compared with the poor person in USA because the former lives in one room tenements without any separate kitchen and plumbing facilities, while the latter has all the basic amenities though they live in dilapidated run-down housing. The Kolkata poor, therefore, need to be viewed in the context of the environment around them.

The current problems of the urban poor are complex and the definition of the urban poor itself is quite subjective. The understanding that the poor are mired in an unalterable situation poses a deep desperation. People of one group could consider themselves as materially deprived when they compare themselves to a more affluent group. Even if they lived above the survival level, the existence of groups with a great level of material possession could cause them to perceive themselves as deprived.

How one defines poverty reflects something about what one feels is the nature of poverty, and what one believes the government's response to it should be. An understanding of poverty can help determine what actions may be taken in order to reduce or eliminate poverty. Adam Smith in 1776, in his famous work *The Wealth of Nations* discussed the basic necessities that are required to remain above poverty status. To him the commodities necessary for the support of life are necessary even for the poor. (Smith, Adam, 1929, reprint).

The term poverty has developed with the modern materialistic society. In history, where social classes were much more deterministic, people did not perceive poverty the way we do today. In the feudal era, for example, one was either poor or a lord, and there was no way to change it. In the great traditions the poor are seen as spiritually pure and more importantly, they were promised easier access than the non-poor to the rewards of the next world or next life. In India's fatalist traditions, the status and existence of rich and poor are predetermined by fate.

Oscar Lewis introduced the term "culture of poverty" as a sub-culture (1968). The poor are psychologically prepared to adapt themselves to an environment poor in resources. The social tools (such as education, values, standards, and economic means) that a second generation of the poor gets, make it almost impossible to quit the poverty environment. Thus a 'cycle of poverty' emerges. Such a cycle has been found in the slums of Kolkata and it makes the

> slum dwellers of Calcutta . . . mostly spatially immobile. The reason for this
> lies in the cycle of poverty that prevails in these slums. These slum dwellers

make extremely meager money due to low education and lack of technical training which gets them only low paying jobs mainly in the informal sector. The slum dwellers mostly live in rented houses for which they have to pay rents between Rs 20-25 (under $1.50) a month. The rent, food and clothing expenses consume most of their income leaving very little expendable money. Thus they eat low calorie diets and very few of them send their children to the secondary school. Therefore the question of moving to a place which is better than their one room household accommodation does not arise. They simply cannot afford the cost of such housing. The question of moving to another location arises only when new employment and possibility of earning more money or bulldozing of slums force them to do so. Proximity to work and amount of rent required are deciding factors for the choice of slum locations. (Dutt, Mittra and Halder 1997, 421)

MEASURING POVERTY

Apart from food and clothing, affordable and decent housing is the most basic concern of the poor. Shelter is a place of protection against a negative external environment. As the poor have limited resources they have to decide on the amount they can spend on their three fundamental needs: food, housing and clothing. Among the fundamental needs, housing is of central importance in both the national economy and the individual standard of living. Slum communities in the Third World cities are growing at an alarming rate. The formation of slum or squatter settlements is largely caused by massive rural-to-urban migration, high fertility, and lack of reasonably high paying employment that can also meet the cost of decent housing.

Poverty has been measured with a view to generalize individual experiences. Such measurement "aids the formulation and testing of hypotheses on the causes of poverty. It presents an aggregate view of poverty over time" (World Bank 2001, 16). Undoubtedly, the poor are most vulnerable and voiceless. There are two approaches to measure poverty. Seebohm Rowntree developed the first one in a classic study of poverty of York, England in 1899 (see World Bank, 2001). It is based on household income and expenditure surveys and the analysis is made quantitatively. This measurement was based on information on both monetary income and consumption. The 1996/97 Calcutta Metropolitan Survey consists of both of those variables.

The second is the World Bank approach, which adds a new dimension to Rowntree's measurement parameters. It not only estimates the consumption, prices, poverty line, estimate for the immediate future, but also country-specific-poverty-lines. There are still others who consider deprivation in the dimension of health and education as important factors in identifying poverty. They include Malthus, Ricardo and Marx. Moreover, "vulnerability is the risk that a household or individual will experience an episode of income and health poverty over time" (World Bank 2001, 19).

The World Bank has estimated that in South Asia, 522 million people were living on less than one dollar a day in 1998. In terms of proportion of population living on less than one dollar a day, South Asia is surpassed only by one other region of the world – Sub-Saharan Africa, where 46.3 percent of their total population in 1998 lived in such poor conditions compared to South Asia's 40 percent. The World Bank highlights the following as the basic poverty characteristics:

      i)   "the lack of income and assets",
      ii)   "sense of voiceless and powerlessness" and
      iii)   "the vulnerability to adverse shocks" (World Bank 2001, 34)

The characteristics i) and iii) can be measured by one-time surveys, but characteristic ii), which is difficult to measure from a one time survey, needs multiple surveys.

As the economy expands, the level of poverty declines. By the same token, when the economy contracts, mean income takes a negative dive. Therefore the general well being and development of a country or region is very much related to the rise and decline in poverty. Kolkata, since India's independence in 1947, has grown economically, and that definitely has its reflections in better living conditions and food intake of the poor. However, Kolkata's relatively slow economic advancement since 1960s contrasts with the fast advancing economies of Bombay (Mumbai) and Delhi.

In all Indian cities, the rich and the middle class live in better housing with more amenities compared to the poor. They earn more money and they have savings as well as expendable money after meeting their basic cost of food, clothing and shelter. Thus, they are less vulnerable when someone in their family falls sick or some emergency expenses are required. Unlike the poor, they have more voice in both political and socio-cultural affairs. They do not feel constant pressure and humiliation because they do not experience deprivation and have a voice. They are generally more educated, better informed, and have a much better outlook intellectually. Their offspring receive better education and end up with more remunerative employment compared to the poor. In contrast to the slum dwellers' 'cycle of poverty', their cycle runs in a continuum – better housing, higher incomes, more money spent on education for their children, offspring getting well educated and employed in better paying jobs. Thus for them (non-slum dwellers), a 'cycle of affluence' pertains. In many instances, housing of the middle class and rich in Kolkata is situated not too far from that of the slum dwellers. Thus, the contrast between the rich and the poor is highly visible existing within the close vision of each other.

A SURVEY OF RICH AND POOR IN KOLKATA

The data derived from the survey of the Calcutta Metropolitan Development Authority in 1996-97 have been used in this study for analysis. This survey which involved 4,500 samples taken on a random basis, covered half of the 138 census wards of Calcutta, and was administered to both slum and non-slum populations. A total of 69 census wards of Calcutta were surveyed, of which eight did not have any slum population, and one ward consisted of 100 percent slum population. The survey also revealed that 39 percent of Calcutta's population lived in slums. Of the slum population, only 15 percent had secondary education and five percent were university graduates. The monthly per capita income was less than 1,200 rupees ($33) for 54 percent of the slum dwellers. Only 12 percent earned more than 2,600 rupees per month. Also, 53 percent of the slum dwellers had a daily calorie intake of less than 2100 (Dutt, Halder and Mittra 1998, 136), which is the minimum acceptable level as determined by the World Health Organization.

ANALYSIS OF THE SURVEY RESULTS

Two components of the survey are used for the analysis. They are:
i. Housing conditions, household asset ownership and community facilities
ii. Consumption expenditure on selected major items during the last 365 days.

The statistical techniques followed include cross-tabulation and Pearson's correlation to analyze the variables. One set of variables derived was the expenditure on non-food items. For the poor in the slum dwellings, expenditure on food accounts for over 50 percent of their income. The remaining amount is spent on housing and for meeting the demands of sickness, though there is some expendable income for clothing and other items such as children's education, family travel and transportation, purchase of major household items and for purchases of gifts for the family or friends. Figures 8-1 through 8-5 contain scatter diagrams at the bottom and correlation results are at the top. Household consumption increases with expenditure on major items (Figure 8-1). If household consumption is low, households do not buy major items. Major items include furniture, cooking materials, sewing machines, refrigerators, radios, pressure cookers, record players, bicycles and motorcars. Figure 8-1 demonstrates a strong and significant positive correlation between household consumption and major item expenditure. The underlying truth is that for those who can afford it, there is an increase in their household consumption with a concomitant increase in the purchase of major items.

Figure 8-2 reflects similar patterns where an increase in household consumption also results in an increase in expenditures on clothing, with a strong positive and significant correlation. Those who have money can buy extra, high-quality clothes which they may not even need, whereas the poor cannot even afford to buy necessary clothes.

Increases in household consumption are also reflected in the increase in the expenditures on education (Figure 8-3). The poor who have limited household consumption expenditure also have a limited amount of money to send their children to schools where payment of tuition and purchase of books are required. The net result is that, the poor in most cases do not finish secondary education though most children are literate. It may be noted that, in Kolkata, as is true throughout India, only primary education is free. This condition aids the perpetuation of the 'cycle of poverty' for the poor who live in the slums as without higher education upward mobility is almost impossible. Conversely, a 'cycle of affluence' remains in operation for the rich and well-to-do who live in non-slum households.

The poor try to spend the least amount of money for their journey to work or journey to school because these are not as necessary as food, shelter and clothing. They try to walk to their work, school, and for shopping. Only when it is imperative do they take mass transport. In the case of Kolkata, only a few use bicycles because of narrow roads, congestion and heavy motorized traffic. As household consumption increases, Kolkatans spend more money in travel and transportation. This also is very much reflected in a very high positive Pearson's correlation between income reflected by high household consumption (income) and traveling/transport (Figure 8-4).

Those who spend less on household consumption goods are presumably poor. They buy few gifts for their families and friends. On the contrary, those who have high household consumption spend a substantial amount of money in the purchase of gifts. Here too, the Pearson's correlation between expenditure on household consumption goods and buying gifts is high and significant (Figure 8-5).

HOUSING CONDITIONS

Housing conditions vary between the rich and well-to-do (non-slum dwellers) and poor (slum dwellers). The nature of the dwelling indicates that most slum dwellers live in slum huts, whereas non-slum dwellers live in flats, in multi-story or one-story buildings. The walls and roofs of huts consist of semi-permanent materials, whereas flats and multi/single story buildings consist of permanent materials. A considerable proportion of single story buildings are also inhabited by slum dwellers. These are those one-story buildings that are constructed with impermanent materials (Figure 8-6).

		MAJOR ITEMS
EXPENDR_PM	Pearson Correlation	0.522**
	Sig. (2-tailed)	0.000
	N	1132

** Correlation is significant at the level 0.01 (2-tailed).

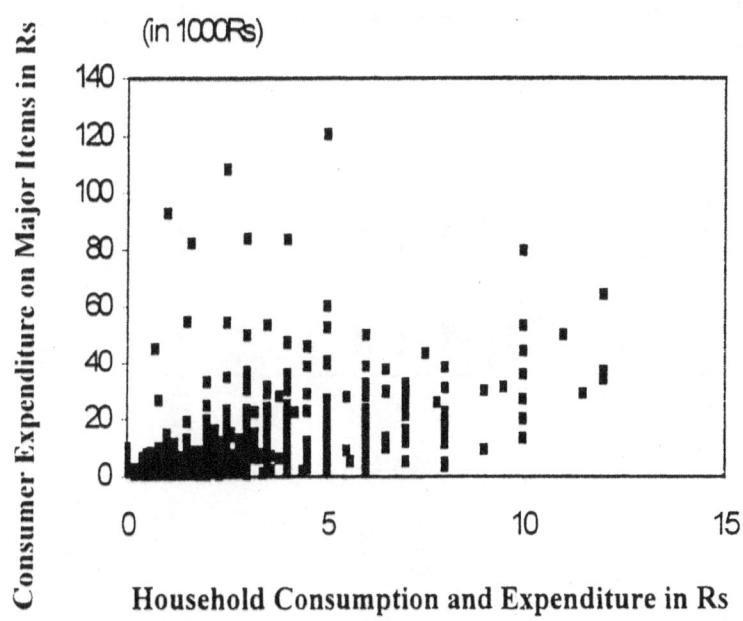

Major Items V.S. Expenditure per Month

Figure 8-1

		CLOTHING
EXPENDR_PM	Pearson Correlation	0.613**
	Sig. (2-tailed)	0.000
	N	1094

** Correlation is significant at the level 0.01 (2-tailed).

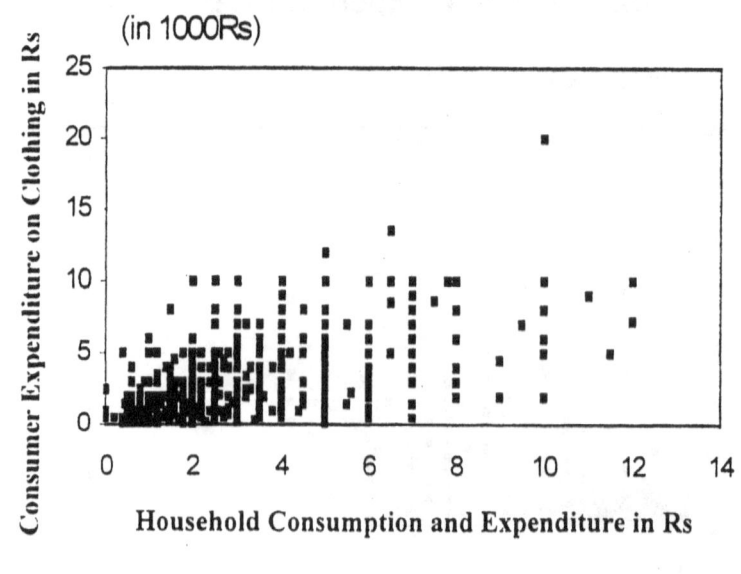

Figure 8-2

		EDUCATION
EXPENDR_PM	Pearson Correlation	0.441**
	Sig. (2-tailed)	0.000
	N	559

** Correlation is significant at the level 0.01 (2-tailed).

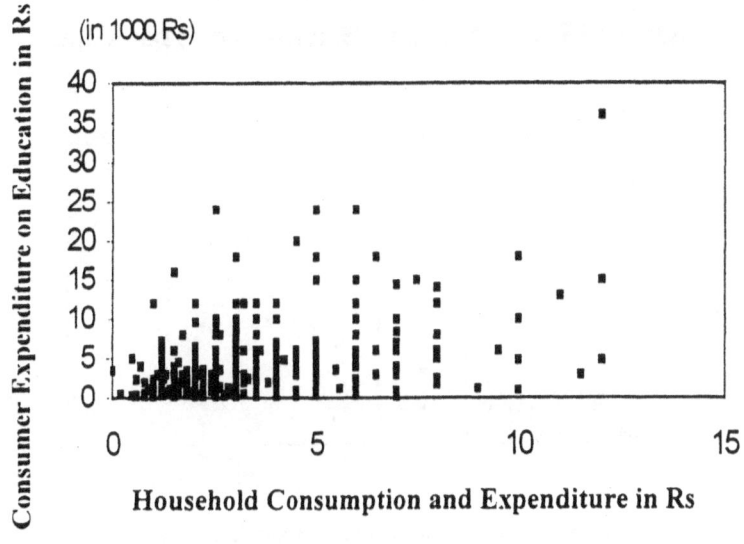

Education V.S. Expenditure per Month

(in 1000 Rs)

Consumer Expenditure on Education in Rs

Household Consumption and Expenditure in Rs

Figure 8-3

		TRAVEL
EXPENDR_PM	Pearson Correlation	0.611**
	Sig. (2-tailed)	0.000
	N	469

** Correlation is significant at the level 0.01 (2-tailed).

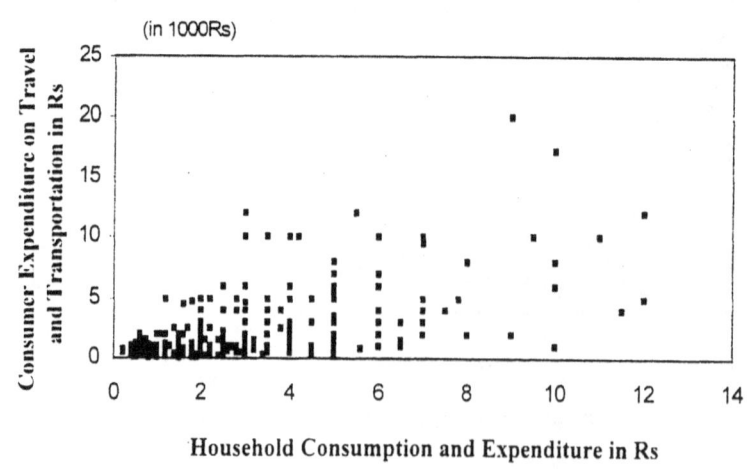

Travel and Transportation V.S. Expenditure per Month

Figure 8-4

		GIFTS
EXPENDR_PM	Pearson Correlation	0.434**
	Sig. (2-tailed)	0.000
	N	692

** Correlation is significant at the level 0.01 (2-tailed).

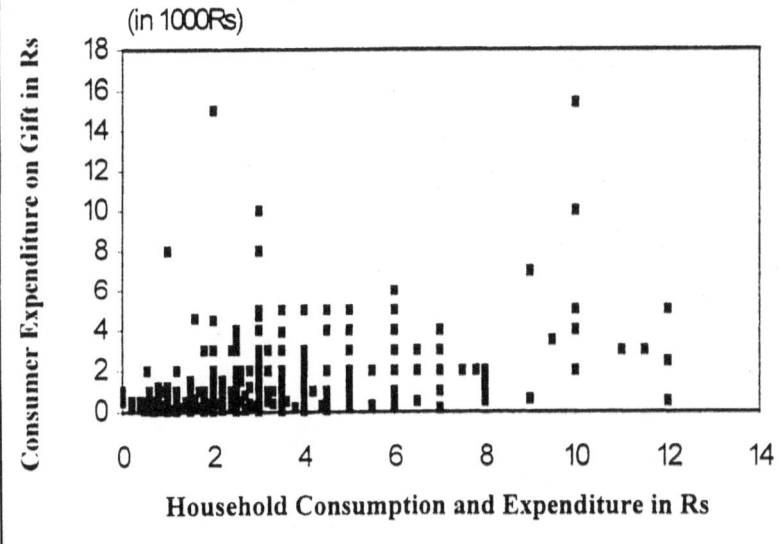

Figure 8-5

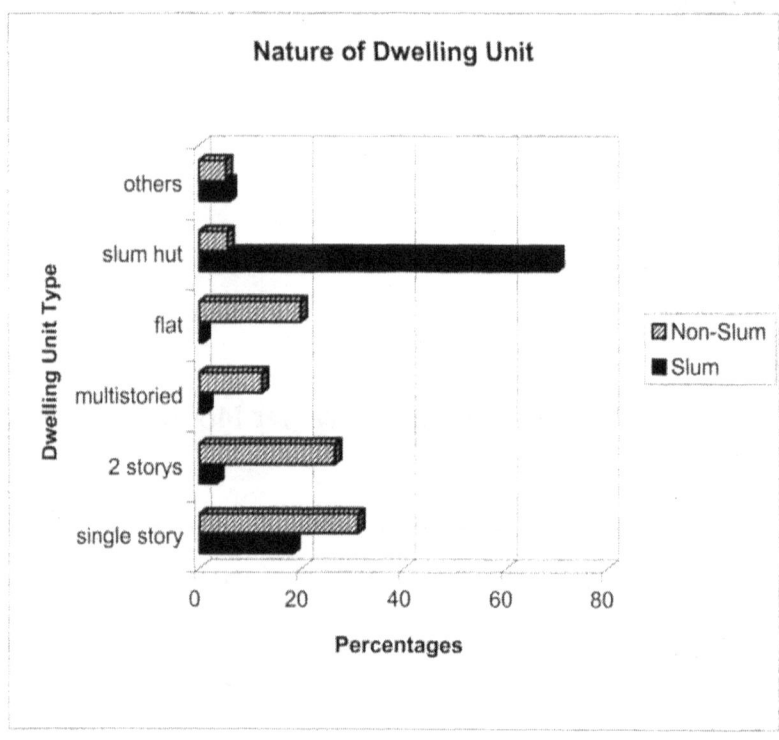

Figure 8-6

House materials are reflected in the wall and roof. The roofs of slum houses consist predominantly of asbestos, tin, tile and wood, because they are available at a reasonable cost and the slum dwellers can use them with the least labor cost (Figure 8-7). Brick, stone and cement are most common for the non-slum houses. Such roofing costs money both for the material and for labor, which non-slum dwellers can afford. Thatched roofing is virtually non-existent in Kolkata slums because law prohibits it. Such a law has been enforced in the city since 1850 because of fire hazard (Roy 1993).

Slum dwellers' households consist of less covered area (floor space) compared to that of non-slums (Figure 8-8). Most slum dwellers occupy areas less than 200 square foot for their living space, whereas most non-slum dwellers occupy over 200 square feet for their household. All 500+ square feet dwellings are occupied by non-slum dwellers. The poor not only live in smaller square footage areas, but most of them have just one room. These rooms are used as multipurpose space, where they cook, sleep, multiply and die. Sometimes, more than one couple in the same household sleeps in a single room. There is a virtual absence of privacy. Most non-slum dwellers live in two to three room households and have separate kitchens and much greater privacy.

Most one-room households occur in slums, while most three or more bedroom houses are in the non-slum areas. The two room households, on the other hand, occur in equal proportion for both slum and non-slum areas (Figure 8-9). In general, slum dwellers not only occupy smaller areas, but they are usually huddled together in single all-purpose rooms.

Bathroom and toilet facilities are some of the rudimentary needs of households and their privacy is highly desirable. Non-slum households consist of 58 percent exclusive-use bathrooms, 38 percent share with others and only four percent use other facilities (Figure 8-10). In the slum households, only nine percent have bathrooms for exclusive use, 75 percent share with others and nineteen percent use other facilities. Thus slum dwellers experience much less privacy compared to the non-slum dwellers when it comes to bathing. Five percent of non-slum households have no bathroom, whereas for the slum households it is seventeen percent. More non-slum households have one or more bathrooms compared to that of slum dwellers (Figure 8-11).

Similarly, 57 percent of non-slum dwellers have their exclusive toilets, 43 percent share with other households, while only eight percent of slum households have exclusive toilets and 92 percent share with others (Figure 8-12). Unlike villagers, few use open space for easing in Kolkata; also very few use service privy. After massive efforts for slum improvement since 1960s, the slum household toilets have been provided with either septic tanks or connected with underground sewage system. This has resulted in 56 percent and 41 percent of slum households being connected with sewer system or provided with septic tanks, respectively. This compares with 42 percent and 54 percent of non-slum dweller households, respectively (Figure 8-13).

Ashok K. Dutt and Animesh Halder

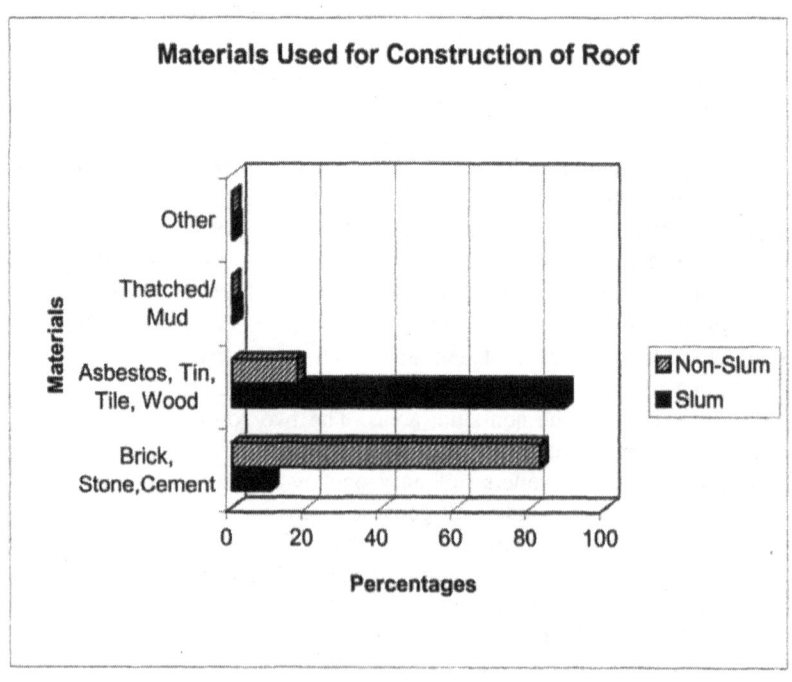

Figure 8-7

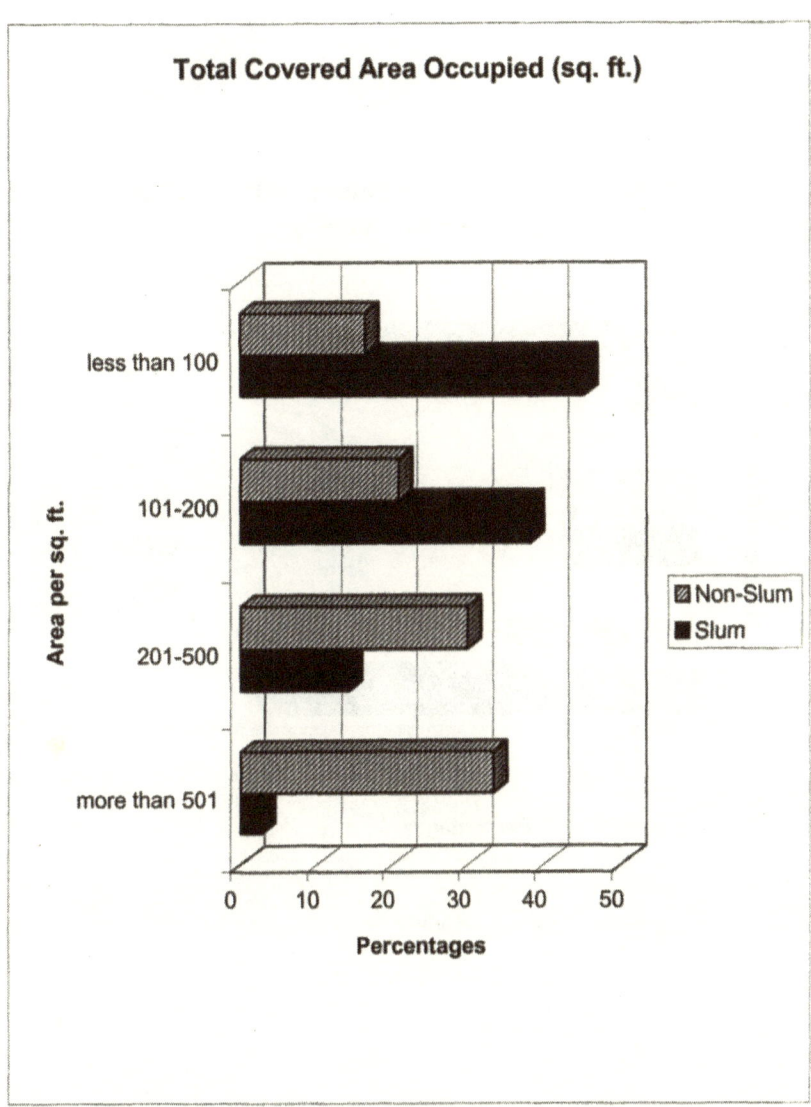

Figure 8-8

Ashok K. Dutt and Animesh Halder

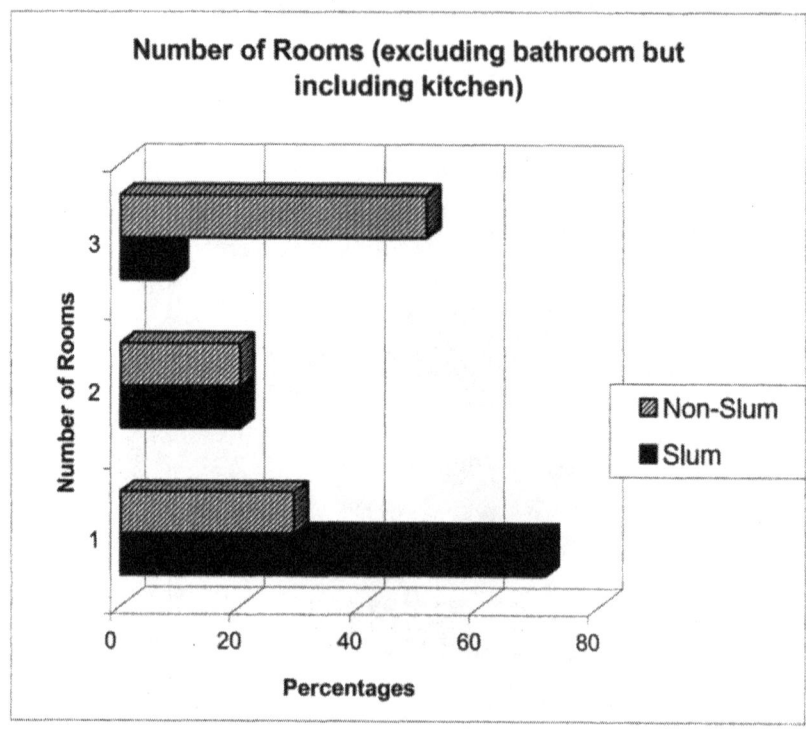

Figure 8-9

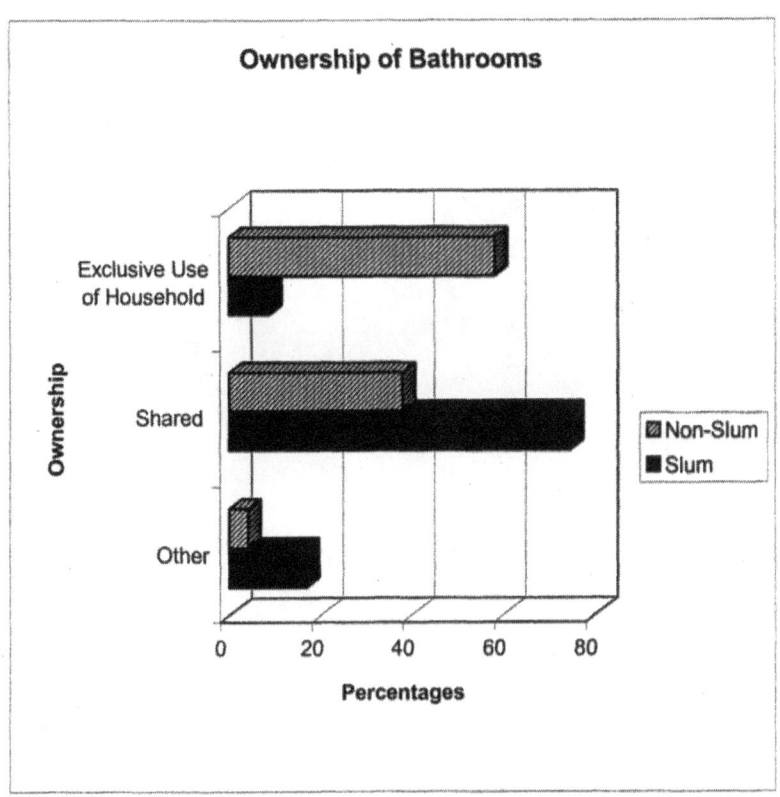

Figure 8-10

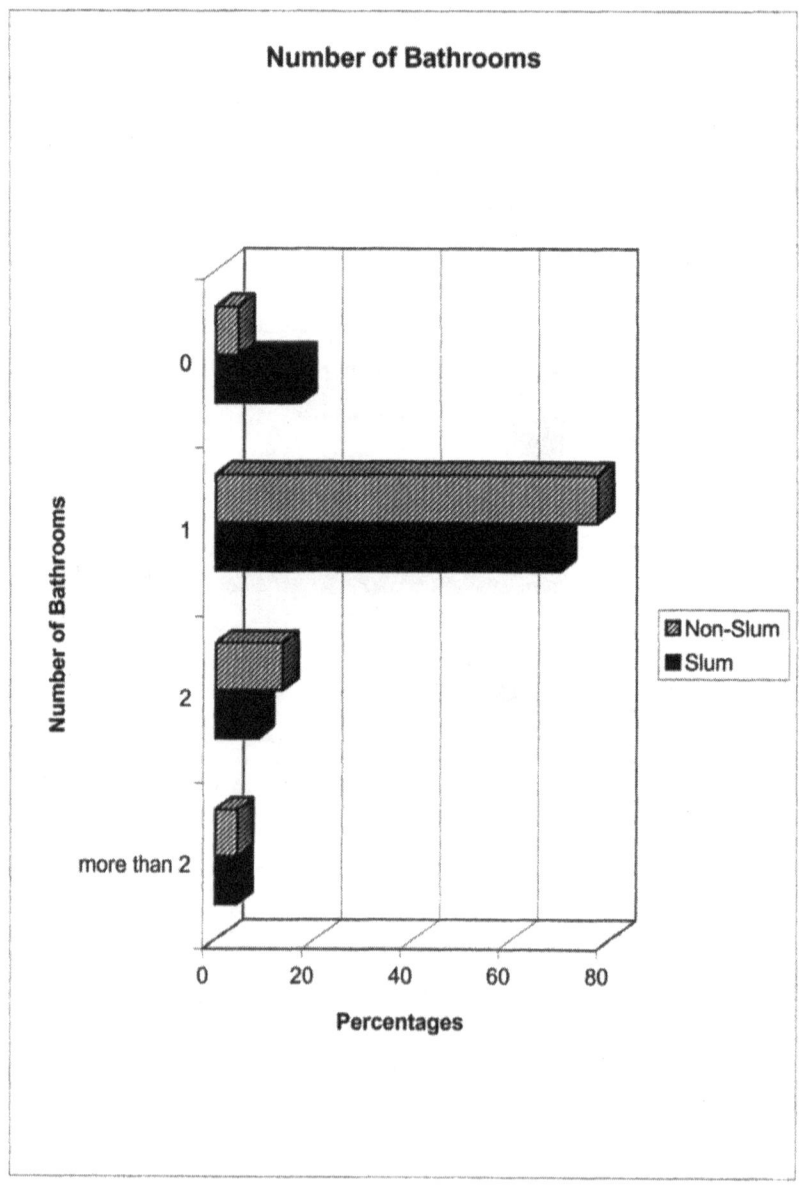

Figure 8-11

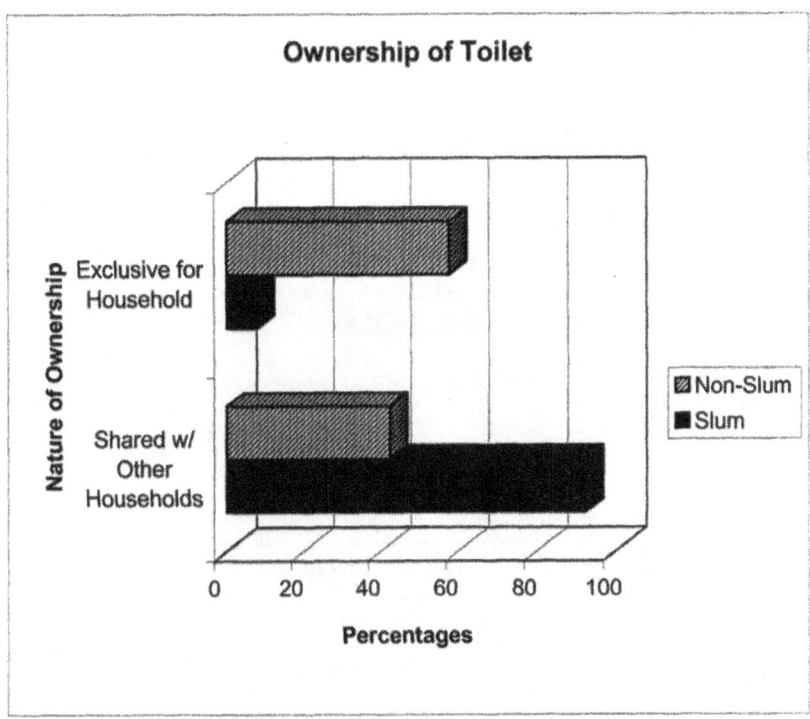

Figure 8-12

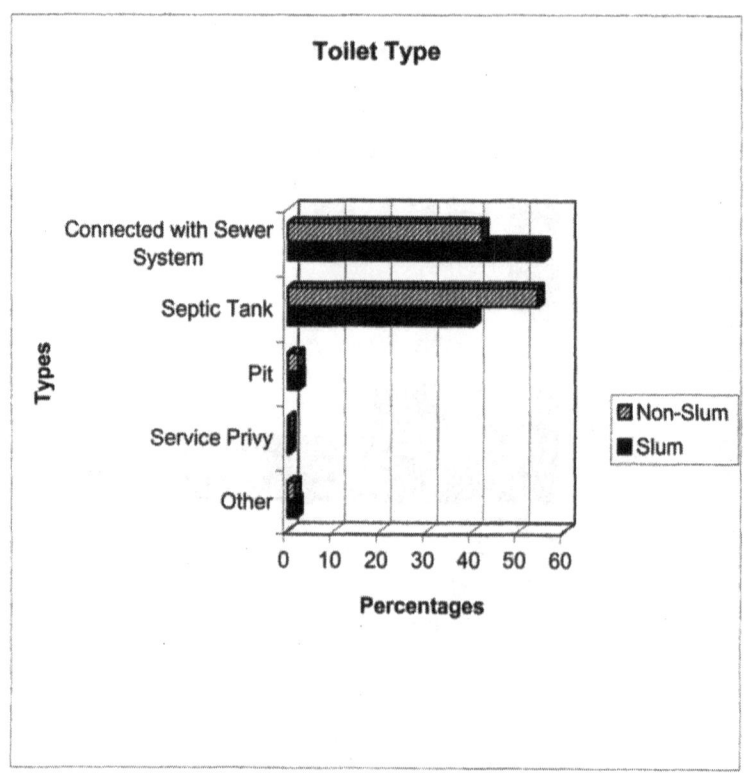

Figure 8-13

Availability of potable water is very important to the households as it is used for cooking, bathing, cleaning and drinking. Its non-availability means inviting water-borne diseases. Almost everyone in Kolkata has access to potable water. 50 percent of non-slum dwellers have individualized facilities from their own tap, tube well or well, whereas 76 percent of slum dwellers use the community taps which have restricted hours of flow and consequently often have long lines (Figure 8-14).

The type of kitchen and fuel that one uses for cooking exemplify slum/non-slum differential very well. Separate individualized kitchens are available to 66 percent of non-slum households compared to 18 percent of the slums. 63 percent of slum households cook in the same room in which they live (indicated as 'living room' by the survey), whereas only 20 percent of non-slum dwellers cook in the same room (Figure 8-15). The use of coal used was universal before the 1960s when air in the evenings was filled with smoke in the congested areas of Kolkata, but in the 1990s only one in every ten households uses coal ovens for cooking in Kolkata. Propane gas and kerosene stoves are more common. The poor living in slums use more kerosene stoves while the rich use propane gas cylinders and stoves. As gas ovens are costly and the propane cylinders need deposits, most poor cannot afford them. As a result, 51 percent of non-slum dwellers use gas and 75 percent of slum dwellers have recourse to kerosene stoves (Figure 8-16).

In regard to lighting, although 91 percent of Kolkata households use electricity for lighting their households, 15 percent in slums and 4 percent in non-slum households still use kerosene (Figure 8-17). Most slum households spend less than Rs. 50 per month for electricity in contrast to over Rs. 91 for non-slum dwellers. Kolkata weather has an unbearable stickiness because of high heat and humidity except during the three winter months, and therefore there is a need for electric fans. Slum dwellers have one or no fan per household, whereas the non-slum dwellers have one or more of them. Similarly, the slums have one or no electric lights for each household compared to two or more for non-slum households (Figure 8-18).

Non Essential Expenditure

It is the non-slum households that largely own non-essential assets, though both groups equally share some types of these assets. The assets that are equally shared are bicycles, black and white television sets, and radios. Drawing comparisons between non-slum and slum households, Fourteen percent and eleven percent own bicycles, 44 percent and 40 percent own black and white TVs, and 68 percent and 44 percent own radios, respectively. These assets are not so expensive for the poor as they can also buy used ones at an affordable price. These old ones are the discarded assets of the rich. Sewing machines and pressure cookers are owned by a considerable number in slums as they add to

Ashok K. Dutt and Animesh Halder

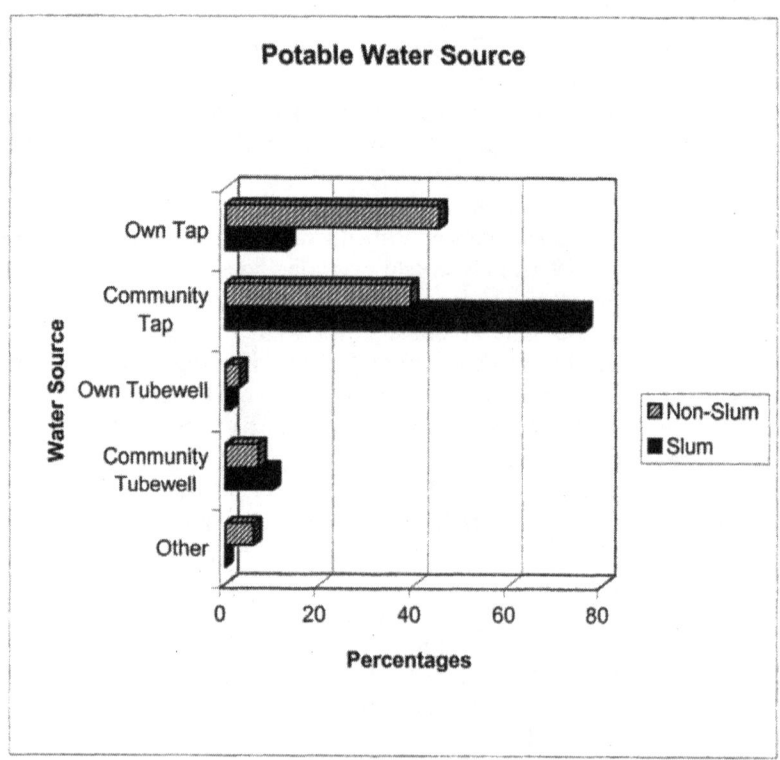

Figure 8-14

Figure 8-15

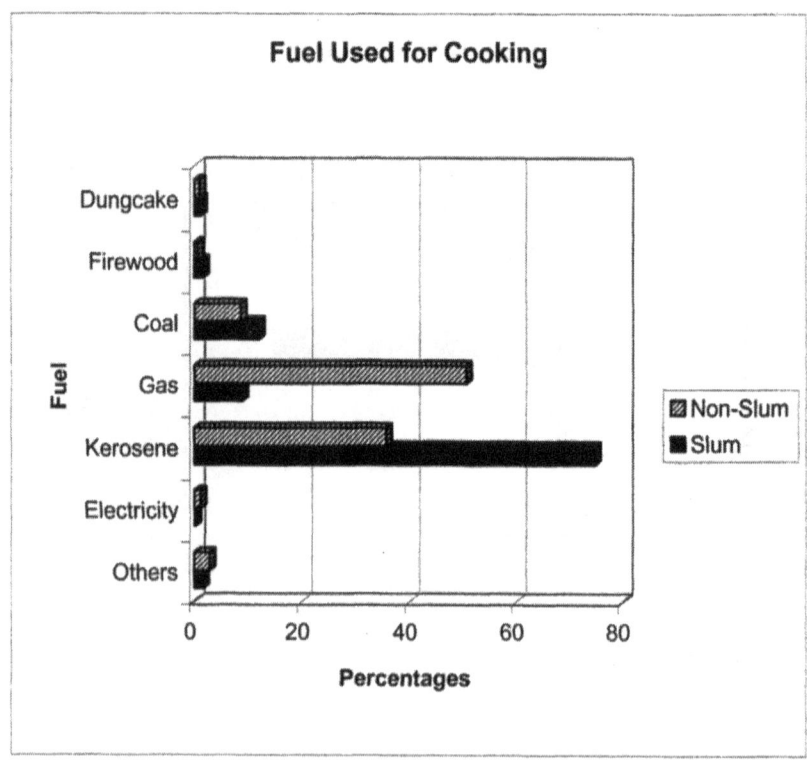

Figure 8-16

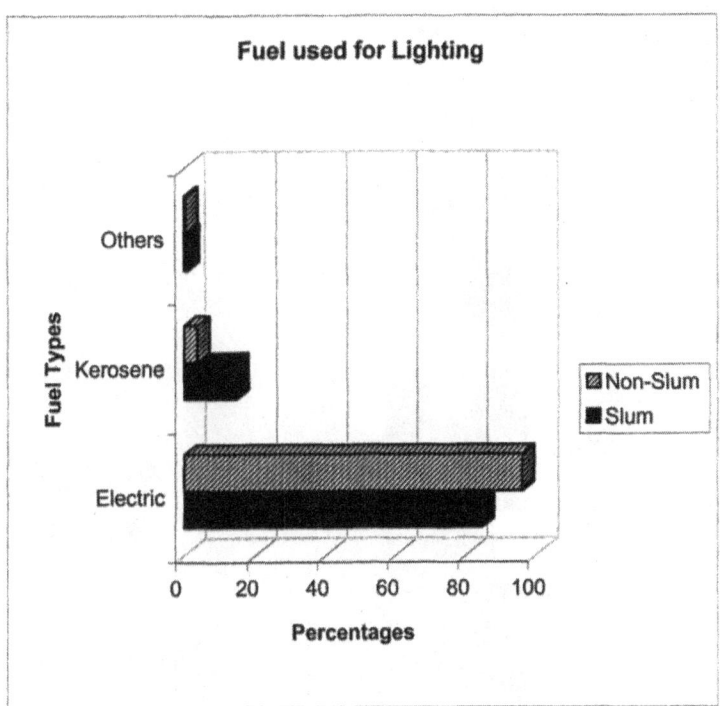

Figure 8-17

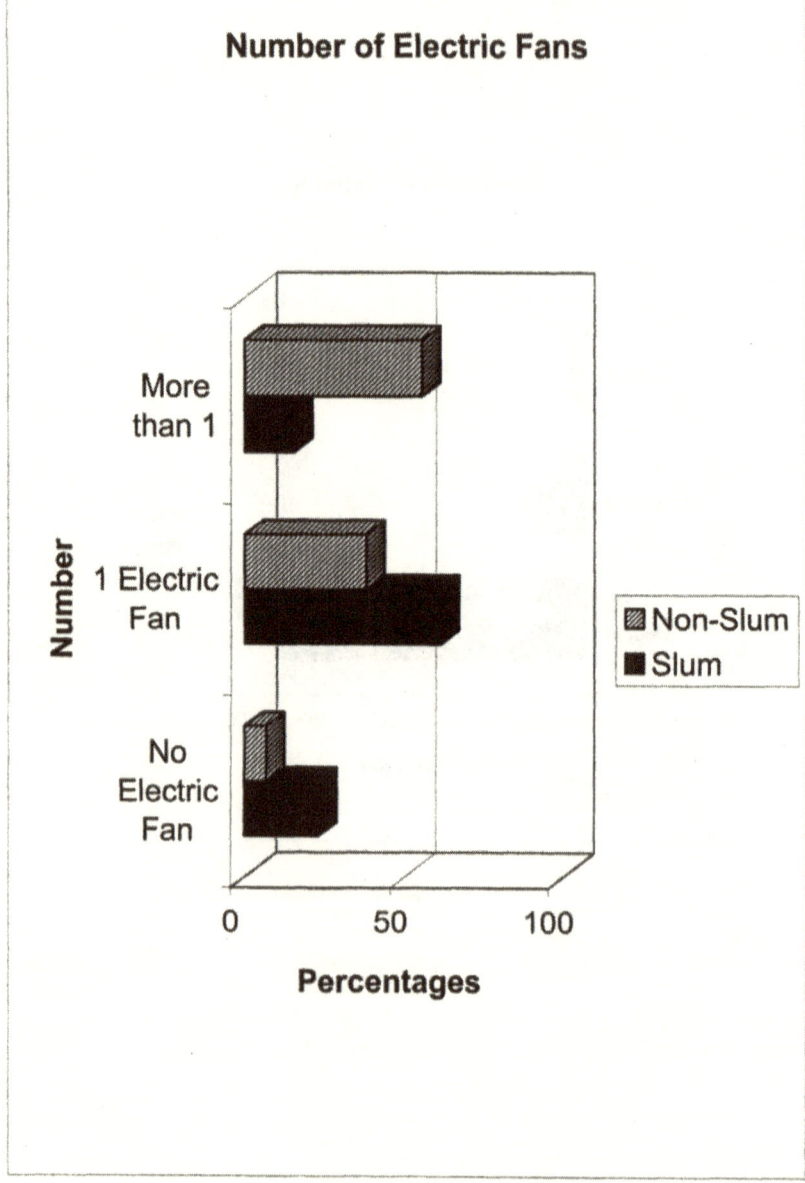

Figure 8-18

the family income by facilitating the making of garments and lowering the fuel cost, respectively. Pressure cookers save the cooking time, thus reducing the fuel use. Still their use surpasses in the non-slum households, where 67 percent of non-slum households own pressure cookers against 30 percent of the slums. Sewing machines are owned by 21 percent non-slum households in comparison to 14 percent of the slums. The rich exclusively own color TV, telephones and automobiles, as 32 percent, 19 percent and 4 percent of the non-slum households own them respectively. It may be reminded that ownership of an automobile is considered an ultimate luxury—only 24 households out of 1000 in Kolkata own automobiles.

CONCLUDING REMARKS

Slum dwellers are mostly poor including a section of lower middle class. The non-slum dwellers, on the other hand, consist primarily of the middle class with a section of the lower middle class and all of the rich. In general terms, slum dwellers are poor and non-slum dwellers are affluent. Both have their discrete and common characteristics that have been depicted in a descriptive model (Figure 8-19). The common housing characteristics include toilets connected with sewer system and septic tanks, use of electricity and at least one electric fan and single story dwellings. Further, the common asset ownership includes black and white television, radio, bicycles, sewing machines and pressure cookers. Non-slum dwellers exclusive housing characteristics include living in flats, multi- and two story dwellings, roofs made from permanent materials, household living space over 200 sq feet, households with three or more rooms, owned bathrooms, separate kitchens and toilets, and tap water. Again, the exclusive asset ownership of non-slum dwellers includes ownership of color TV, telephones and automobiles. There is no asset which is only owned by the slum dwellers and not by the non-slum dwellers. However, exclusive slum housing characteristics include huts, living household space less that 100 sq feet, flimsy roofing materials, shared toilets and bathroom, no separate kitchen, households consisting of one or two rooms.

Because of the lack of vertical mobility, the slum dwellers chances of moving into non-slum households is slim, therefore their housing characteristics and asset ownership remain permanently set for them.

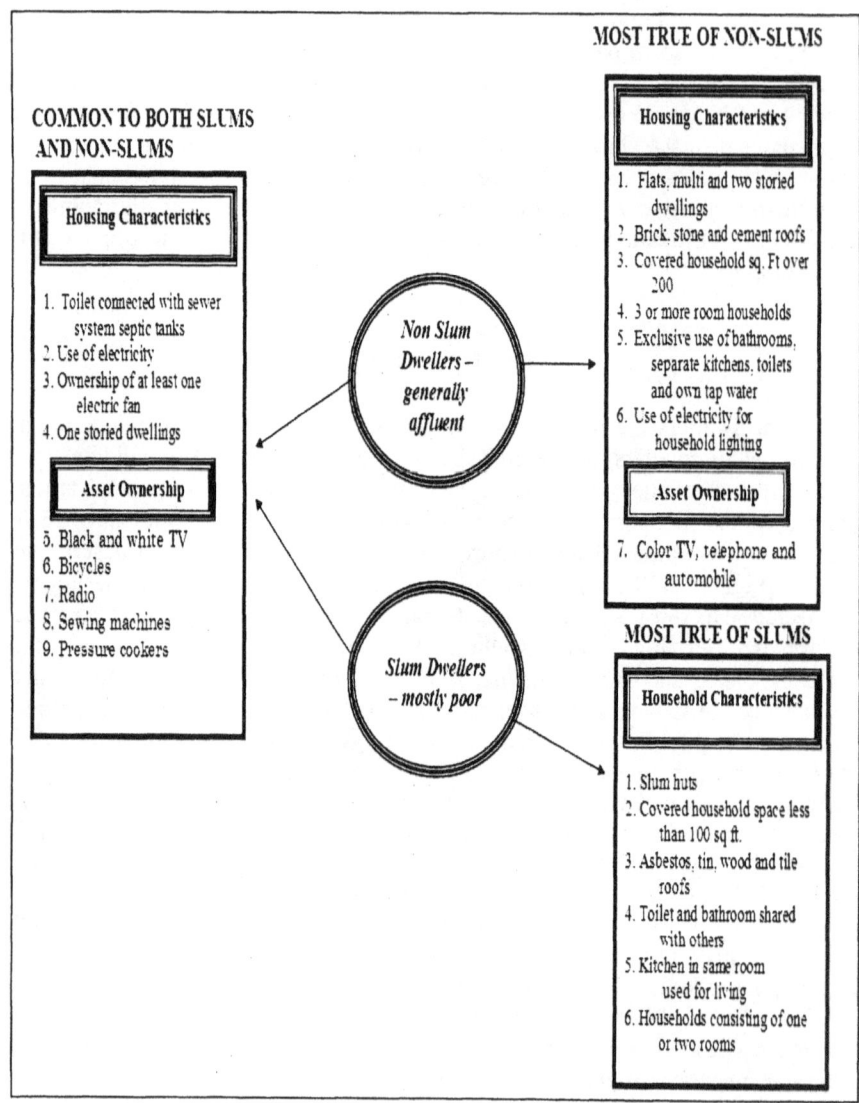

Figure 8-19
Descriptive Model Showing Housing and Asset
Ownership by Kolkata Slum and Non Slum Households

REFERENCES

Chakrabarti, A. M and A. Halder, (1991). *Slum Dwellers of Calcutta: Socio EconomicProfile – 1989-1990.* Calcutta: Calcutta Metropolitan Development Authority.

Dutt A. K., S. Tripathi, and A. Mukhopadhyay. (1994). "Spatial Spread of Daily Activity Patterns of Slum Dwellers in Calcutta and Delhi", pp. 337-352 in A. K. Dutt, et al., (eds.) *The Asian City: Process of Development, Characteristics and Planning.* Dordrecht, Netherlands: Kluwer Academic Publishers.

Dutt, A.K., A. Halder, and C. Mittra, (1998). "Shifts in Slum Upgrading Policy in India with Special Reference to Calcutta", pp. 125-150 in Noble A. G., et al. (eds.) *Regional Development and Planning for the 21ˢᵗ Century: New Priorities, New Philosophies.* Aldershot: Ashgate.

Dutt, A., C. Mittra, and A. Halder (1997). Slum Location and Cycle of Poverty: Calcutta Case. *Asian Profile* 25:5; 413 – 425.

Jagannathan, N. V and A. Halder. (1988). Case Study of Pavement Dwellers in Calcutta: Occupation, Mobility and Rural-Urban Linkages. *Economic and Political Weekly.* 2602-2604.

Lewis, Oscar (1968) *A Study of Slum Culture: Background for La Vida*, New York: Random House.

Mishra, B. R. (1959). *Report on Socio-Economic Survey of Jamshedpur.* Patna: Patna University, Department of Commerce.

Mukhopadhyay, A. and Ashok K. Dutt. (1993) Slum Dwellers' Daily Movement Pattern in a Calcutta Slum. *GeoJournal.* 29:2: 181-186.

Mukhopadhyay, A. and Ashok K. Dutt and Animesh Halder (1994) "Sidewalk Dwellers of Calcutta," pp. 337-352 in A. Dutt, et. al., (editors) *The Asian City: Process of Development, Characteristics and Planning.* Dordrecht, Netherlands: Kluwer Academic Publishers.

Nangia, Sudesh. (1984). *Innovative Approaches to Help Slum, Squatter and Rural Households Improve Their Dwellings in India.* Bangkok: Monograph Prepared for ESCAP/UNIDO, Division of Industry, Human Settlement and Technology, 7-10.

Nangia, Sudesh. (1988). "Slums of Urban India" Pp. 131-141 in Costa, F. J., et al. (eds.) *Asian Urbanization, Problems and Process.* Stuttgart: Gebrüder Borntraeger.

Narayan, Deepa et al. (2000). *Voices of the Poor: Can anyone hear us?* New York: Oxford University Press.

Planning Commission, Government of India. (1983). *Shelter for the Urban Poor and Slum Improvement IV.* New Delhi: Planning Commission 11-23.

Rao, K. R., and M. S. A. Rao. (1984). *Cities and Slums: A Study of a Squatters' Settlement in the City of Vijayawada.* New Delhi: Concept Publishing Company.

Roy, M. B. (1993). *Calcutta Slums: Public Policy in Retrospect*. Calcutta: Minerva Associates PVT Ltd.

Sen, S, N. 1960. *The City of Calcutta: A Socioeconomic Survey – 1954-55 to 1957-58*. Calcutta: Bookland Private Ltd.

Sheelin, Mallikarjun K. (1996). *The Geographical Analysis of Slums in Hubli-Dharwad Municipal Corporation Area*. Dharwad: Karnatak University. Unpublished Ph. D. Thesis.

Smith, Adam (1929) *An Inquiry into the Nature and Causes of the Wealth of Nations*, London, J. M. Dent & Sons Ltd. (First published in this edition 1910. Reprinted 1929).

Wiebe, P. D. (1975). *Social Life in Indian Slum*. Durham, Carolina Academic Press.

World Bank. (2001). *World Bank Report 2000/2001: Attacking Poverty*. New York: Oxford University Press.

9 Globalization and the Restructuring of Urban Space in Mexico City

Adrian Guillermo Aguilar and Concepción Alvarado

From the standpoint of their economic function, major cities have always been associated with a concept of centrality because, among other things, they concentrate agglomeration economies, huge quantities of information, and market areas. During the current phase of globalization, urban centrality has been maintained, although it is possible to observe certain territorial variations; for example, the central business district tends to become fragmented into various nodes of productive activities.

The economic globalization process has introduced a territorial dynamic involving both urban dispersion and concentration. Territorial dispersion of economic activities at the metropolitan, regional, and national levels has been facilitated and due to the development of telecommunications and computing processes this in turn contributes to a demand for new forms of territorial centralization involving top-level management functions and control operations (Sassen 1998:392). In other words, productive processes are fragmented throughout space, and this favors, among other things, the process of suburbanization and urban dispersion of routine, rather unspecialized productive and service activities which can be located in the more peripheral zones. But on the other hand, we can observe a re-concentration of administrative and top managerial functions as well as functions related to decision-making and technological innovation within productive processes as a result of the increasing "centrality" of major cities. Thus, within large metropolises there is no longer a direct relationship between centrality and the presence of a single central business district (CBD). In the recent past, the central city was still synonymous with this business district. However, at present the spatial manifestation of the central business district can take on various territorial forms; in this sense, we can speak of a new form of "metropolitan centrality" which is usually expressed in the existence of various urban subcenters that stand out within the built urban area. For example, there can be a few relatively large subcenters, or an entire network of smaller subcenters.

Some of the most important features that indicate this new centrality in major cities are as follows: in the first place, a large number of traditional CBDs have undergone major transformation and renovation processes due to economic and technological changes; secondly, there has been a tendency towards the formation of a network of suburban centers whose number and size vary widely, and whose connections are closely related to improvements in road infrastructure; and thirdly, as of telematics and the constant intense economic transactions that take place in these cities, local globalized spaces are formed, which in turn are manifestations of what Sassen (1998:394) calls a "transterritorial centrality" whose clearest expression are the financial links between the so-called world cities such as New York, London, Paris, and Tokyo.

In this context, this chapter analyzes the extent to which urban centrality has been modified within the built area of Mexico City, to the degree that it presents a multinodal structure in the concentration of its main economic activities. This analysis is important because it provides us with elements for describing this type of transformation in a major metropolis in a developing country, and also for comparing this process with what has taken place in other metropolises of the developing world.

I. From Monocentrism to the Multinodal Metropolis

Several urban analyses have attempted to show that the monocentric model apparently is no longer valid for exploring the recent evolution of the urban structure in larger metropolises. It seems evident that the current structure of major cities has a rather polycentric configuration which is nothing like the predominance of a single, important center (see Richardson 1988; Berry and Kim 1993; Kloosterman and Musterd 2001).

As regards the individual metropolitan area, the predominance of a major commercial core, or central business district (CBD) has increasingly been challenged by the growth of subcenters in the suburbs or in peripheral locations. The clearest example of this would be the concept of edge city[1] proposed by Garreau (1991) (see Champion 2001:658).

A monocentric structure is related, above all, to the structure of cities in developed countries that underwent an industrial phase where, for example, there were railroad terminals in central areas, and the links between the center of the city and the periphery were dominated by trains with a radial pattern starting out in the central business district, which was gradually modified to the extent that automobile use opened up new residential areas in the urban periphery. It is believed that the modification of the principles of the monocentric model occurred mostly between 1925 and 1965. Technological advances in transportation facilitated shifts in the location of the population and economic activities, particularly in the case of manufacturing and wholesale trade, creating suburban locations of all types of businesses (Kloosterman and Musterd 2001:625).

Therefore, after the boom experienced by urban form subsequent to World War II related to a single, large urban core, this model was later limited by suburbanization, decentralization, and dispersion processes. These changes produced a reduction in commuting times between the center and the periphery in the largest metropolitan areas. In general, in large, dispersed metropolitan areas in developed countries we find alternative employment in urban subcenters, around which there is a wide variety of residential neighborhoods. The population that commutes from the periphery to the center of the metropolis sooner or later seek to escape urban congestion, changing their place of residence and workplace to the periphery; this type of adjustment is easier to effect in this kind of city (Berry and Kim 1993:1). However, in major cities in developing countries, due to the accelerated urbanization process, it is not likely that we will find many alternate subcenters for jobs. For that reason, such labor shifts from the center to the periphery without a doubt characterize, to a great extent, the intra-metropolitan mobility of the working population.

Currently many of the major urban regions are considered multinodal, with third-, fourth-, and fifth-generation subcenters that are located within and beyond the edge cities along high-technology corridors or constitute communities planned as large-scale and private. The new city is an "a la carte" city: it is mainly composed of three overlapping networks: (i) the residential network which is made up of places that are part of the family and its personal life; (ii) the consumption network, which includes shopping centers, recreational facilities, and perhaps a secondary residence; (ii) the productive network, which includes the workplaces of one or both spouses, and the suppliers of firms. Each of these networks has its own particular spatial logic (Berry and Kim 1993:2).

The intraurban deconcentration of productive activities has also affected the pattern of commuting that characterized the monocentric model, where the population essentially traveled from the suburbs to the central areas. The new structure gave way to cross-commuting to the center of the city, and these movements can easily be observed on the main rapid roads of major cities due to road congestion in both directions.

For its part, the monocentric model was grounded on two basic premises: first, that the dominant form of production was manufacturing and transportation of goods; and secondly, it was assumed that from each household only one member of a family would travel from the home to the workplace. For that reason, other non-work-related trips were not taken into account. Nevertheless, in the past decades, data management and transmission, as well as the production of services, have replaced the production and handling of goods as the dominant urban activity (Kloosterman and Musterd 2001:625).

In particular, business-related services generally have different kinds of requirements: more than the cost of moving merchandise from one place to another, their location is determined by the need to have face to face contacts. Those services that are not highly dependent on this type of contact surely select a cheaper peripheral location. It is also worthwhile to stress that the territorial fragmentation of work facilitated by information technologies increasingly tends to scatter the spatial distribution of the population and its economic activities. This has already been observed in multinodal structures.

With regard to the second point, at present in order to select an adequate place of residence it is necessary to consider at least the location of the workplace of two family members instead of just one. And with the more decentralized location of jobs, this becomes a more complex process because most of the time it implies cross-commuting, due to which the principles of the monocentric model are fractured even more. Moreover, other, non-work-related trips have become very important: shopping excursions, taking the children to school, recreational activities, among others. All of this affects spatial mobility patterns in urban areas.

However, central location in the city is still very significant. This statement is true, above all, for financial activities and the exchange of information and innovations, for which personal contacts are extremely important. Obviously, those business groupings or centers are no longer the only ones to be found in the central urban space. Rather, a new spatial division of labor at the intraurban level has given way to new, significant economic groupings, especially around important intersections, along certain rapid roads, or in new shopping centers, all of this within an acceptable range of daily travel. In this case, physical form is an important feature, since the new groupings tend to evidence one of the following forms: an urban corridor in a radial pattern, or compact subcenters that may be identified in the different metropolitan rings.

The Polycentric Metropolis. Polycentrism basically denotes the existence of many centers in a particular area: this concept has come to constitute a basic feature of urban structure in major cities, since conditions there are more conducive to a strong trend among economic activities to group together in the various subcenters of urban activity.

In order to discuss the concept of polycentrism, several central aspects can be proposed. These aspects should be analyzed in more profound research. In the first place, polycentrism refers to two major levels: an intraurban pattern of groupings of population and productive activities at the level of the individual metropolitan area; in this case, we observe employment subcenters that compete in size with the central business district. And secondly, an interurban pattern of the same kind: here the concept of "region" containing a number of cities, none of which is dominant, is important. This is what Dieleman and Faludi (1998:365) call a polynucleated metropolitan region. For an analysis of the ways in which such as regions can be formed, see Champion (2001:664).

What are the main features of a polycentric urban region (PUR) that distinguish it from a traditional monocentric model (MM)? In the first place, the most obvious distinction involves spatial patterns of employment and services. In an MM, functions geared to serving the urban region are located in the single center comprised of the central business district and the manufacturing area around it. In the PUR model, in contrast, these functions are distributed around a certain number of centers which are distinguished from the MM's local suburban centers by the location of high-level services and employment in the basic sector.

In the second place, the aspect that is less evident in a PUR is the number and size of centers. For example, in the United States the case of new subcenters is pointed out when referring to edge cities or employment zones of the Los Angeles Airport. In the case of Dallas-Fort Worth, employment is concentrated in a multitude of small groupings and in a variety of concentrations and corridors. In the words of Waddell et al. (1993:15), the urban landscape that is observed in evolution is "multinodal, multiaxial, and multiform." This suggests a multiplicity of points at which the resident population may have easy access to services and employment, leading to a different spatial pattern.

In the third place, this change from an MM to a PUR will be accompanied by changes in the geography of land prices and, with this, of residential areas. That is to say, in a PUR there will be a series of high-value peaks, each extending towards the exterior until it intersects with extensions of another peak. The larger the number of high-value peaks that we find, the more uniform land prices will be.

In the fourth place, in a PUR multiple centers are not identical. They vary in size and reveal that some nodes are more accessible than others. Even more importantly, these subcenters vary in terms of their nature and image. The main moving forces behind the development of these centers are competition and specialization within the world economy. For example, according to Kunzmann (1996), for the case of the European city-region there are subcenters of international finance, tourist circuits, airports, a technopole with research and development, a modern productive complex, an edge city, and a gentrified urban island, as well as suburban offices (Champion 2001:666). Thus, the urban landscape of a PUR is much more complex and fragmented than that of a monocentric model.

Several empirical studies have examined the decentralization of metropolitan spatial structures in developed countries. Most have underlined the existence of various subcenters characterizing polycentrism. Research points towards a differentiation in polycentric patterns; for example, we can consider the conclusions of the most important work done along these lines (see Gordon and Richardson 1996:289-295; Cervero and Wu 1997:865):

1)   McDonald and Prather (1994) explain employment dispersion in Chicago in terms of the dominance of three suburban employment centers aside from the CBD; these centers are: O'Hare Airport, Schaumburg, and DuPage, a central county.

2)   Waddell and Shukla (1993), for their part, in a study of Dallas-Fort Worth describe a dispersed development pattern in which the role of corridors and small groupings is much more important than that of major urban subcenters.

3)   White, Binkley, and Osterman (1993) focused their study of Milwaukee on a four-zone region (the central city, the inner suburbs, the outer suburbs, and the periphery) and presented a general analysis of decentralization very similar to that of Gordon and Richardson (1996), although the outer suburbs have seven subcenters.

4)   Clark and Kuijpers-Linde (1994) indicated a contrast between the high degree of interdependence among Los Angeles subcenters (an archipelago, or nodes within an urban sea, and more separated subcenters, each of which has its own sphere of influence and market area, in the Randstad Holland).

5)   Giuliano and Small (1991) identify 30 subcenters in Los Angeles (the five-county region); their criterion was based on contiguous areas with employment densities of more than 12 workers per acre and total employment of more than 10,000 persons.

6)   Cervero and Wu (1997), in their analysis, report that the city of San Francisco has evolved towards a polycentric metropolis with four distinct urban subcenter hierarchies. The first level groups together the largest centers with the highest density, which tend to be located in the central city; one of the second-level centers with the highest growth rate, Silicon Valley, is located in the southern part of the region; the next two levels are mostly located along highways and in the metropolitan periphery.

Generalized dispersion does not imply uniform distribution of employment and activities. What has appeared to have occurred throughout time is that there are increasingly fewer pronounced peaks that can be observed in any three-dimensional map of employment density, and a greater number of larger peaks. This statement does not necessarily imply that agglomeration economies are diminishing, but rather that they are more accessible in a wider range (Gordon and Richardson 1996:291).

For the purposes of this chapter, it is important to point out several of the most significant conclusions reached in a study on the city of Los Angeles: despite the fact that for many decades, the proportion of employment, not only in the CBD but also in the city's main subcenters, has been reduced, the trend towards a declining number of subcenters, and a smaller proportion of employment in the subcenters, however they are defined, has continued. Only 12 percent of the region's jobs are located in subcenters, including the CBD. Such proportions are not consistent with the average interpretations of the hypothesis of polycentrism that implies a noticeable grouping of metropolitan-region jobs in the subcenters (Gordon and Richardson 1996:293).

II. The Restructuring of Urban Space in Mexico City

Mexico City has been a continually expanding metropolis, especially since the second half of the twentieth century. For several decades now, it has incorporated areas adjacent to it, and it continues to include rural spaces leading to the creation of new urban and suburban settlements. In 1950, the Mexico City Metropolitan Zone had a population of 3.3 million; in 1970, that figure reached 9.0 million; in 1990, it then had 15.2 million; and in the year 2000, it reached almost 18 million inhabitants. During this period, Mexico City has gradually decreased its growth rate since, whereas from 1950 to 1970 it attained more accelerated growth patterns, with an average annual rate of a little more than five percent, during this past decade, 1990-2000, its growth slowed down to 1.6 percent (see Aguilar and Ward 2003).

In terms of its urban structure, at least until the 1970s Mexico City was considered a monocentric city where there was a single commercial and business center of major importance which, to a great extent, coincided with the historical downtown area. However, in time the urban image was no longer dominated by a single center. Rather, various subcenters have appeared in the suburbs or in peripheral locations, which compete with the commercial and business center (CBC). In spite of the rise of these urban subcenters and their competition with the CBC, we should not overlook the fact that the traditional commercial and business area is still very important for the functions and global structure of Mexico City.

With the transition of Mexico City towards a more polycentric structure, cross-commuting was stimulated to a very great degree, and this has helped accentuate even further the development of various subcenters, increasingly encouraged by the intensive use of automobiles in the city. As a result of this new urban morphology, we can observe different territorial forms such as, for example, the urban corridors that follow the city's most important roads and serve as lines linking economic activity flows and interpersonal relations among all the individuals who travel along the spaces of this large city. The presence of subcenters in the city's morphology leads to a complex, increasingly more fragmented and segregated urban landscape that dominates urban functionality. This new look has helped identify several well-differentiated and important spaces, as will be seen later on in this article.

Recent spatial differentiation within the city has been stimulated, among other things, by direct foreign investment (DFI), which grew considerably as of the economic opening up. Moreover, DFI has played a significant role in structuring urban spaces for offices and shopping centers in the best, most accessible locations, as well as private housing developments with attractive amenities such as golf courses.

In the 1994-1997 period, the Central Region[2] of Mexico attracted 71 percent of all direct foreign investment in the country, with a marked concentration of investment (97%) in the two entities that contain Mexico City: the State of México and the Federal District. That is to say, despite the important economic base existing in other regions of this country, foreign capital shows a strong preference for the main urban center in Mexico. To be more precise, almost half of all direct foreign investment (49%) was aimed at the manufacturing sector; of this, 95 percent was located in the State of México and the Federal District, and following manufacturing in importance were commercial activities (18%) and financial services (16%) (Aguilar 2002:663).

We should also note that Mexico City's urban structure is enviable and hard to equal among some cities of the country's urban system. To have an idea of the magnitude of investments that have been made in Mexico City, this has been the territorial unit that has concentrated the greatest amount of federal government investment (FGI) among the country's 32 states. For example, between 1959 and 1998, the FGI made in the Mexico City Metropolitan Area, the Federal District, and seven metropolitan municipalities, accounted for 93 percent, on average, of all the FGI allocated in the country (Sobrino 2000:224). This government investment was used for primary construction of the roads network, as in the case of the "Miguel Alemán" Viaduct, the "Adolfo López Mateos" Peripheral Highway, the Inner Circuit, and the Tlalpan Highway, among others. These roads were, and still are, along with the rapid roads and the subway, the ones to join together Mexico City's urban and suburban spaces. Due to these interconnecting roads, the city's urban space has been enlarged in numerous directions (particularly towards the north and west), especially towards places where there is an important flow of intraurban trips.

Federal government investment was also allocated to constructing nine subway lines and a city train service, which are concentrated and converge predominantly in the central portion of Mexico City. Besides this infrastructure, work was also carried out in perimetral aqueducts and deep drainage. All of this infrastructure and equipment endowed Mexico City with services unmatched by any other city in the country, and this contributed, among other things, to the fact that at the end of the twentieth century this urban center came consolidate itself as an internationally important city.

Another service that has played a fundamental role in linking together Mexico City and the rest of this nation and for this city's international projection are the optical fiber lines installed in certain parts of the urban environment of this large metropolis. The installation of fiber optical lines made it possible to connect to the U.S. telecommunications network, and this led to a 436 percent increase in telephone calls between 1990 and 1998; massive access to Internet, for example, the users of this service between 1995 and 1998 went from 94,000 to more than 1.3 million, respectively (Parnreiter 2000:90-91). This enhancement of telecommunications in Mexico was closely related to the privatization of Teléfonos de México in 1990, precisely when the city was about to institutionalize its economic opening up with the signing of NAFTA. Telmex's privatization implied the endowment of infrastructure for the rapid, secure, and mass transmission of data and, with this, inclusion in the global telecommunications network. For example, the number of telephone lines doubled from 1990 to 1999, and 38 percent of these are located in Mexico City. Unfortunately, this type of telecommunications service is concentrated in four delegations of the Federal District: Cuauhtémoc, Miguel Hidalgo, Venustiano Carranza, and Benito Juárez (ibid.). This is a significant feature indicating the importance of the traditional CBC. The processes of urbanization, suburbanization, and productive decentralization that have taken place in Mexico City have had significant implications for the city's image and functionality. Thus, we can observe a central area and different urban subcenters with distinct land uses: trade and services, as well as industrial and residential. These different land uses result in a compact, fragmented urban morphology. Following is a more detailed description of the main land uses and their most relevant features.

1. The Commercial and Business Center (CBC)

Mexico City includes the Historical Downtown Area which, to a great extent, concentrates the city's traditional commercial and business center (Monnet 1995:47 and Coulomb 2000:535). The central city is composed of four delegations (political units): Benito Juárez, Cuauhtémoc, Miguel Hidalgo, and Venustiano Carranza. There have been certain indications of depopulation in these central delegations: between 1950 and 1960, their population decreased some 5 percent to 10 percent, and by 1970 these four delegations had lost approximately a third of their population (Monnet 1995:40). The trend towards lower population in the four central delegations has continued until the year 2000; at present, the most populated political-administrative units in the Federal District are the Iztapalapa and Gustavo A. Madero delegations, whose population is more than one million each (Garza 2000b) (see Table 9-1).

In the center of Mexico City, we observe two very well-differentiated activity poles: to the west is Paseo de la Reforma, especially where it intersects with Insurgentes Avenue, known as the city's business area; and to the east, the Historical Downtown Area. Reforma became a business center in the 1960s, here there is a hypercenter with a maximum concentration of activities. It includes major corporate offices of national and international firms, as well as banks and insurance companies, hotels, and airlines. Insurgentes, in turn, concentrates major department stores, restaurants, services for firms, and private schools. Between Reforma and Insurgentes there is a well-differentiated, secondary axis called the "Zona Rosa," or "Pink Zone," where we find the heart of the business section, the center for restaurants and for entertainment.

The Historical Downtown Area was the city's only central space until the 1960s, when the Reforma business center was established. The Historical Downtown Area housed approximately 4,200 buildings, a third of which are historical monuments (Monnet 1995:24). Some of these buildings were remodeled so that they could house institutions such as museums, the offices of some government ministries, banks, and restaurants. There are other historical buildings that were used in a very precarious fashion for ground-floor stores, homes, warehouses, or offices on the upper floors. There is also another type of property, which are the vacant lots or others used for parking. The Historical Downtown Area includes three well-differentiated poles: i) to the north is the traditional neighborhood called "Tepito," where population density is high and activities are mostly in the areas of formal and informal industry and trade; ii) to the east we find the "La Merced" market, where activity centers around wholesale and retail sales of foodstuffs; iii) to the center of the city we find the Main Square, or "Zócalo," which is the most important segment of the Historical Downtown Area; between the Zócalo and the Eje Central (towards the west) there are businesses, services, and administrative offices (of the President's Office, the Supreme Court of Justice, etc.), the location of the main branches of banks established long ago and major stores. To the west of here, there is a transitional zone between Balderas Avenue and Eje Central, where there are entertainment centers visited by inhabitants from the lower socioeconomic levels (Coulomb 2000 and Monnet 1995).

2. Business and Services Land Use

Aside from the traditional commercial and business center and the Downtown Historical Area of Mexico City, there are also other areas or urban subcenters which compete, to some degree, with the old downtown area. This is the case of recent commercial and service centers that have arisen, especially, in the western and southern parts of the city.

Recent, modern commercial and services land uses, along with high-income residential land uses, are drastically changing the urban landscape since they are causing a greater spatial segregation of the population. In this type of land use, it is possible to clearly identify areas specifically devoted to corporate centers, where there are extraordinarily luxurious and "intelligent" office buildings of major national and/or transnational firms, such as Santa Fe-Interlomas, Paseo de la Reforma, and South Insurgentes Avenue. In addition, these exclusive spaces include shopping malls distinguished by a selective number of commercial firms that can be found in most of these malls. Here, investors homogenize tastes for apparel, in eating patterns, and in the entertainment centers frequented by a select group of people[3] (Hiernaux 1999:65). There are also areas designated for housing institutions of elementary, secondary, and higher education. Examples are the Universidad Iberoamericana, Westhill and Monteverde in Santa Fe, and the Universidad Anáhuac in Tecamachalco, among others.

As part of this urban landscape, the presence of very high-level residential land use is significant. In these areas, which are well-differentiated within the urban morphology, we find modern apartment buildings and single-family homes, where dwellers enjoy services typical of a First World city, that is, ample green areas, parking lots, sports clubs, and places for entertainment. These developments, or gated communities, evidently contribute to a separation between two important nuclei of the population: that devoted to certain global activities, and the other nucleus, devoted to a market for national and/or local activities. These qualitative and quantitative differences evidence the process of spatial segregation that certain areas of this large metropolis are undergoing.

The concentration of this infrastructure is undoubtedly linked to the centralization of urban renovation and modernization projects in which commercial and financial service activities predominate (Kuri 1998:67). Some of these urban corridors mentioned by Kuri can be observed in spaces reproducing U.S. commercial areas, but on a much smaller scale. Examples of these commercial centers are: Perisur (1981), Centro Coyoacán (1989), Pabellón Polanco (1990), Interlomas (1992), Galerías Insurgentes (1993), Galerías Coapa (1993), Plaza Santa Fe (1993), Centro Comercial World Trade Center (1994), Centro Insurgentes (1994), and Pabellón Altavista (1995). Another more recent example is the Las Américas Exhibition Center (2002), to the west of the city where we find the Race Track of the Americas and Exhibition Center, which are now in operation and where hotels, banks, and shopping centers are currently being constructed.

3. Industrial Land Use

The industrial spaces that arose during the industrialization boom of Mexico City were located mainly to the northern zone in the following delegations: Azcapotzalco (Tabacalera and the PEMEX Refinery) and Gustavo A. Madero (Vallejo) (Icazuriaga). Later on, as was mentioned by Icazuriaga (1992:82), industry in the early 1970s began to shift towards the city's periphery, for example, towards municipalities in the State of México in the northern part of the city, in the first place to Tlalnepantla, Naucalpan, and Ecatepec, as well as, in a second stage, towards Cuautitlán, Tultitlán, Cuautitlán Izcalli, La Paz, Romero de Terreros, Coacalco, and Tecámac.

This boom was quite localized in both time and space in the Federal District, in other words, for four decades, Fordist industrial activity was a very important undertaking. However, as of the 1980s, industry began to show signs of decentralization (Aguilar 1996, 2002; Icazuriaga 1992; Garza 2000a).

At present, new urban establishments can be identified in the Federal District, as well as in its periphery; we are referring to the so-called industrial parks known as "ecological parks," where there have been created industries that do not need great quantities of water and which are considered "clean" in environmental terms. Around these industrial parks there is a quite a lot of housing, where industrial use lives alongside low-income housing use. An example of this is the Iztapalapa delegation, with the Ecological Industrial Complex and the Finsa Industrial Park, as well as Cuchilla del Moral, Granjas Esmeralda, and Escuadrón 201.

4. Residential Land Use

The construction of residential areas is inherently related to real estate promoters (Hiernaux 1991:297 and 1999:62; Schteingart 1988:115), who are the major building agents of urban space[4]. That is to say, the results of the actions taken by these promoters are reflected spatially in the image of the city within it, but also around it. Real estate promoters provide living quarters for different socioeconomic groups, from the highest to the lowest. Residential developments of different levels tend to polarize the city's internal and external space, since the best-equipped areas in terms of infrastructure are those occupied by high-income inhabitants (Hiernaux 1991:291, 1999:69-74; Aguilar and Ward 2003).

The areas devoted to high-income groups in Mexico City and its periphery are located mainly in the south of the city, as well as in the west, such as the urban corridor found in the Southern Periférico (Peripheral Highway) including the Pedregal neighborhood. Other exclusive areas are Santa Fe-Interlomas, Bosques del Pedregal, Lomas de Chapultepec, and La Herradura, among others. Many of these places are blocked off and have guards to protect them, among other things, from the insecurity afflicting the city. This type of closed area enjoys all kinds of services, and is located next to commercial and service centers, where the inhabitants of these areas find everything they need for their social activities, such as restaurants, movie theaters, and shopping centers, without the necessity of looking for other recreational areas.

Other examples of residential land use are geared to the middle class, and take the form of single-family homes and apartments. Here distribution is wider than the previous case, since this kind of housing can be found in large areas throughout the city. An example of this type of housing are Villa Coapa (in the south of the city), where there is also a significant number of businesses and services aimed at the middle class population. Another example is the Condesa neighborhood, which in the last decade of the twentieth century has been revitalized by the Government of the Federal District, as well as by private enterprise, and especially by restaurateurs, in order to make this area amenable to the middle- and upper-middle-class population of the area. The Roma and Del Valle neighborhoods (in the center of the city) are undergoing marked substitution of housing land use for business and service land use; there we find a combination of a great number of apartment buildings and single-family homes for the middle class with business and service land use that is increasingly gaining ground over the housing.

The open, peripheral areas of housing use designated for the lower-income population are located mainly towards the east in the delegations of Iztapalapa and Iztacalco, and towards the south in Magdalena Contreras within the Federal District, as well as in a significant number of metropolitan municipalities in the State of México adjoining the Federal District. These areas are located in the municipalities of Valle de Chalco Solidaridad, Nezahualcóyotl, Ecatepec, and Tlalnepantla, to mention just a few. The majority of these human settlements were originally illegal (Duhau and Schteingart 1997:32). Nevertheless, with the passage of time they have been incorporated into urban growth and have changed their status to regular, or legal settlements.

So as to have a notion of the impact of the growth of residential land uses in the municipalities of the State of México adjoining the Federal District, above all Ecatepec, Tultilán, Coacalco, and Cuautitlán Izcalli, we can mention that the INFONAVIT (Institute of the National Fund for Workers' Housing) built 64 percent of social interest (low-cost) housing during the 1984-1993 period (Maya and Cervantes 2002). Another important fact is that in the municipality of Ixtapaluca, which is located to the east of the Federal District in the State of México, the growth of social interest residential land uses in Mexico City has shifted in the past few years. In 2002, a total of 12,945 social interest housing units were built.

The municipality of Ixtapaluca has become an important destination since it is currently receiving a significant number of inhabitants that were driven out of the Federal District due to the cost of housing and the lack of social interest housing. That has obliged thousands of Mexico City dwellers to move to the conurbated municipalities because they have failed to find dignified housing in the great metropolis. This municipality has important roads that connect the population with Mexico City; those roads are mostly the Mexico-Puebla Highway (both the federal highway and the toll road), and Tláhuac-Chalco Avenue.

The massive construction of this type of housing constitutes a serious problem for the Government of the State of México because for every peso invested in housing, the state government has to contribute thirty cents in order to endow the area with services such as transportation, roads, drainage, and water. The endowment of these urban services poses a grave problem for the Government of the State of México because the majority of the inhabitants living in these spaces only return there at night, while in the morning they go to the Federal District to carry out their productive and recreational activities, turning these spaces into "dormitory cities."

III. The Formation of Urban Subcenters in Mexico City

In this section, we present a statistical analysis of the concentration of employment and population in a pattern of subcenters in the Mexico City Urban Area. The purpose of this examination is to analyze the pattern of territorial distribution of these subcenters in relation to the total magnitude of the concentration of employment and different types of economic activities in the city; and to ascertain how important each of these subcenters is and also the type of economic activities that it concentrates; in order to provide elements for discussing whether Mexico City's urban structure is multinodal.

To begin with, we can affirm that Mexico City's current urban structure is not very similar to a monocentric model. Rather, it is characterized by a decentralized employment pattern that has tended to disperse and/or concentrate in a limited number of urban subcenters and corridors.

In this article, we use employment data by economic sector from the year 1999 in terms of Basic Geostatistical Areas (BGA), which are the smallest analytical units in the urban area. In Mexico City there were a total of 4,730 urban BGAs in the year 2000, while in 1990 a total of only 3,455 had been identified. That is equivalent to an increase of 1,275 BGAs in that ten-year period, 70 percent of which were located in the State of México. This makes clear the marked urban expansion of the periphery of the city, particularly in this state.

In order to define the formation of urban subcenters, we considered as a principal criterion the total number of employed persons in each BGA, without taking into account the total resident population. The main idea is to identify employment nuclei that are distinguished from their adjacent areas due to the concentration of jobs: in this case, the minimum criterion utilized was 5,500 jobs per BGA and an attempt was made to include adjacent BGAs that also had a strong concentration of employment in order to form continuous areas with a marked agglomeration of employment (see Figure 9-1). That explains why several subcenters are comprised of various BGAs.

At one time, the possibility was also considered of using the employment density variable (employment/land surface). However, after an initial analysis of the statistical data, we found that the variable was not very useful because there is a high variation in the size of the BGAs. For example, there are very large BGAs with high employment concentrations that have medium values; and there are also very small BGAs with high employment concentrations that have very high density values. Both of these situations distort the definition of subcenters.

In the end, a total of 35 urban subcenters were identified, and classified into five groups according to their total employment numbers. The first group included only the city's Historical Downtown Area as the main center, so as to distinguish the original nucleus from the rest of the subcenters. These 35 subcenters are identified in Table 9-2, and were named according to the principal neighborhood or avenue where they are located.

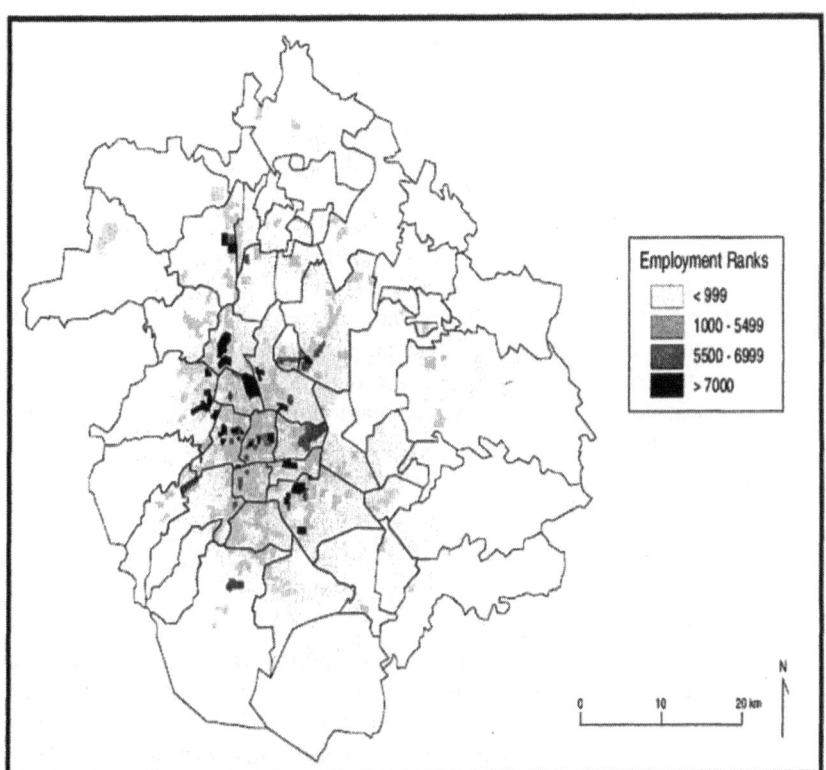

Figure 9-1
Total Urban Employment by BGA's in 1999

1. Characteristics of the Urban Subcenters

In Table 9-1, we can see the main characteristics of the urban subcenters that have been identified. Based on the data presented, the following aspects are important:

1)   Employment concentrated in these 35 subcenters represents only 23 percent of total employment in the urban area of the Mexico City Metropolitan Zone. In other words, approximately a fourth of employment is agglomerated in these subcenters, and although this concentration is very significant, the data reveals that most employment is to be found outside these centers in a very dispersed pattern within the limits of the urban area. The most important employment concentrations are found, for example, in the Historical Downtown Area (Group One; 60,395 jobs) and in zones very close to and peripheral to that area. This indicates the significant role still played by this central zone of the city in terms of job concentration. In fact, the subcenters in the central area are the ones that are comprised of a greater number of BGAs. For example, there are eight in the Historical Downtown Area and five in Paseo de la Reforma. Therefore, these are very large subcenters, but with a major concentration of employment.

2)   In terms of the land surface occupied by these urban subcenters, a clear relationship does not seem to exist among groups of subcenters and their land surface. Yet we can observe that the urban subcenters in groups I, II, and III are the largest, with more than 200 hectares up to a maximum of a little more than 600 hectares, whereas those in groups IV and V are within a range of less than 100 hectares (with certain exceptions).

3)   With regard to their territorial distribution, we find that a significant number of subcenters, constituting about a third (thirteen of these) are located in the central city (the four central delegations). In the second place, in the inner suburbs, also called the first metropolitan ring, we find the most important proportion with a total of sixteen subcenters; and in the outer suburbs, or second ring, the remaining six urban subcenters are located. This distribution shows how the central city groups together some of the city's largest business and service concentrations, as is the case of the Historical Downtown Area and a prolongation reaching Paseo de la Reforma and the Polanco neighborhood, aside from a corridor along South Insurgentes Avenue, and the major space occupied by the International Airport. Within the first metropolitan ring, an important concentration is to be found towards the north of the city, with urban subcenters representing vast industrial concentrations. And there is another important concentration towards the southeast of this ring, near the Main Wholesale Market (Central de Abastos). In the third ring, the absence of a marked variety

of subcenters is notable, except for industrial areas along the highway to Querétaro, such as Tlalnepantla or Cuautitlán Izcalli. In short, in a diameter of twelve kilometers as of the Main Square, or Zócalo, in downtown Mexico City, a great majority of the largest urban subcenters with the greatest employment concentrations can be found. That is to say, in terms of the entire urban area, a decentralized urban subcenter structure has not developed; rather, outside the first metropolitan ring, the structure is very dispersed. Above all, our attention is called to the fact that there is an absence of subcenters in the metropolitan periphery (see Figure 9-2).

4)   If we examine the proportion of jobs with regard to the population residing within the limits of each subcenter, we can observe that, above all, there is a very low presence of population throughout the entire land surface of these urban subcenters amounting to only one percent of the Mexico City Metropolitan Zone's total population. In general, the employment-population ratio is very low, although in some urban subcenters in the central zone of the city we can find the greatest number of inhabitants, with an average proportion of eight jobs for each resident (see Table 9-1).

2. Urban Subcenters and Employment by Economic Sector and Subsector

For our analysis of urban subcenters in terms of employment concentration by major economic sectors, we classified subcenters according to the economic sector in which most of the occupied population works. With this criterion in mind, we identified seventeen manufacturing subcenters, four business subcenters, and fourteen service subcenters. In all of these cases, the occupied population was greater than 50 percent in the economic sector in which they were classified, with the exception of three subcenters which can be classified as mixed. There, the dominant sector included more than 45 percent of the occupied population, and the second most important sector accounted for over 35 percent of the occupied population. If we only take into account total employment by sector, we find that in all 35 subcenters, manufacturing employment is the most important, with 34 percent of the total, followed in importance by services with 21 percent, and business with 16 percent (see Figure 9-3 and Table 9-2).

Manufacturing Subcenters.

In terms of their spatial distribution, the majority of these seventeen manufacturing subcenters are concentrated in the northern part of the city where practically all the subcenters located in that zone (except Ciudad Satélite Oriente) specialize in manufacturing. The other significant concentration is located towards the southeast, where we find three of these subcenters: Granjas México, Escuadrón 201, and Lomas Estrella. The latter three (in the inner

Table 9-1

Urban subcenters in Mexico City by BGAs, by groups, 1999. General features

Name	No. BGAs	Population 2000	Employment 1999	Area in ha	Employ./ha density	Employ./pop. Ratio	Km. to downtown
Group 1							
1. Historical Downtown Area	8	14,758	60,395	215	281	4.1	0.74
	8	14,758	60,395	215	281	4.1	
Group 2							
2. Industrial Naucalpan	5	15,299	64,450	298	216	4.2	10.84
3. Vallejo	4	9,112	53,923	669	81	5.9	7.46
4. Mariano Escobedo	5	9,641	45,757	157	292	4.7	7.90
5. Paseo de la Reforma	5	9,570	38,011	145	262	4.0	6.88
6. Industrial Tlalnepantla	3	9,746	36,871	404	91	3.8	14.02
7. Insurgentes Sur	4	13,528	35,269	142	249	2.6	6.79
8. Industrial Xalostoc	5	8,950	30,802	538	57	3.4	30.57
9. Marina Nacional	2	3,504	30,328	61	497	8.7	4.34
	33	79,350	335,412	2414	139	4.2	
Group 3							
10. Granjas México	3	14,562	28,661	180	160	2.0	4.92
11. Main Supply Market	2	2,153	26,606	292	91	12.4	8.54
12. Industrial Cuautitlan Izcall	3	1,009	24,871	378	66	24.6	25.97
13. Polanco	2	7,060	19,898	99	202	2.8	7.11
14. Los Reyes Iztacala	1	4,481	15,324	210	73	3.4	11.98
	11	29,265	115,360	1158	100	3.9	
Group 4							
15. Escuadrón 201	2	3,613	13,929	106	131	3.9	8.83
16. Palmas	1	1,165	11,685	38	305	10.0	7.20
17. Cuchilla del Moral	1	3,647	11,106	21	541	3.0	8.65
18. La Morena	1	4,728	9,922	26	389	2.1	5.84
19. Industrial Vallejo	1	1,222	9,005	99	91	7.4	8.48
20. Cd. Satélite Ote	1	4,054	8,812	59	150	2.2	12.72
21. Lomas de Sotelo	1	1,965	8,076	85	95	4.1	8.86
	8	20,394	72,536	434	167	3.6	
Group 5							
22. Lomas Estrella	1	7,501	7,904	79	100	1.1	13.23
23. Modelo	1	2,615	7,504	31	239	2.9	11.24
24. Bosques de Reforma	1	0	7,336	13	567		11.06
25. Ferrocarril Hidalgo	1	95	7,384	72	102	77.7	4.67
26. Airport	1	0	6,712	738	9		7.02
27. Tultitlán	1	2,717	6,751	58	116	2.5	23.31
28. Camarones	1	5,631	6,565	68	96	1.2	7.95
29. La Merced	1	932	6,422	13	477	6.9	1.65
30. Sta María Insurgentes	1	4	6,403	26	247	1600.6	3.47
31. Hipódromo	1	3,923	6,008	28	213	1.5	4.16
32. Sta fe	1	946	5,891	143	41	6.2	14.00
33. Guadalupe Inn	1	3,281	5,826	48	123	1.8	10.03
34. San Juan de Aragón	1	29	5,874	65	90	202.5	6.19
35. Federal Cuernavaca	1	3,295	5,711	233	25	1.7	19.68
	14	30,969	92,290	1617	57	3.0	
Total subcenters		174,316	675,993	5,837.6	116	3.9	
Total MCMZ		17,580,834	2,899,746				
%		1	23				

Source: Author's calculations. SCINCE (2000), INEGI and CIEN (1999), INEGI.

suburbs), along with the Cuautitlán-Izcalli and Tultitlán subcenters in the north of the city (in outer suburbs) are really nuclei of more recent consolidation, which in turn represent a very limited industrial "deconcentration."

In terms of the presence of certain manufacturing subsectors, four of these are the most important in all the manufacturing subcenters: food, beverages, and tobacco, with 18 percent of the occupied population; textiles and clothing, with 20 percent; chemicals with 21 percent; and metal products with 24 percent. Those four subsectors account for 83 percent of the population occupied in manufacturing in manufacturing subcenters (see Table 9-4a).

If we consider the distribution of these subcenters within the urban area, as well as their manufacturing specialization, we can distinguish certain relevant characteristics:

Southeastern Zone
This includes the subcenters of Granjas México, Escuadrón 2001, and Lomas Estrella. There, we find specialization particularly in chemicals and textiles and clothing, and to a lesser extent in metal products; in all, 35,089 jobs are concentrated there.

Northeastern Zone
This includes the subcenters of Industrial Xalostoc, San Juan de Aragón, and Ferrocarril Hidalgo. There, we find specialization in chemicals, food, and metal products. In all, a total of 33.808 jobs are concentrated there.

Northern Zone
This includes the following subcenters: Vallejo, Industrial Tlalnepantla, Industrial Cuautitlán-Izcalli, Los Reyes Iztacala, Industrial Vallejo, Tultitlán, and Santa María Insurgentes. There, we find specializations, above all, in metal products and chemicals, with a total concentration of 108,448 jobs. Evidently, this is the most important concentration of industrial employment along the exit area of the Mexico-Querétaro highway.

Northwestern Zone
This includes the following subcenters: Industrial Naucalpan, Lomas de Sotelo, Modelo, and Camarones. There, we find specialization in the subsectors of textiles and chemicals, with a total concentration of 66,787 jobs.

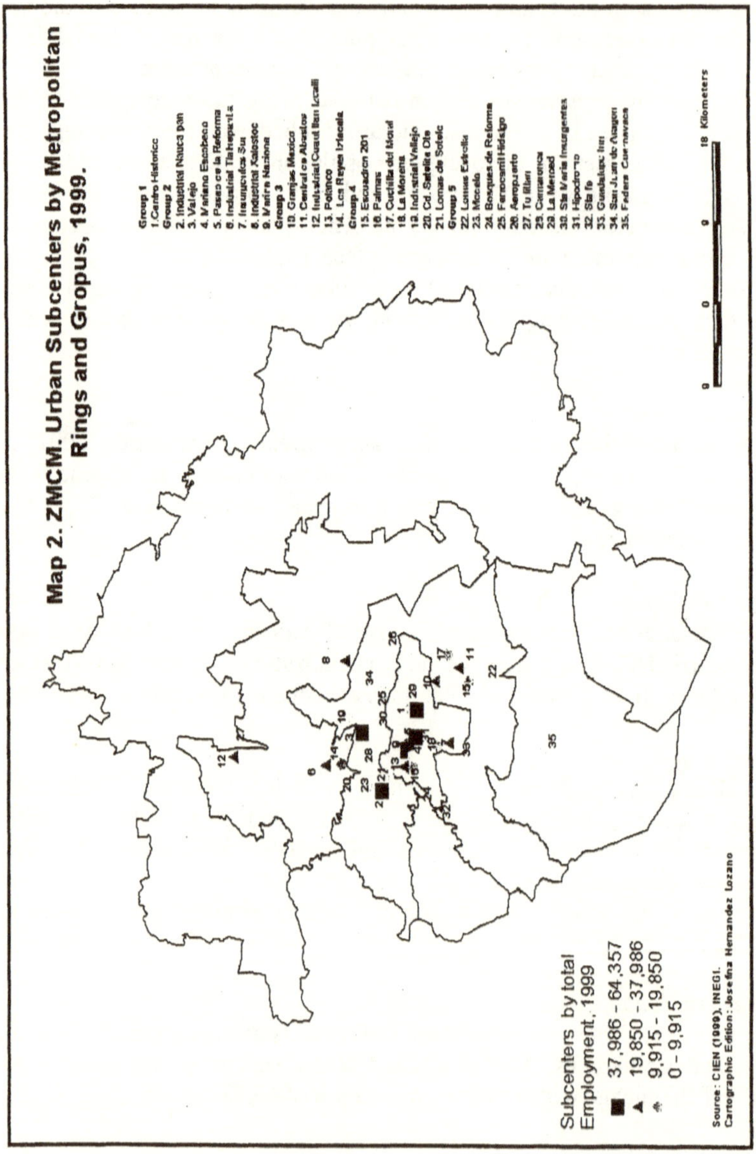

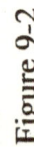

Map 2. ZMCM. Urban Subcenters by Metropolitan Rings and Gropus, 1999.

Group 1
1. Centro Histórico

Group 2
2. Industrial Nauca pan
3. Vallejo
4. Merlano Escobeco
5. Passo de la Reforma
6. Industrial Tlalnepant a
7. Insurgerotes Sur
8. Industrial Xalostoc
9. Merlano Nabonar

Group 3
10. Granjas México
11. Central de Abastos
12. Industrial Cuaut ban Izcalli
13. Polanco
14. Los Reyes Ixtacala

Group 4
15. Escuadron 201
16. Palmas
17. Cuchilla del Moral
18. La Morena
19. Industrial Vallejo
20. Cd. Satélite Ote
21. Lomas de Sotelc

Group 5
22. Lomas Estrella
23. Merada
24. Bosques de Reforma
25. Ferrocarril Hidalgo
26. Aeropuerto
27. Tu llan
28. Cerrasanca
29. La Merced
30. Sta María Insurgentes
31. Hipodromo
32. Srfa
33. Guadelupe Ine
34. San Juan de Aragon
35. Federe Cuernavaca

Subcenters by total
Employment, 1999

■ 37,986 - 64,357
▲ 19,850 - 37,986
◆ 9,915 - 19,850
   0 - 9,915

Source: CIEN (1999), INEGI.
Cartographic Edition: Jeseña Hernandez Lozano

0   9   18 Kilometers

Figure 9-2

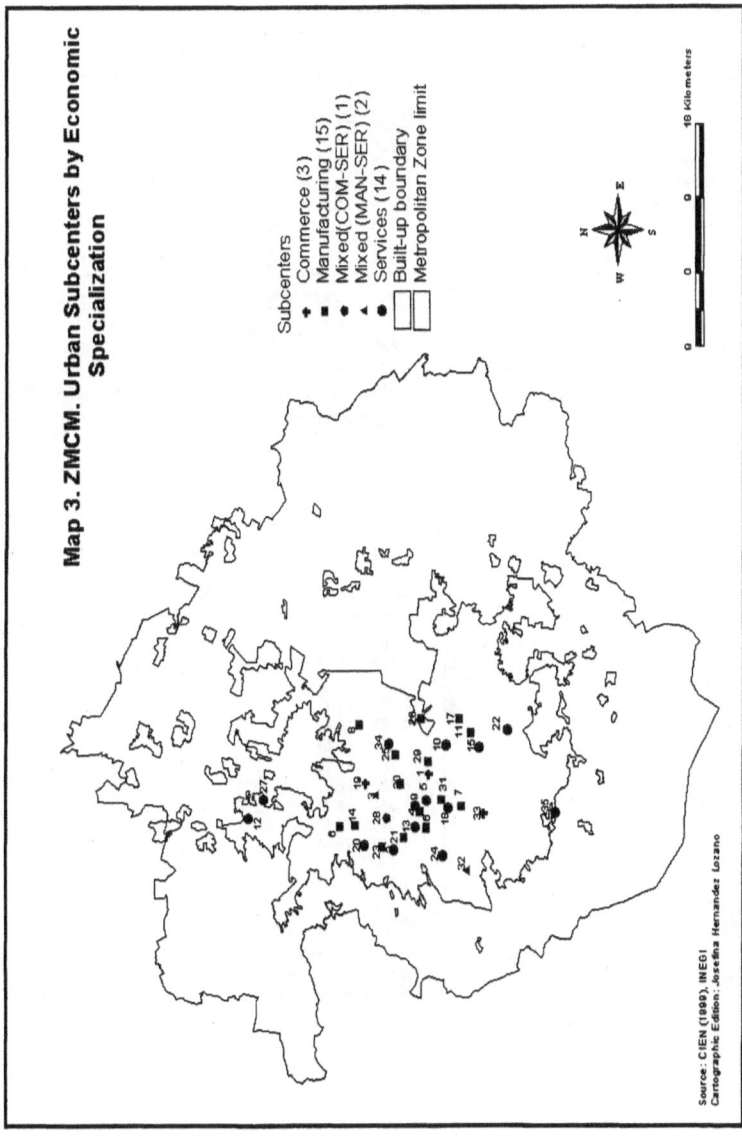

Map 3. ZMCM. Urban Subcenters by Economic Specialization

Subcenters
+ Commerce (3)
■ Manufacturing (15)
● Mixed(COM-SER) (1)
● Mixed (MAN-SER) (2)
▲ Services (14)
▢ Built-up boundary
▢ Metropolitan Zone limit

Source: CIEN (1999), INEGI
Cartographic Edition: Josefina Hernández Lozano

Figure 9-3

Table 9-2

Mexico City Metropolitan Zone. Urban subcenters in Mexico City by BGAs, by groups, 1999. Sectoral employment

Name	Manufacturing	%	Business	%	Services	%	TOTAL	SPECIALTY
Group 1								
1.Historical Downtown Area	9,447	15.7	**30,193**	50.0	20,689	34.3	60,395	Business
Group 2								
2. Industrial Naucalpan	**50,552**	78.5	9,591	14.9	4,214	6.5	64,450	Industry
3. Vallejo	42,087	78.2	8,795	16.3	2,946	5.5	53,923	Industry
4. Mariano Escobedo	13,888	30.4	8,017	17.5	23,804	52.1	45,757	Services
5. Paseo de la Reforma	3,497	9.2	6,173	16.3	28,316	74.5	38,011	Services
6. Industrial Tlalnepantla	18,903	51.4	8,018	21.8	9,877	26.8	36,871	Industry
7. Insurgentes Sur	1,287	3.7	5,025	14.3	**28,939**	82.1	35,269	Services
8. Industrial Xalostoc	24,989	81.4	3,651	11.9	2,069	6.7	30,802	Industry
9. Marina Nacional	7,233	23.9	1,291	4.3	21,776	71.9	30,328	Services
Group 3								
10. Granjas México	21,380	74.8	2,471	8.6	4,727	16.5	28,661	Industry
11. Main Supply Market	3,249	12.3	19,733	74.4	3,537	13.3	26,606	Business
12. Industrial Cuautitlan Izcalli	18,677	75.4	3,895	15.7	2,208	8.9	24,871	Industry
13. Polanco	7,443	37.5	2,131	10.7	10,276	51.8	19,898	Services
14. Los Reyes Iztacala	12,529	82.3	2,078	13.6	621	4.1	15,324	Industry
Group 4								
15. Escuadrón 201	10,161	73.4	2,006	14.5	1,674	12.1	13,929	Industry
16. Palmas	1,488	12.8	1,166	10.0	9,008	77.2	11,685	Services
17. Cuchilla del Moral	1,230	11.1	329	3.0	9,533	85.9	11,106	Services
18. La Morena	286	2.9	431	4.3	9,198	92.8	9,922	Services
19. Industrial Vallejo	4,147	46.4	1,526	17.1	3,269	36.6	9,005	Mixed (IND-SER)
20. Cd. Satelite Ote	80	0.9	4,662	53.2	4,016	45.9	8,812	Mixed (BUS-SER)
21. Lomas de Sotelo	4,364	54.5	1,111	13.9	2,533	31.6	8,076	Industry
Group 5								
22. Lomas Estrella	3,548	45.2	850	10.8	3,450	44.0	7,904	Mixed (IND-SER)
23. Modelo	6,472	87.3	439	5.9	500	6.7	7,504	Industry
24. Bosques de Reforma	63	0.9	1,608	22.0	5,642	77.2	7,336	Services
25. Ferrocarril Hidalgo	4,694	64.4	2,023	27.7	575	7.9	7,384	Industry
26. Airport	19	0.3	1,123	16.8	5,553	82.9	6,712	Services
27. Tultitlán	6,277	94.3	235	3.5	141	2.1	6,751	Industry
28. Camarones	5,399	83.5	791	12.2	279	4.3	6,565	Industry
29. La Merced	40	0.6	5,757	90.9	533	8.4	6,422	Business
30. Sta María Insurgentes	5,828	92.4	321	5.1	156	2.5	6,403	Industry
31. Hipodromo	120	2.0	1,046	17.5	4,823	80.5	6,008	Services
32. Sta fe	4	0.1	1,512	25.8	4,349	74.2	5,891	Services
33. Guadalupe Inn	240	4.1	688	11.8	4,882	84.0	5,826	Services
34. San Juan de Aragon	4,125	71.4	1,223	21.2	433	7.5	5,874	Industry
35. Federal Cuernavaca	1,180	20.8	773	13.6	3,724	65.6	5,711	Services
TOTAL subcenters	294,926	43.8	140,682	20.9	238,270	35.4	675,993	
TOTAL MCMZ	*866,223*		*902,912*		*1,130,611*		*2,899,746*	
%	*34*		*16*		*21*		*23*	

Source: Author's calculations. SCINCE (2000), INEGI and CIEN (1999), INEGI

Business and Services Subcenters

Business Subcenters. In the first place, we refer exclusively to urban subcenters that are specialized in business, and there are only four which can be divided into two groups: those located in the center of the city, the Historical Downtown Area and La Merced (market); and those located in the first suburban ring, the Main Supply Market, and Ciudad Satélite Oriente (mixed with services) (see 9-3b). There is a marked identification of the first group of these subcenters with traditional business activities conducted in the center of the city (Historical Downtown Area and La Merced), where retail trade predominates. According to total employment for this business subsector, the center of the city continues to have, without a doubt, the greatest concentration of this type (30,193 jobs).

On the other hand, the Satélite Oriente subcenter stands out among the considerable housing developments in the northwest part of the city, and there we also find a predominance of retail trade. In this subcenter, the total number of business jobs is not very high (4,662). In part, this can be explained because it is a mixed center and another important proportion of employment is devoted to service activities. In fact, if we observe some of the industrial subcenters, we find that several have a higher number of business jobs than this nucleus. Lastly, we observe the most intense wholesale trade activity in the Main Wholesale Market of Mexico City, which is the last business subcenter towards the southeast of the urban area (see Table 9-3b).

Aside from the Historical Downtown Area and the Main Wholesale Market, neither of which was established recently, the rest of the subcenters really represent a very limited number with very little employment concentration. This tends to evidence a very dispersed business structure.

Services Subcenters.

In this type of subcenter, we can identify a high predominance of the producer services subsector, since in fourteen of the seventeen subcenters we find that the population is mostly occupied in this subsector. Secondly, the population occupied in the restaurant and hotel subsector is important in five of these subcenters; outstanding due to its particular function is the subcenter composed of the Mexico City International Airport (see Table 9-3c). According to their location, we can identify six groups: (i) the first one along Paseo de la Reforma, in the section going from its boundary with the Historical Downtown Area to the First Section of Chapultepec Park including the Pink Zone; (ii) the second group is located in the Polanco neighborhood, with nearby extensions to Marina Nacional and Palmas, including the subcenters of the same name and Mariano Escobedo; (iii) the third group can be identified along Insurgentes Avenue, although in a discontinous fashion, for certain sections evidence more intense activity than others; in this case we are talking about several subcenters include Hipódromo, La Morena, South Insurgentes, and Guadalupe Inn; (iv) in a

Adrian Guillermo Aguilar and Concepción Alvarado

Table 9-3A								
Mexico City Metropolitan Zone. Manufacturing subcenters in Mexico City by BGAs, by groups, 1999.								

Name	Food, beverages, and tobacco		Textiles and clothing		Chemicals		Metal products		Total
2. Industrial Naucalpan	2,395	4.74	17,601	40.69	10,044	23.22	13,218	30.56	43,258
3. Vallejo	17,067	40.55	2,207	6.39	5,928	17.17	9,332	27.02	34,534
6. Industrial Tlalnepantla	2,387	12.63	2,399	16.78	3,525	24.65	5,990	41.89	14,301
8. Industrial Xalostoc	5,777	23.12	2,721	14.23	6,419	33.58	4,201	21.97	19,118
10. Granjas México	2,078	9.72	10,408	54.61	2,821	14.80	3,752	19.69	19,059
12. Industrial Cuautitlán Izcalli	3,693	19.77	2,274	13.41	5,756	33.94	5,234	30.87	16,957
14. Los Reyes Iztacala	442	3.53	2,154	21.78	2,022	20.45	5,270	53.30	9,888
15. Escuadrón 201	1,091	10.74	1,578	22.01	2,143	29.89	2,358	32.89	7,170
19. Industrial Vallejo	318	7.67	1,952	50.05	535	13.72	1,095	28.08	3,900
21. Lomas de Sotelo	499	11.43	1,519	35.84	1,042	24.59	1,178	27.80	4,238
22. Lomas Estrella	16	0.45	752	24.58	2,058	67.28	233	7.62	3,059
23. Modelo	50	0.77	3,218	51.85	2,321	37.40	617	9.94	6,206
25. Ferrocarril Hidalgo	2,124	45.25	910	22.06	371	8.99	721	17.47	4,126
27. Tultitlán	669	10.66	656	11.00	2,369	39.73	2,269	38.05	5,963
28. Camarones	1,365	25.28	1,289	27.15	1,290	27.17	804	16.93	4,748
30. Sta María Insurgentes	2,440	41.87	1,187	21.34	309	6.18	1,068	21.34	5,004
34. San Juan de Aragon	144	3.49	226	5.64	1,638	40.88	1,999	49.89	4,007
Subtotal	42,555	20.70	53,051	25.81	50,591	24.61	59,339	28.87	205,536
Total 35 subcenters	54,262	22.01	60,218	24.43	62,651	25.41	69,393	28.15	246,524
Total MCMZ	154,514	17.88	150,455	22.02	178,683	26.15	199,560	29.21	683,212
% 35 subcenters/MCMZ	35.12		40.02		35.06		34.77		36.08
% 17 subcenters/35 subcenters	78.43		88.10		80.75		85.51		83.37
Source: Author's calculations. CIEN (1999), INEGI.								

Table 9-3B. Mexico City Metropolitan Zone. Business subcenters in Mexico City by BGAs, by groups, 1999.

Name	Wholesale	Retail	Total
Group 1			
1.Centro Histórico	6,683	23,510	30,193
11. Central de Abastos	15,841	3,892	19,733
20. Cd. Satelite Ote	193	4,469	4,662
29. La Merced	277	5,480	5,757
Total subcenters	22,994	37,351	60,345
Total 35 subcenters	69,028	71,654	140,682
Total MCMZ	249,329	654,336	903,665
% 35 subcenters/MCMZ	27.69	10.95	15.57
% 4 subcenters/35 subcenters	33.31	52.13	42.89
Source: Author's calculations. SCINCE (2000), INEGI and CIEN (1999), INEGI			

Table 9-3C. Mexico City Metropolitan Zone. Urban subcenters in Mexico City by BGAs, by groups, (1999). Employment in services, by subsector

Name	Producer[1]	Education	Hotel and Rest	Repairs	Other[2]	Total
1.Historical Downtown Area	4,784	1,677	6,640	1,999	732	15,832
4. Mariano Escobedo	10,566	1,402	9,388	363	2,593	24,312
5. Paseo de la Reforma	13,264	3,387	8,114	466	3,106	28,337
6. Industrial Tlalnepantla	7,826	55	840	290	805	9,816
7. Insurgentes Sur	21,800	1,313	2,974	620	2,086	28,793
8. Industrial Xalostoc	1,445	34	193	255	133	2,060
9. Marina Nacional	21,020	48	197	141	323	21,729
13. Polanco	7,386	842	1,054	43	911	10,236
14. Los Reyes Iztacala	264	40	132	117	68	621
16. Palmas	7,790	44	425	9	691	8,959
17. Cuchilla del Moral	9,430	6	28	2	67	9,533
18. La Morena	8,884	98	58	119	30	9,189
19. Industrial Vallejo	226	18	347	78	2,573	3,242
20. Cd. Satelite Ote	982	445	1,441	1,012	101	3,981
21. Lomas de Sotelo	1,954	125	279	58	81	2,497
22. Lomas Estrella	3,090	246	86	15	0	3,437
24. Bosques de Reforma	5,172	162	78	6	261	5,679
26. Airport	839	9	1,639	7	3,059	5,553
31. Hipodromo	3,214	709	580	87	275	4,865
32. Sta fe	3,036	1,135	120	2	21	4,314
33. Guadalupe Inn	2,854	283	1,273	29	557	4,996
35. Federal Cuernavaca	1,058	26	528		136	1,748
Total subcenters	**136,884**	**12,104**	**36,414**	**5,718**	**18,609**	**209,729**
Total 35 subcenters	**147,241**	**12,665**	**43,447**	**7,294**	**20,985**	**231,632**
Total MCMZ	**481,171**	**205,945**	**211,595**	**126,984**	**69,633**	**1,095,328**
% 35 subcenters/MCMZ	31	6	21	6	30	21
% 17 subcenters/35 subcenters	93	96	84	78	89	91

Source: Author's calculations. SCINCE (2000), INEGI and CIEN (1999), INEGI

[1] Professional, technical, and specialized; financial institutions, insurance and bonds and rental and real estate management.

[2] Services related to agriculture and animal husbandry and rental of real estate

fourth group we find two subcenters towards the west of the city that were recently created, for example, Bosques de Reforma and Santa Fe; (v) in a fifth group are represented the only subcenters towards the southeast of the city, that is, Cuchilla del Moral and Lomas Estrella; and lastly (vi) in a sixth group, all that is included here is the subcenter of the federal highway to Cuernavaca, in the extreme south of the city, representing in an exceptional way a peripheral location of an outer suburb.

From an analysis of these subcenters, we can conclude the following: producer services exhibit a marked tendency towards concentration, above all in nuclei and urban corridors in the most expensive areas of the city; the pattern of location of these subcenters indicates a slight trend towards concentration in the west and south of the urban area, particularly along important roads such as Paseo de la Reforma, Mariano Escobedo, Palmas, and South Insurgentes. This shows a strong tendency to favor urban corridors; the consolidation of these centers is, above all, a product of a displacement of other urban functions such as residential ones, from central urban zones, with very few subcenters in peripheral areas that do not extend beyond the outer suburbs. In addition to producer services, and restaurants and hotels, it is noteworthy that the rest of the services have a very dispersed structure in the urban area, for their proportion of the occupied population does not stand out in all the subcenters specialized in services.

3. Changes in the Concentration of Employment in Urban Subcenters, 1989-1999

In this section, we shall present data based on a comparison of changes in employment concentrations in the urban subcenters of Mexico City for ten years, from 1989 to 1999. We will do this for the purpose of evaluating to what extent these nodes exhibit a tendency towards concentration or dispersion in overall terms, or by economic sector. Based on this analysis, we find that there are two aspects that are the most relevant (see Table 9-4).

In the first place, during the period we can observe, in global terms, an increase of more than 230,000 jobs in the 35 subcenters that have been identified; this indicates that those nodes maintain a significant degree of centrality which, in the majority of cases, tends to be reinforced.

In the second place, if we analyze the concentration of activities by economic sector, we find diverse tendencies. Business activity shows a gain of over 30,000 jobs in the reduced number of subcenters devoted to this specialty. Manufacturing activity exhibits both negative and positive trends: 6 of the subcenters lost a total of more than 15,000 jobs, while the rest of the industrial subcenters experienced a gain of more than 93,000 jobs. Obviously, the subcenters located along the Mexico-Querétaro Highway were the ones to benefit the most. Lastly, service activity registered the largest increments during

Table 9-4. Mexico City Metropolitan Zone. Urban subcenters in Mexico City by BGAs, by groups, 1989-1999. Growth of Employment

Name	Employ 1999	Employ 1989	Diff. Employ	Diff. Pop.
BUSINESS				
1. Historical Downtown Area	60,395	46,332	14,063	-6,246
11. Main Supply Market	26,606	10,962	15,644	2,153
29. La Merced	6,422	5,926	496	-401
	93,422	**63,220**	**30,202**	
INDUSTRY				
2. Industrial Naucalpan	64,450	10,041	54,409	-10,259
3. Vallejo	53,923	53,565	358	-5,599
6. Industrial Tlalnepantla	36,871	31,098	5,773	-278
8. Industrial Xalostoc	30,802	24,678	6,124	-919
10. Granjas México	28,661	35,824	-7,163	-18,487
12. Industrial Cuautitlan Izcalli	24,871	13,407	11,464	-194
14. Los Reyes Iztacala	15,324	16,742	-1,418	-6,293
15. Escuadrón 201	13,929	15,987	-2,058	-253
21. Lomas de Sotelo	8,076	7,899	177	43
23. Modelo	7,504	7,405	7,504	2,615
25. Ferrocarril Hidalgo	7,384	7,883	-499	17
27. Tultitlán	6,751	97	6,654	600
28. Camarones	6,565	10,202	-3,637	-2,440
30. Sta María Insurgentes	6,403	5,803	600	-9
34. San Juan de Aragon	5,874	6,406	-532	-19
	317,388	**247,037**	**70,351**	
SERVICES				
4. Mariano Escobedo	45,757	33,038	12,719	-2,253
5. Paseo de la Reforma	38,011	29,376	8,635	-1,645
7. Insurgentes Sur	35,269	15,023	20,246	-1,722
9. Marina Nacional	30,328	8,444	21,884	-747
13. Polanco	19,898	14,290	5,608	-719
16. Palmas	11,685	2,658	9,027	-501
17. Cuchilla del Moral	11,106		11,106	3,647
18. La Morena	9,922	1,839	8,083	-1,057
24. Bosques de Reforma	7,336	4,918	2,418	-1,383
26. Aeropuerto	6,712	3,982	2,730	-327
31. Hipodromo	6,008	4,587	1,421	-897
32. Sta fe	5,891	858	5,033	-129
33. Guadalupe Inn	5,826	3,721	2,105	-15
35. Federal Cuernavaca	5,711		5,711	699
	239,461	**122,734**	**116,727**	
MIXED (INDUSTRY-SERVICES)				
19. Industrial Vallejo	9,005	7,374	1,631	37
20. Cd. Satelite Ote	8,812	9,045	-233	-4,239
22. Lomas Estrella	7,904	7,258	7,904	7,501
	25,722	**23,677**	**2,045**	
Total subcenters	**675,993**	**442,005**	**233,988**	
Total MCMZ	**2,906,996**	**1,916,164**		
%		**23**		

Source: Author's calculations. SCINCE 1990, INEGI and CIEN 1989, INEGI.

this period: all the subcenters were "winners," for a total of over 116,000 jobs.

From the above we can conclude that the 35 subcenters play a very important role as centers of economic activity that tends to be reinforced. However, at the same time, from the perspective of economic sectors, the number of manufacturing subcenters is being reduced and only some of them are maintained as the most specialized in this activity. On the other hand, tertiary activity shows a marked tendency towards dispersion, not only in all the subcenters, but also throughout the urban space.

CONCLUSIONS

The analysis presented shows that in the last decades of the twentieth century, the urban structure of the metropolitan area of Mexico City has shifted from a single, important central business district to a more polycentric form. In other words, a multinodal scheme can best explain the distribution of urban employment as opposed to a monocentric model, although in a limited way. Based on an analysis of urban employment distribution in Mexico City in terms of BGAs, we defined 35 urban subcenters which represent the most important employment concentrations in relatively small spaces. In turn, these nodes are important enough to have a bearing on major modifications of the urban structure. All the subcenters located in the central city specialize in services and business with urban forms similar to nuclei, corridors, and high-density zones. In this case, we should point out the Historical Downtown Area, Paseo de la Reforma, South Insurgentes, the Pink Zone, Polanco, and the International Airport. In the first metropolitan ring we find the subcenters that represent industrial districts: these are the largest in terms of land surface and are located north of the central city. In these inner suburbs there is greater dispersion, mainly towards the north and the southeast. Within the central city, we can identify a polycentric structure comprised of several important subcenters, although in a relatively reduced urban zone, considering the distance from the Main Square, or Zócalo, where the Historical Downtown Area still has slight primacy. In the first metropolitan ring, although we can note greater dispersion of subcenters and marked polycentrism towards the north and southeast, a fundamental role has been played in the consolidation of these subcenters by the presence of major roads, along which these subcenters have been developed. A clear example of this is the exit area of the highway to Querétaro. Therefore, even though we can identify a multinodal structure, this structure has been developed in a very restricted urban space that is located, more or less, in a radius of twelve to fifteen kilometers from the central business district.

Beyond the central areas, employment concentration is characterized by marked urban dispersion in all of the city's space. Very noticeable is the almost total absence of recent and important subcenters in the second ring and metropolitan periphery, above all towards the east. That indicates accelerated residential urbanization in several zones of the metropolitan periphery that basically function as "dormitory cities," which were not endowed with important employment concentration nodes. The limited presence of jobs in these peripheral spaces is greatly responsible for motivating labor movements towards the central zones.

Notes:

1. The edge city was defined as a new spatial form on the basis of five criteria: a space in which there are at least 46,000 square meters of office space; a concentration of at least 55,200 square meters of commercial space; more jobs than homes; the population perceives this territory as a specific place; a place where there had not been anything like a city thirty years previously.

2. This region includes the states of Querétaro, Hidalgo, Puebla, Tlaxcala, Morelos, México, and the Federal District (Mexico City).

3. There are certain trademarks that are repeated in all of these malls: examples are clothing firms (JC Penny, Benetton, Ferrioni, and Hugo Boss), articles for the home, restaurants (McDonald's and Sushi Itto), and a concentration of movie theaters (Cinemex and Cinépolis). This homogenization in consumption patterns dominates the scene of the urban fabric of Mexico City and its periphery.

4· The construction of residential areas can be either exclusive or mass. In both cases, its expression is the same: to add more built spaces (be they horizontal or vertical) to the central city and/or its urban or suburban subcenters.

REFERENCES

Aguilar. A.G.. (2002): "Megaurbanization and Industrial Relocation in Mexico's Central Region." *Urban Geography*. 23(7):649-673.

Aguilar, A.G. and P. Ward (2003). "Globalization, Regional Development, and Mega-City Expansion in Latin America: Analyzing México City's Peri-Urban Hinterland", *Cities*. 20(1):3- 21.

Berry, B.J.I, and H. Kim (1993). "Challenges to the Monocentric Model.". *Geographical Analysis* 25:1-4.

Cervero, R. and K.L. Wu. (1997). "Polycentrism, Commuting, and Residential Location in the San Francisco Bay Area." *Environment and Planning A*. 29(5):865-877.

Champion, Anthony G. A. (2001). "Changing Demographic Regime and Evolving Polycentric Urban Regions: Consequences for the Size, Composition and Distribution of City Populations." *Urban Studies*. 38(4):657-677.

Clark, W.A.V. and Marianne Kuijpers-Linde. (1994). *Commuting in Restructuring Urban Regions.* Abingdon, England: Carfax.

Coulomb, R. (2000) "Gobernabilidad democra'tica y sostenibilidad financiera para el centro histo' rico de la ciudad de Me'xico." *L'ordinaire latino-ame'ricain*: Issue on Centros histo'ricos, 181: 65–80.

Dieleman F. M. and A. Faludi. (1998). "Randstad, Rhine-Ruhr and Flemish Diamond as one Polynucleated Macro-Region ?" *Journal of Economic and Social Geography.* 89(3):320-327.

Duhau, Emilio and Martha Schteingart, 1997 Las Colonias Seleccionadas, Suelo y Vivienda. In: Schteingart, Martha, Julio Boltvinik et al. *1997 Pobreza, Condiciones de Vida y Salud en la Ciudad de México.* México DF: El Colegio de México..

Garza, G. (2000a) "Superconcentración, crisis y globalización del sector industrial, 1930-1998", Garza, G. (ed.), *La Ciudad de México en el fin del segundo milenio.* México: El Colegio de México, Gobierno del Distrito Federal, México D.F., 170-177.

Garza, G. (2000b). "Ámbitos de Expansión Territorial", in Garza, G. (ed.), *La Ciudad de México en el fin del segundo milenio. México*: El Colegio de México, Gobierno del Distrito Federal, México D.F., 237-246.

Giuliano, G., and Small, K. A. (1991). "Subcenters in the Los Angeles region." *Regional Science and Urban Economics.* 21(2): 163-182.

Gordon, Peter and Harry W. Richardson (1996), "Beyond Polycentricity: The Dispersed Metropolis, Los Angeles, 1970-1990," *Journal of the American Planning Association.* 62(3):289- 295.

Hiernaux, D. (1991) "Servicios urbanos, grupos populares y medio ambiente en Chalco, Mexico". in: Schteingart, M. and L. DÕAndrea (eds.). *Servicios Urbanos, Gestion Local y Medio Ambiente.* Colmex/CERFE, Mexico.

Hiernaux, Daniel (1999) 'Les mots de la planification du territoire au Méxique', in *Amérique latine: les discours techniques et savants sur la ville dans la politique urbaine.* 'Les mots de la ville' Project, Working Paper No. 37, Paris: MOST-UNESCO

Icazuriaga, Carmen (1992) *La metropolización de la ciudad de México a través de la instalación industrial, México*: Cuadernos de la Casa Chata.

Kloosterman, R. C. and S. Musterd. (2001). "The Policentric Urban Region: Towards a European Metropolitan Region? *Urban Studies.* 38(4):623-633.

Kunzmann, K. (1996) "Euro-megalopolis or themepark Europe? Scenarios for European spatial development." *International Planning Studies.* 1:143-163.

Kuri, Ariel Rodríguez. "Desabasto, hambre y respuesta política, 1915." In *Instituciones y ciudad. Ocho estudios históricos sobre la ciudad de México,* edited by C. Illades and K. Ariel Rodríguez. Mexico City: FP-SONES-Uníos. 2000.

McDonald, J.F. and P.J. Prather. (1994). "Suburban Employment Centres: The Case of Chicago." *Urban Studies*. 31(2):201-218.

Monnet, Jérôme (1995). *Usos e imagenes del centro histórico de la ciudad de México*. Mexico City: DDF / CEMCA.

Parnreiter, Christof: (2000) "Mexico City: The Making of a Global City?" In: Saskia Sassen (ed): *Cities and Their Cross-Border Networks*. UNU-Press.

Richardson, Harry W. (1988). "Monocentric versus Polycentric Modes: The Future of Urban Economics in Regional Science." *Annals of Regional Science*. 22:1-12.

Sassen, S. (1998). "The Impact of New Technologies and Globalization on Cities." in F. Lo and Y. Yeung (eds.), *Globalization and the World of Large Cities*. Tokyo: United Nations University.

Schteingart, Martha (1988) "Mexico City," pp. 268-293 in Mattei Dogan and John D. Kasarda (editors), *Mega-Cities (The Metropolis Era, Volume 2)*. Newbury Park, CA: Sage Publications.

Sobrino, Jaime. (2000) "Participación económica en el siglo XX." In Gustavo Garza (eds): *La Ciudad de México en el fin del segundo milenio*. El Colegio de México, México DF.

Waddell, P., B.J.L. Berry and I. Hoch. (1993). "Housing Price Gradients: the Intersection of Space and Built Form" *Geographical Analysis*. 25(1):5-19.

Waddell P. and V. Shukla (1993). "Manufacturing Location in a Polycentric Urban Area: A Study in the Composition and Attractiveness of Employment Subcenters." *Urban Geography*. 14(3):277-296.

White, Sammis B.; Lisa S. Binkley and Jeffrey D. Osterman (1993) "The Sources of Suburban Employment Growth." *Journal of the American Planning Association*. 59(2):193-204.

10 Poverty in Winnipeg: A Study in Urban – Social Geography

R.C. Tiwari

Winnipeg, the capital of the Province of Manitoba accounts for 67 percent of the provincial population of 1.1 million. A multi-ethnic and a multi-cultural city which once had distinct ethnic neighborhoods but with "Canadianization" of younger population and their desire to be suburbanites, the degree of segregation has relatively decreased. However, the landmarks like denominational churches and food delis remain a reminder of earlier ethnic concentrations. In the inner-city[1] the new immigrants from South-East Asia have started to add to the functional diversity by opening groceries and/or restaurants. The most visible group, Aboriginals (also known as People of the First Nations or Native Indians), are arriving from the Reserves in ever increasing numbers. They too display the same desires and wishes of new immigrants to urban areas to become "suburban Canadians." In Winnipeg the ethnic dimension is slowly giving way to the economic dimension and a consequence of this process is that the economically disadvantaged are left to agglomerate in the inner city. Therefore, poverty is not limited to one ethnic group nor is it uniformly distributed. The aim in this study is to briefly discuss poverty in general and its main measurement, that is, average family income and then briefly describe two groups living in poverty, single parent families and Aboriginals. The antecedent of this choice of variables lies in the studies of social area analysis, which uses three constructs, economic status or social status, family status or urbanization and ethnic status or segregation to portray the social geography of a city. Though income can be used as surrogate for social status, here both social status and income are used to get a better understanding of the social structure of the city. However, the distribution of single parent family and the distribution of

Aboriginals are being used as surrogate for family and ethnic status. Interdependency between these variables exists and is recognized. The data for Winnipeg has been obtained from various Statistics Canada reports and the city's census tracts and neighborhoods are used as measuring units.

POVERTY[2]

The term poverty does "not have one meaning, but a series of meanings linked through nothing more than a series of resemblances." Spicker (1999:159) identifies eleven clusters and Figure 10-1 shows the inter-related nature of the various meanings. However, central to all these meanings is *"unacceptable hardship"* for people living in a society.

Earlier Alcock (1993:4) stated "poverty refers not just to state of affairs but to an unacceptable state of affairs. The imperative of action is intrinsic in this concept. Poverty is a problem, or it is nothing. What it can not be is not a problem." Booth in his studies on London had introduced the concept of "line of poverty" (Gordon, et al. 2000). As Booth was in shipping business the idea was borrowed from the plimsoll line. It was Rowntree who turned line of poverty in to poverty line (Veit-Wilson 2002). In general terms poverty line specifies the dollar figure, and people earning below that number are supposed to be living in poverty. Statistics Canada developed the Low Income Cut-Off Lines (LICO) in 1959 and since then the LICO has been widely used as an unofficial measure of poverty. Statistics Canada questions the use of the LICO as the poverty line. Ms. Maryanne Webber, Director, Income Statistics, Statistics Canada, in a letter to *Winnipeg Free Press*, dated 15 December 1998 stated that:

> The LICO is based on the proportion of income that the average family spends on food, shelter and clothing plus 20 percent. The LICO tells us how many families have too little income to cover what the average family spends on food, shelter and clothing plus 20 percent, taking into consideration differences in family size and community size. Should you wish to label this "poverty" it is your choice. But it is important to note that this not in any sense an official definition of poverty and it certainly is not Statistics Canada's.

However, the National Council of Welfare and many other social policy groups regard the LICO as poverty lines and use the terms poor and low income interchangeably. Statistics Canada takes pains to avoid references to poverty lines. Regardless of the terminology, the cut-offs are a useful tool for defining and analyzing the significantly large portion of the Canadian population with low incomes.(National Council of Welfare 2002:150)

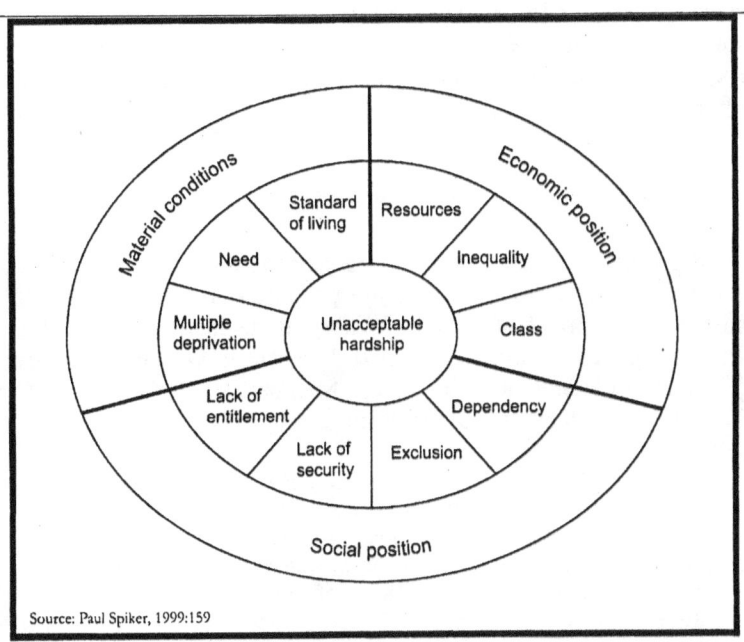

Source: Paul Spiker, 1999:159

Figure 10-1
Family Resemblances Between Different Concepts of Poverty

In this paper LICO is also used to define people living in poverty. Figure 10-2 shows the distribution of income in Winnipeg by neighborhood and also shows LICO for different family sizes. Table 10-1 shows the distribution of poverty in Canada.

The poverty rates for Manitoba in 1999 are slightly higher than the national average. In Manitoba, the poverty rates are 18.5 percent for all persons, 23.8 percent for children under 18 years; and for both those 65 years of age and older and for single mothers the rate is 65 percent. Needless to say Manitoba, classifies as a 'have-not' province. Table 10-2 shows the poverty trends for Winnipeg.

CHILD POVERTY

Child poverty is sometimes discussed separately but is really an extension of parental poverty, and for years Winnipeg had the dubious distinction of being the child poverty capital of Canada. While this distinction may now be with another Canadian city, child poverty is still present in Winnipeg. In November 1989, in a fit of moral indignation, the Members of Parliament in Canada, unanimously passed the following resolution:

> That this House express its concern for more than one million Canadian children currently living in poverty and seek to achieve the goal of eliminating poverty and seek to achieve the goal of eliminating Poverty among Canadian children by the Year 2000 (All party resolution passed by the House of Commons on 29 November 1989)

The year 2000 came and went but poverty stayed. According to the mover of the motion, Ed Broadbent, a lack of political commitment on the part of Government was really responsible for the inaction (Novick 1999:7). What it may also indicate is that poor people seldom vote and if they do, they vote for the "wrong" party. Table 10-3 shows child poverty in Canada and Manitoba

The child poverty rate for 1996 for Winnipeg was 23 percent. However, much of the poverty in Winnipeg is concentrated in the inner city as indicated in the map showing percentage distribution of household poverty and child poverty (see Figure 10-3).

Ringem (1988) identifies two types of poverty—absolute and relative but there is only one measurement—income. Therefore, distribution of income in Winnipeg is briefly discussed below.

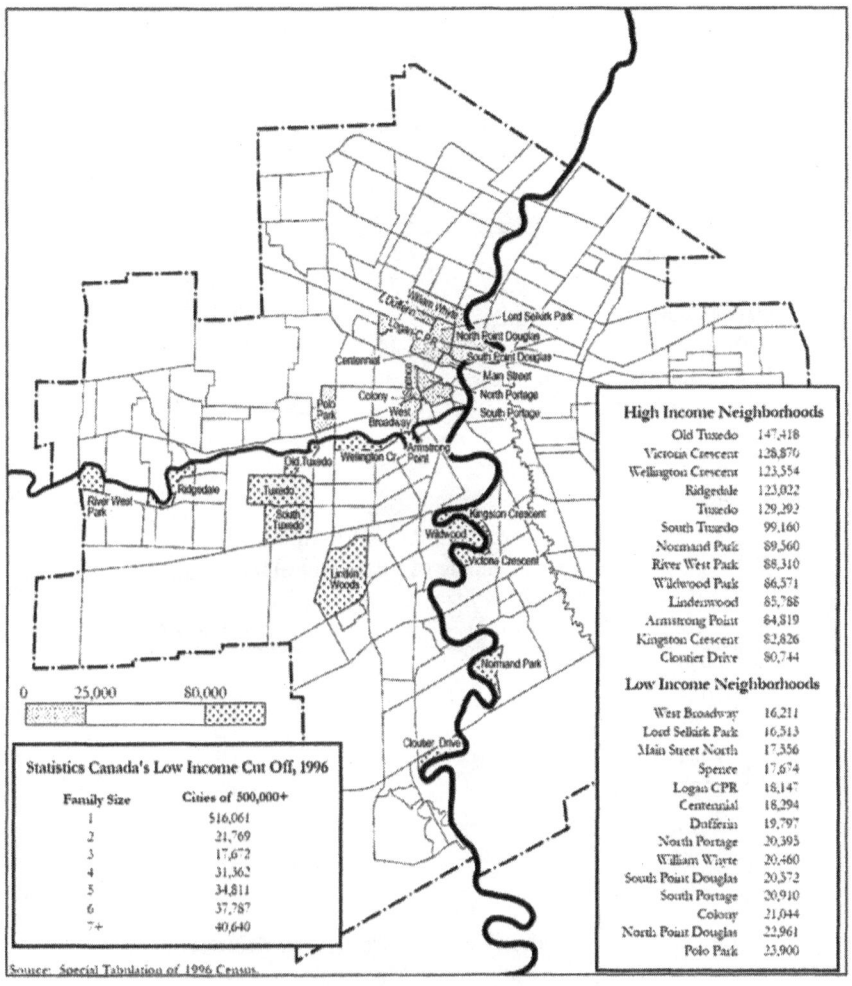

High Income Neighborhoods

Old Tuxedo	147,418
Victoria Crescent	128,870
Wellington Crescent	123,554
Ridgedale	123,022
Tuxedo	129,292
South Tuxedo	99,160
Normand Park	89,560
River West Park	88,310
Wildwood Park	86,571
Lindenwood	85,788
Armstrong Point	84,819
Kingston Crescent	82,826
Cloutier Drive	80,744

Low Income Neighborhoods

West Broadway	16,211
Lord Selkirk Park	16,513
Main Street North	17,356
Spence	17,674
Logan CPR	18,147
Centennial	18,294
Dufferin	19,797
North Portage	20,395
William Whyte	20,460
South Point Douglas	20,572
South Portage	20,910
Colony	21,044
North Point Douglas	22,961
Polo Park	23,900

Statistics Canada's Low Income Cut Off, 1996

Family Size	Cities of 500,000+
1	$16,061
2	21,769
3	17,672
4	31,362
5	34,811
6	37,787
7+	40,640

Source: Special Tabulation of 1996 Census.

Figure 10-2
Distribution of Income in Winnipeg

R.C. Tiwari

Table 10-1
Poverty Rates in Canada for Selected Age Groups and Selected Years
(based on pre-tax income)

Year	All Persons	Children under 18	Aged 65 and Above	Single Parent Families	
				Female	Male
1981	15.9	16.3	33.0	52.6	18.6
1985	17.6	19.3	28.0	60.9	26.2
1991	16.4	18.8	21.9	59.5	22.0
1999	16.2	18.7	17.7	51.8	18.0

Source: National Council on Welfare, 2002:27.

Table 10-2
Household Poverty Trends in Winnipeg, 1971-96
(as a percentage of all households)

Year	Households in Poverty (overall)	Households in Poverty in Inner City
1971	20.6	32.6
1981	21.3	36.2
1986	21.8	39.5
1991	23.9	44.3
1996	28.4	50.8

Source: Leszubski, D., et al, 2000

Table 10-3
Percentage of Children Living in Poverty in Selected Years,
Canada and Manitoba

Year	Canada	Manitoba
1989	15.2	22.6
1996	31.6	27.1
1999	18.7	23.8

Source: National Council on Welfare, 2002:23, 133

Distribution of Income in Winnipeg

Income is an important indicator of social status. Shevky and Bell derived social status by using education and occupation (Humphreys and Dutt 2002) but in Winnipeg distribution of average family income more or less depicts the distribution of social status. (Figure 10-4 shows the distribution of social status.) Not only this distribution describes the areas with high social status but earlier studies of distribution of income and social status show high class residential areas are more or less "fixed" in certain neighborhoods. Figure 10-2 shows the distribution of average family income in selected neighborhoods for 1996 (the figures for 2001 are as yet not available). Winnipeg, like so many other cities, is a socially divided city; however, the divisions may have been created by physical barriers, such as the two rivers and the railway lines. The other side of tracks is not a simple statement. It is loaded with socio-cultural connotations. As can be seen the southwest part of Winnipeg along with the areas located on the rivers show high income while the inner city has low income.

The "well-off" people live in the southwestern sector while poor people are concentrated in the inner city. Many well-off people have moved out of the city and live in peri-urban area.

Distribution of Single Parent Families

Shevky and Bell's construct of "urbanization" was basically an indicator of traditional vs. non-traditional families (Humphreys and Dutt 2002). The tradition in which mothers stayed home to look after the young children but this tradition has given way to a tradition where many mothers with young children regularly work. The non-traditional, if one can say so, are the single parent families. By analyzing the maps of distribution of single parent families in Winnipeg for the years 1976 to 1996 (Figure 10-5) one observes greater concentration of single parent families in and around the inner city. Table 10-4 shows the percentage of single parent families and the percentage of single parent families headed by females.

In 1989 Linda Taylor had observed that:

Single-parent families headed by a female form one of the largest poverty groups in Canada today. In the same year Statistics Canada reported that 41.8% of these families lived below the poverty line, a rate nearly four times higher than two parent families. (Linda Taylor "Poverty and Single Mothers" *Specifics*, Winter 1991/92:18)

Taylor quoted from an estimate done for some other study that in Winnipeg and Manitoba in 1989, 98% of single parent families led by females were living below the poverty line.

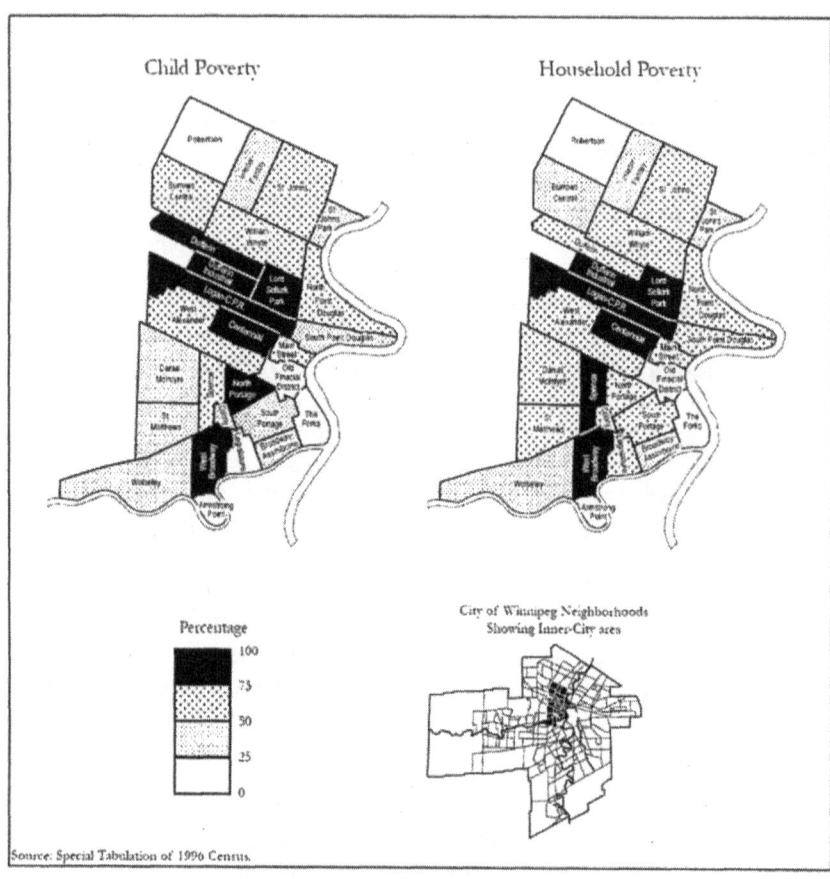

Figure 10-3
Distribution of Household and Child Poverty

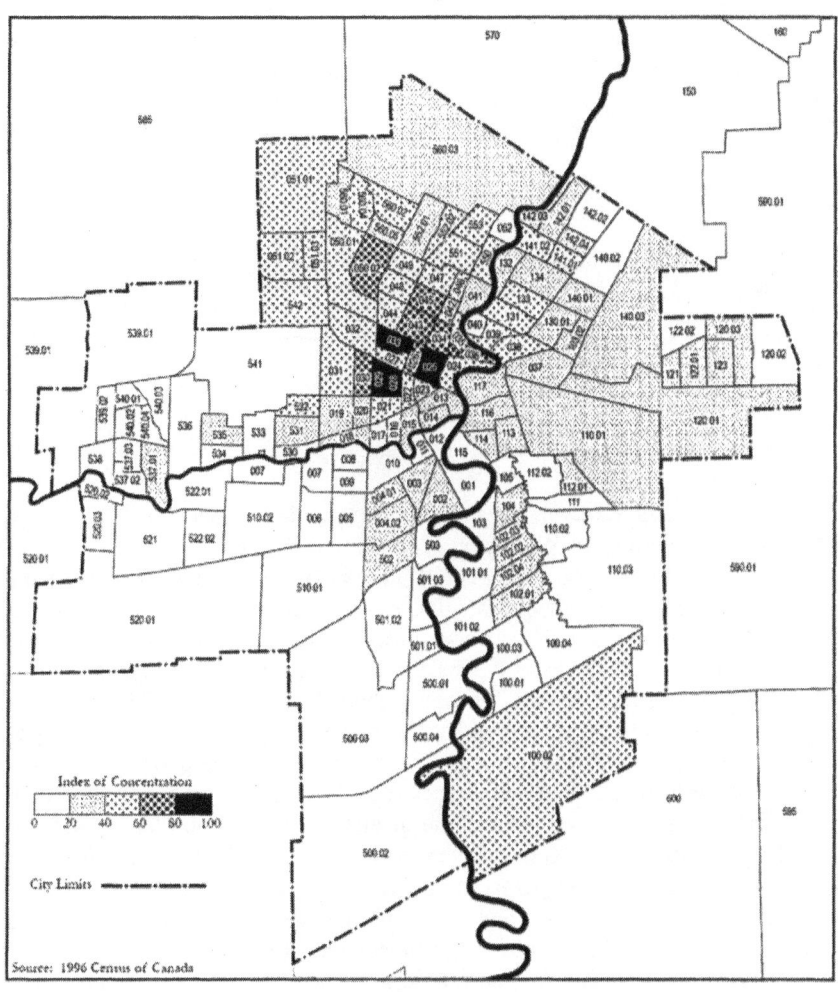

Figure 10-4
Distribution of Social Status
(based on income)

As shown in Table 10-4, the percentage of female headed single parent families is quite consistent. The only change is that there is a gradual sub-urbanization of single parent families. This may also be due to a grudging acceptance of divorce in the society and changing mores in which fathers have started to get custody of the children, possibly increasing the percentage of single parent families in the suburbs.

Table 10-4
Single Parent Families and Single Parent Families Headed by Females

Year	Single Parent Families as a % of All Families	% of Single Parent Families Headed by Females
1986	13.92	84.79
1991	14.82	84.29
1996	15.82	84.96

Source: Source: National Council on Welfare Reports, 2002.

The social conditions in the inner city are quite serious and there are 150 Food Banks operating in Winnipeg. A great many of them are located in the churches and community centers. The Winnipeg Harvest which supplies food to most of the food banks does not give out the locations of the food banks. Therefore, observations here are drawn from one food bank located in the Knox United Church in the inner city. The food bank is run by volunteers and the Winnipeg Harvest supplements the food gathered by the Church. The organizers keep details on a filing card which has the name and other details including the number of children and whether or not the person is a single parent. There were over 1,500 cards, which is broadly indicative of the number of people who come to this food bank. However, most of the details are rightly confidential and from our observations a few inferences can be drawn. First, every race and ethnic group was represented; however, the dominant group was Aboriginal. Second, the users of this food bank lived in the immediate vicinity. The Church was surrounded by a number of apartment blocks and the managers/owners rent to the people on welfare because social welfare agencies pay rent directly to the managers/owners. Thirdly, the dominant group collecting food were Aboriginal single females with children. That was not a surprise.

ABORIGINALS OR NATIVE INDIANS

Winnipeg is a multi-ethnic and a multi-cultural city. As stated earlier, voluntarily segregated residential areas can still be recognized. But it will be fair to say that the younger generation is becoming "Canadian." Hence the choice of residential area is no longer determined by socio-cultural factors but by socio-

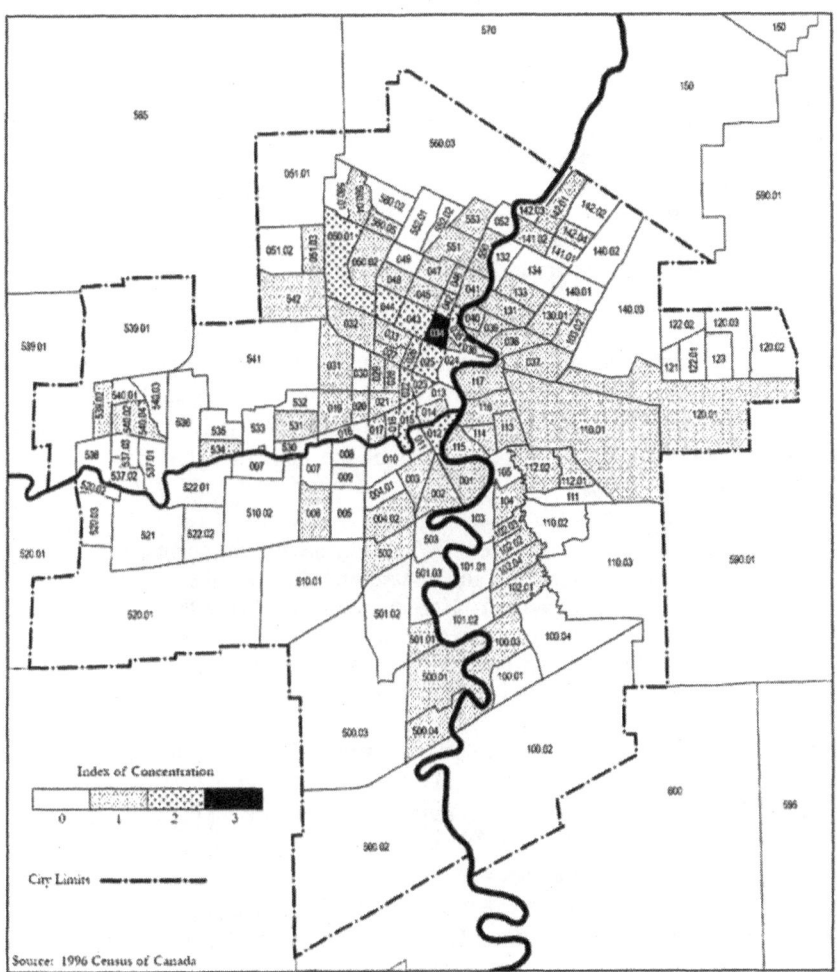

Figure 10-5
Distribution of Single Parent Families

economic factors. However, discriminations of various types, though illegal, are quite common and in some ways are retarding the assimilation process. It is interesting to quote James Grey's observation on racial discrimination in earlier Winnipeg:

> Racism . . . was not something that covered the community like a paint. It was more like a laminate. Or, to switch the metaphor, ours was a society with a well-defined pecking order of prejudice. On the top were the race proud Anglo-Saxons, who were prejudiced against everybody else. On the bottom were the Jews, against whom everybody discriminated. (James Grey 1966: 132)

The most dominant group remains British but this dominance has gradually declined. Earlier dominance is best illustrated by the following statement made by the young Hungarian boy (about 12 years of age) who at the turn of the last century lived with his family in the North End (traditionally a poor area where the new immigrants found a place to live) the hero of John Marlyn's book, *Under the Ribs of Death*:

> "The English," he whispered. "Pa' the only people who count are the English. Their fathers got all the best jobs. They are the only ones nobody ever calls foreigners. Nobody ever makes fun of their names or calls them 'bologny eaters', or laughs at the way they dress or talk. Nobody," he concluded bitterly, "cause when you are English it's the same as being Canadian." (Marlyn 1957:24)

Further in the novel the young boy gives us some idea about his ambition for his future when he is telling a mate of his " 'I jus' don't wanna go to jail,' Sandor cried. 'It's awright for you. You got nuthin ta lose. But I got plans. Some day I am gonna work.' " (Marlyn 1957:57). Today one can substitute Hungarian for Aboriginal and the observations still hold true.

At the turn of last century Jews were the disadvantaged people, but today Aboriginals occupy that position. The Social Planning Council of Winnipeg in 1986 had reported that:

> Natives are disadvantaged in all socio-economic categories compared to the general population. They earn less, have lower levels of education, and are employed more often. Their plight is particularly acute in the economically depressed inner city where their per capita representation is twice that of the city as whole. Although some progress has been made in housing, the trends indicate that the economic gap between Natives and non-natives is widening.

Aboriginals or Indians have been migrating from the Reserves, which are 55 in number in this province. The vast majority of these reserves are situated on low productivity land. An Aboriginal migrant coming from the reserve is moving from a hunting - gathering society to a post-industrial society. The gap between the two societies is wide. In Third World countries the migrants of this kind are accommodated in the informal sector, but there is no informal sector in Winnipeg. The new Aboriginal immigrant is not adequately trained to participate in a post-industrial economy, hence unemployment is very high. Though Aboriginals are provided with welfare, which is totally inadequate, a majority of them have no work or prospect of employment so a large percentage of them end up in the "watering holes" (bars) located on the Main Street. Failing to have funds for fun, people are ready to pawn their goods. Figure 10-6 shows the distribution of pawn shops in Winnipeg. The spatial adjacency of poor neighborhoods and the location of pawn shops needs no explanation.

Although some changes have come, a lot remains to be done before equality will be achieved. Statistics Canada has recorded the number of Aboriginals, however, these numbers should only be taken as an indicator of a general trend. The population growth rate for Canada between 1996 and 2001 was 3.89 percent but the growth rate for Aboriginals was 18.16 percent; similarly the growth rate for the Province of Manitoba was 0.31 percent but for the Aboriginals it was 14.24 percent. For the City of Winnipeg the growth rate was 0.6 percent and for the Aboriginals the rate is 21.86 percent. This is an indication of a Third World society surrounded by a First World society. Figure 10-7 shows the percentage distribution of provincial population in Canada and distribution of Aboriginal population as a percentage of the provincial population. The province of Manitoba has the largest percentage followed by the Province of Saskatchewan. Figure 10-8 shows the distribution of Aboriginals in Winnipeg in 1996. Comparing this distribution with earlier distributions it becomes clear that concentration remains in the inner city but as the Aboriginals improve their economic conditions they too follow the path to suburbs.

A study of age-sex structure can show general characteristics of that population as well as indicate sex-ratios. Figure 10-9 shows the age-sex structure of Aboriginal and non-Aboriginal population of Winnipeg in 2001. For non-Aboriginals the sex-ratio is 95.5 males per 100 females and for Aboriginals this ratio is 87.6. Population pyramids reflect the demographic transition stages for non-Aboriginals and Aboriginals. The population pyramid for Aboriginal resembles population pyramids of developing countries, where there is a greater percentage of younger population and relatively small percentage of old age people. As stated earlier, Aboriginals are migrating to the city, but physical distance plays an important part in this process with the reserves which are

R.C. Tiwari

Figure 10-6
Distribution of Pawnshops

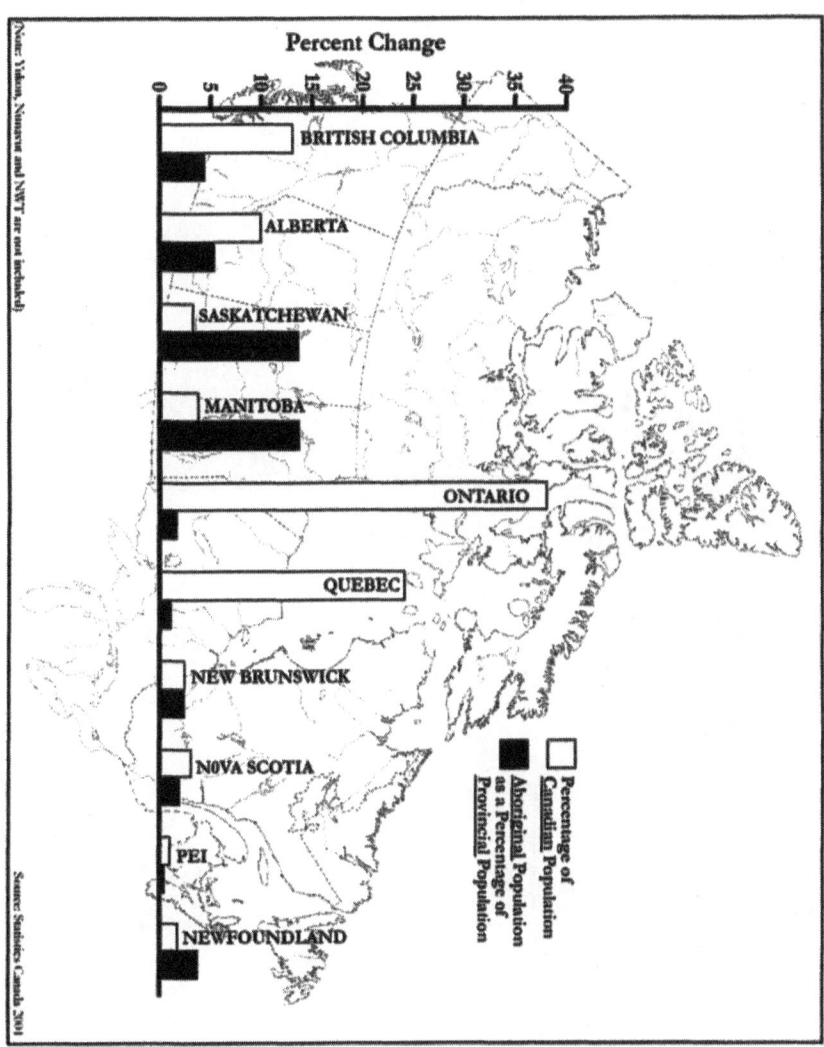

Figure 10-7
Distribution of Provincial Population and Aboriginals

R.C. Tiwari

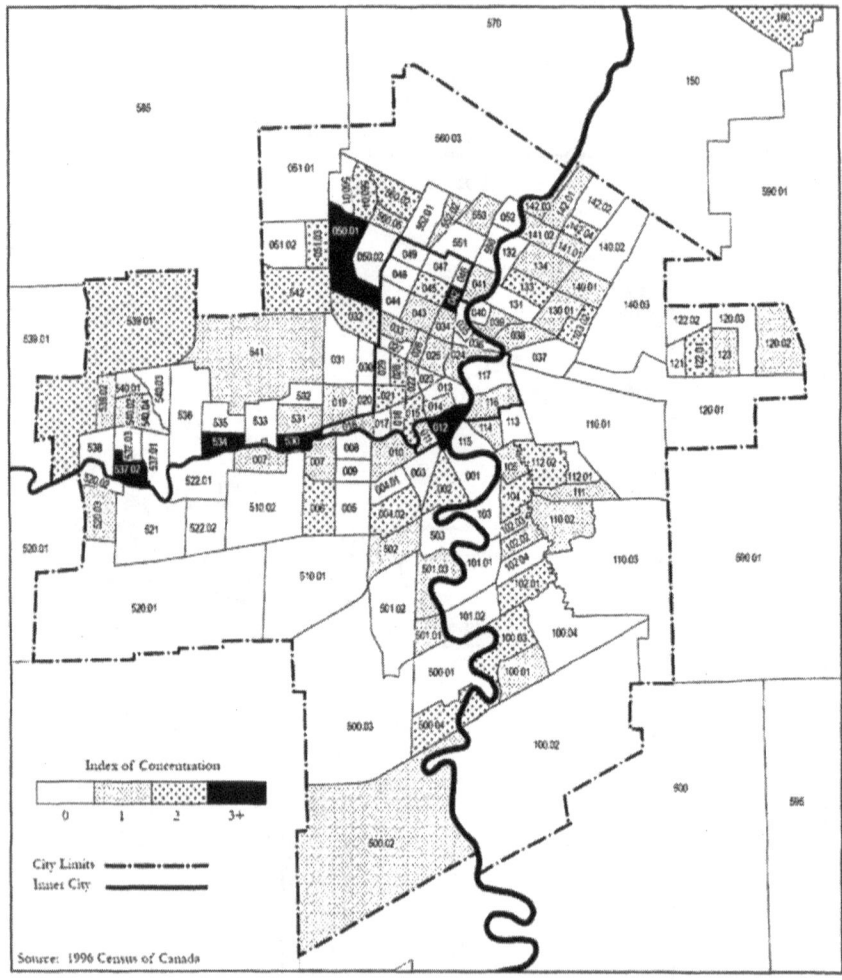

Figure 10-8
Concentration of Aboriginals

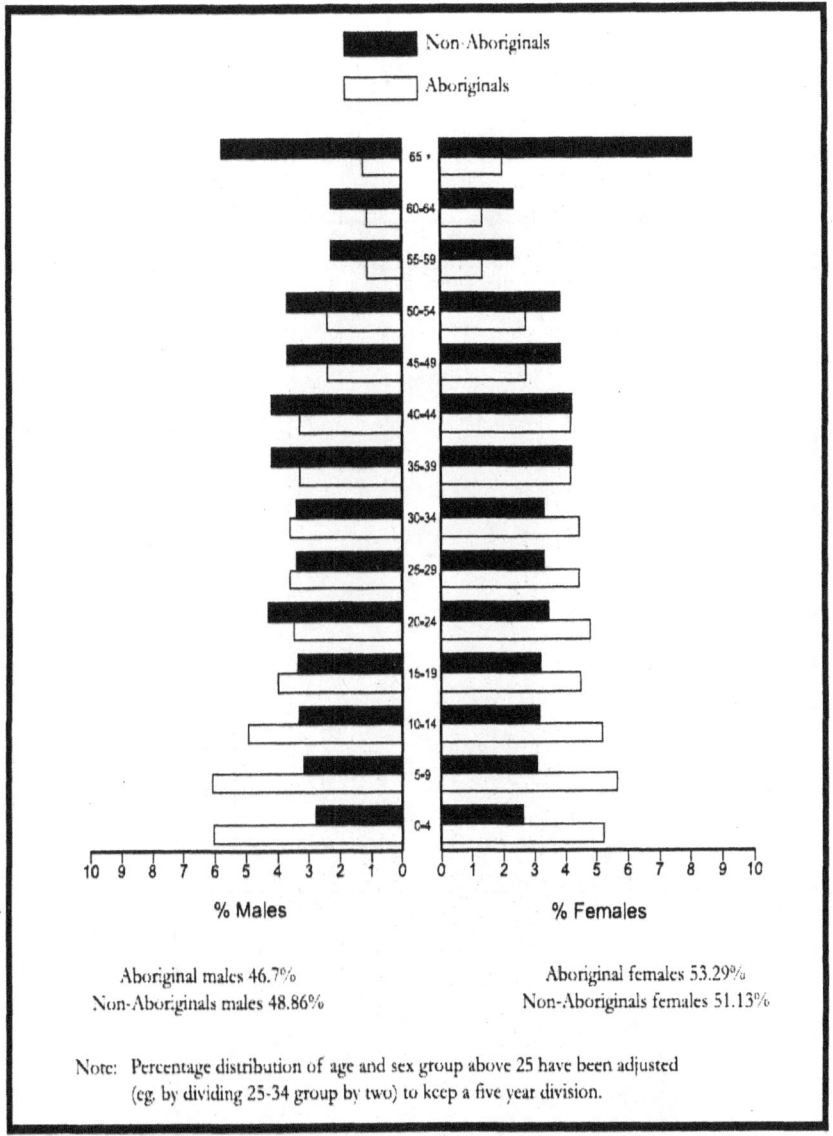

Figure 10-9
Age and Sex Structure of Aboriginals and Non-Aboriginals in Winnipeg

R.C. Tiwari

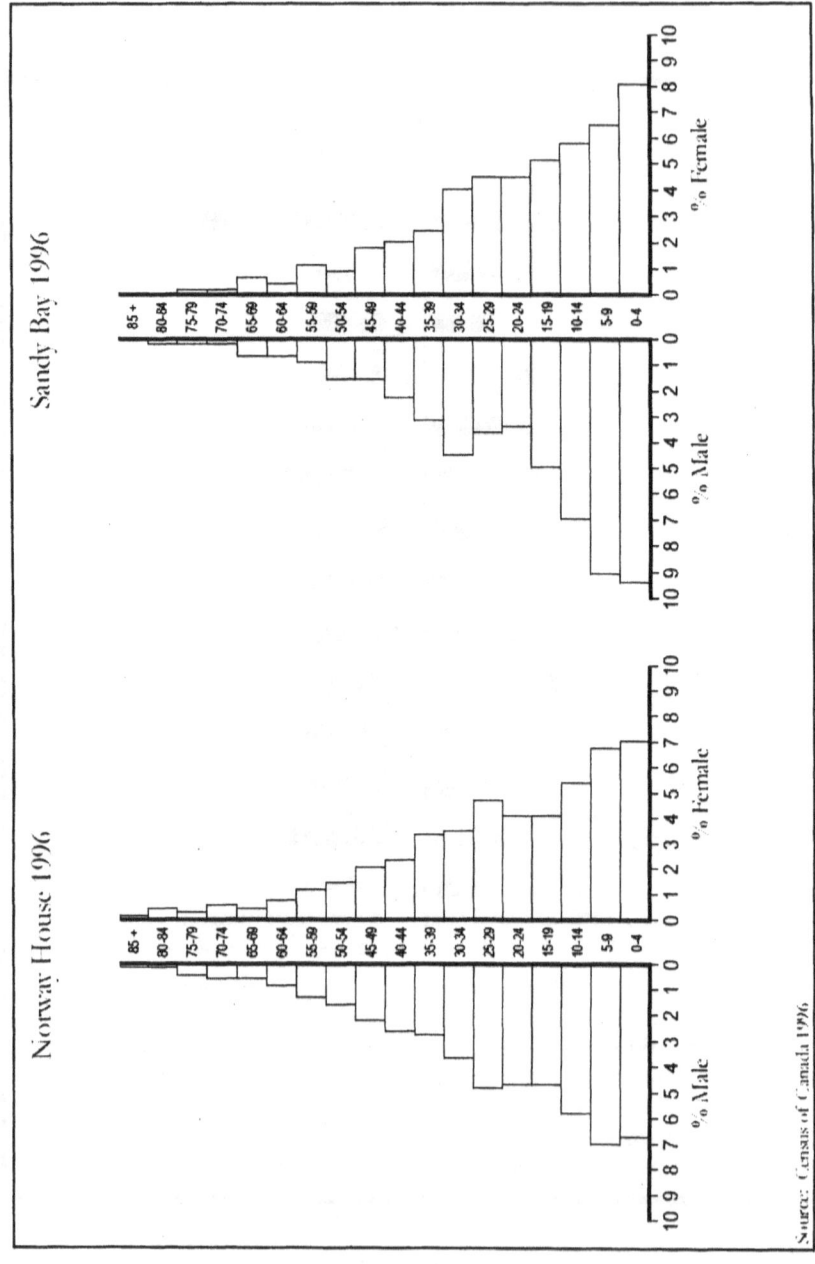

Figure 10-10
Age and Sex Structure of Two Selected Reserves

nearer to Winnipeg contribute more to migration streams. For example, Sandy Bay Indian Reserve which is located only 90 miles north of Winnipeg contrasts with Norway House which is an isolated Indian Reserve located about 350 miles away and only accessible by air. These two reserves display quite a difference in their population pyramids. (Figure 10-10) The pyramid for Sandy Bay reflects the gap where male migrants have left the reserve, while Norway House reflects a more balanced population distribution. There is also "circular migration" between Sandy Bay and Winnipeg. Although circular migration has yet to be studied in detail, attempts are being made to study inter-urban and intra-urban mobility. An interim report on Aboriginal mobility (inter-urban) was published in March 2003. For this study 525 newly arrived Aboriginal migrants in Winnipeg were interviewed. Like any new urban migrants, these migrants are young (males and females), single and ever hopeful to better themselves. Not unexpectedly, the places connected by highways tend to contribute more persons to the immigrant stream. The main reasons are indicated for moving are for family reasons (42.8%), for employment (23.5) and for educational opportunities (13.9%). (The term 'family' should be interpreted in a very broad sense because this may include friends, neighbors, as well as close and distant family members. However, this does indicate that new migrants do have some connection with the urban area.) As new Aboriginals migrants arrive from the Reserves and participate in the urbanization process, earlier migrants, having made good in the city, are on their way to join the movement towards suburbs. Thus these processes of urbanization and sub-urbanization of Aboriginals are interesting phenomenon. However, the speed by which these processes are taking place is creating its own problem of adjustment.

CONCLUSIONS

Canada is an affluent country, with poverty of a large sector of society being an aberration. In 1989, Parliament unanimously agreed to eradicate child poverty by 2000. However, good thoughts failed to be converted in "good deeds" and poverty kept on creeping upwards. The publication of the United Nations Development Program (UNDP) Human Development Index (HDI) had unfortunate and unforeseen consequences. The index had very little to do with poverty, nevertheless the index was used to deflect criticism of social welfare policies (It would be interesting to observe performances of the "politicians" as the UNDP 2003 Human Development Index has put Canada as number eight in the world). Social welfare payments are totally inadequate, but are enough to soothe the conscience of the well-off sector of the society. It may also be an appropriate time to re-evaluate the relationship between minimum wage and the increase in the numbers of working poor.

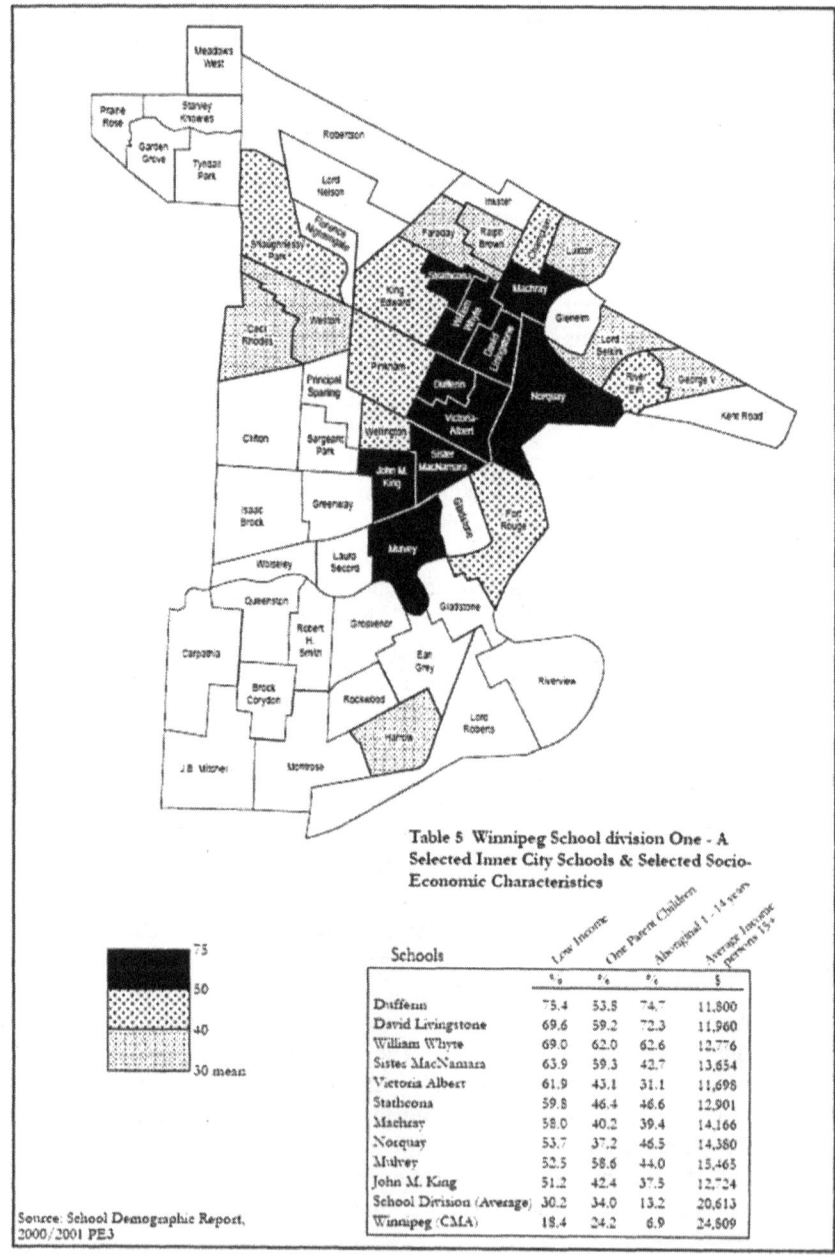

Table 5 Winnipeg School division One - A
Selected Inner City Schools & Selected Socio-
Economic Characteristics

Schools	Low Income %	One Parent Children %	Aboriginal 1 - 14 years %	Average Income persons 15+ $
Dufferin	75.4	53.8	74.7	11,800
David Livingstone	69.6	59.2	72.3	11,960
William Whyte	69.0	62.0	62.6	12,776
Sister MacNamara	63.9	59.3	42.7	13,654
Victoria Albert	61.9	43.1	31.1	11,698
Strathcona	59.8	46.4	46.6	12,901
Machray	58.0	40.2	39.4	14,166
Norquay	53.7	37.2	46.5	14,380
Mulvey	52.5	58.6	44.0	15,463
John M. King	51.2	42.4	37.5	12,724
School Division (Average)	30.2	34.0	13.2	20,613
Winnipeg (CMA)	18.4	24.2	6.9	24,809

75
50
40
30 mean

Source: School Demographic Report, 2000/2001 PE3

Figure 10-11
School Division 1—Low Income

Winnipeg remains a socially divided city and its inner-city is sometimes referred to as an "Urban Reserve," and is attracting Aboriginals in increasing numbers. However, migrants including Aboriginals who are qualified and have good jobs go directly to suburbs. The absence of informal sector makes it difficult to enter the job market at the very lowest level. Education and training are considered essential for improving socio-economic conditions but the enormity of the problem can be appreciated by studying Figure 10-11. The spatial concentration of low income families, of single parent families and of Aboriginals puts a lot of strain on already limited resources. So, social landscape of Winnipeg is of a socially divided city. The ever increasing sub-urbanization of people and jobs is contributing to the intensification of social divisions. The inner city is in the process of developing in to a 'conflict zone' and if the governments at various levels do not pay serious attention to the problems of the inner city this city is in for some big surprises.

Notes:

1. There is no agreement as to what constitutes inner city of Winnipeg. The Core Area Initiative Program, a tri-level government program for the improvement of the central city and provided money for the improvement so it was not geographical (spatial) but political reasons to include four additional census tracts in the Core Area Program but these tracts are separated by the two rivers and are not really part of the inner city and are not included here.
2. There is a wealth of literature on poverty so only selected references are made here. Gordon & Spicker (eds) and Bradshaw and Sainsbury (eds.) could be referred along with the two volumes by Himmelfarb.

REFERENCES

Alcock, P. (1993). *Understanding Poverty*, London: McMillan Press.

Bradshaw J. & R. Sainsbury. (2000) *Researching Poverty* Aldershot: Ashgate.

Gordon, D. and P. Spicker (1999). *The International Glossary of Poverty*. London: Zed Books.

Gordon, David, et.al. (2000) *Poverty and Social Exclusion in Britain*. Joseph Rowntree Foundation 2000

Grey, James. (1966) *The Winter Years*. Winnipeg: General Publishing.

Himmelfarb G. (1985). *The Idea of Poverty*. New York: Vintage Books.

Himmelfarb,G. (1992). *Poverty and Compassion*. New York: Vintage Books.

Humphreys, Adrien G. and Ashok K. Dutt. (2002). *Urban Ecological Research Methods Applied to the Cleveland, Ohio Metropolitan Area*. Lewiston NY: Edwin Mellen Press.

Institute of Urban Studies. (2003). *First Nations / Metis / Inuit Mobility Study Interim Report One*. March.

Lezubski, D. et.al. (2000) "High and Rising: The Growth of Poverty in Winnipeg" in Jim Silver (ed.) *Solutions that Work: Fighting Poverty in Winnipeg*. Winnipeg: Canadian Centre for Policy Alternatives.

Marlyn, John. (1957). *Under the Ribs of Death*. Winnipeg: New Canadian Library.

Novick, M. (1999). *Fundamental First: An Equal Opportunity from Birth for Every Child*, Campaign 2000 Discussion Paper. Toronto.

Peters, Evelyn. (2000). "Aboriginal People and Canadian Geography: A Review of Recent Literature." *Canadian Geographer*. 44(2):44-55.

Peters, Evelyn (2001). "Geographies of Aboriginal people in Canada" *Canadian Geographer*. 45(1):138-144.

National Council of Welfare. (2002). *Poverty Profiles, 1999*. Summer.

Ringem, S. (1988). "Direct and Indirect Measures of Poverty" *Journal of Social Policy*. 17(3):351-65.

Skelton, Ian. (2002). "Residential Mobility of Aboriginal Single Mothers in Winnipeg: An Exploratory Study of Chronic Moving." *Journal of Housing & the Built Environment*. 17:127-144.

Social Planning Council of Winnipeg. (1997). *Acceptable Living Level of Living (ALL)*. Winnipeg. September.

Social Planning Council of Winnipeg. (1999). *Barriers to ALL*. Winnipeg. March.

Spicker, Paul. (1999). "Definitions of Poverty: Eleven clusters of Meaning" in David Gordon and Paul Spicker (eds.) *The International Glossary on Poverty*. London: Zed Books.

Taylor, Linda. (1992). "Poverty and Single Mothers" *Specifics*. Winter.

Townsend, P. (2000). "Post 1945 Poverty Research and Things to Come" pp. 3-35 in Bradshaw & Sainsbury (eds.), *Researching Poverty*. Aldershot: Ashgate / Joseph Rowntree Foundation.

Veit-Wilson, J. (2002). "Researching Poverty and the Poor." *Journal of Social Policy*. 31(3):537-544.

Webber, M. (1998). Letter. *Winnipeg Free Press*. 15 Dec.

Index

Figure is indicated by *f.* Table is indicated by *t.*

About the Contributors

Adrian Guillermo Aguilar is Professor of Geography and Director, Geography Institute, Universidad Nacional Autonoma de Mexico.

Concepción Alvarado is with the Geography Institute, Universidad Nacional Autonoma de Mexico.

John E. Benhart is Professor Emeritus of Shippensburg University of Pennsylvania. He has published widely in on the topics of geographic education and environmental planning.

James Bennett received his M.S. in Geoenvironmental Studies from Shippensburg University. He is currently working as a planner in Cumberland County, Pennsylvania.

Frederick Boateng is a Graduate Assistant in The Department of Geography and Planning, the University of Akron, Akron OH 44325-5005.

Gerhard O. Braun is Professor of Urban Studies / Metrostudies (TEAS) at Free University of Berlin, Germany. He currently serves as Chairman of the Department of Geography and as President of the IGU-Commission on "Monitoring Cities of Tomorrow".

Ashok K. Dutt, is Professor Emeritus of Geography, Planning and Urban Studies at the University of Akron has published 21 books, over 80 journal articles and about 70 book chapters.

H.S. "Manie" Geyer is Professor of Regional Planning and Chair of Urban and Regional Planning at the Northwest University, Potchefstroom Campus. Prior to joining academia, he served as head of the Planning Division of the Soweto metropolitan government in Johannesburg. He has consulted and published widely in the fields of urbanization, urban policy, and planning.

Animesh Halder formerly served as a Director in the Calcutta Metropolitan Development Authority where he worked in the areas of slum development planning, conducted socio-economic studies on the urban poor, and implemented poverty alleviation programs. In addition to his extensive work as a planner, he has also as a Lecturer in several universities including Calcutta University. He currently is a freelance planning consultant.

Rebecca S. Hawthorne received her M.S. in Geoenvironmental Studies from Shippensburg University. She is currently Open Space Coordinator for Cumberland County, Pennsylvania.

Ioan Ianos is Professor in the Human Geography Department, Faculty of Geography, University of Bucharest; He is also serves as the General Director for Higher Education in the Education and Research Ministry.

Deborah P. King received her M.A. in Geography from the University of Georgia. Currently she is an Instructor in the Department of Geography and Planning, the University of Akron, Akron OH 44325-5005.

Thomas Kontuly is Professor of Geography at the University of Utah and an Investigator with the Institute for Public and International Affairs. Much of his extensive research has focused on urbanization, migration, and employment in Europe.

Richard Morrill is Professor Emeritus at the University of Washington. His interests include most of human geography, with a particular focus on inequality. One of the original 'space cadets' at Washington, he remains deeply committed to geography as a science.

Allen G. Noble is a Distinguished Professor Emeritus of Geography and Planning, the University of Akron, Akron, OH 44325-5005. He is the editor of co-editor of several books on India, as well as the author of numerous journal articles on South Asia.

George M. Pomeroy is Associate Professor of Geography at Shippensburg University of Pennsylvania. His research interests are in the area of urban geography, urban and regional planning, South Asia, and China.

R.C. Tiwari is currently a senior scholar in the Department of Environment and Geography, University of Manitoba. Prior to joining the Department in 1966, he had taught geography in schools and college in India, East Africa, and England.

His current research interests are urban social geography; the work of Sir Patrick Geddes; and, geography of princely cities of India.

Gerald R. Webster is Professor and Chair of the Department of Geography at the University of Wyoming. His interests are broad and include political geography, urban geography, and the changing electoral landscape of the American South.

www.ingramcontent.com/pod-product-compliance
Lightning Source LLC
Chambersburg PA
CBHW051341130726
47899CB00016B/537